AF575492

Praise for *Ecotherapy-Informed EMDR*

"*Ecotherapy-Informed EMDR* by Jennifer Marchand is a refreshing and essential guide for therapists seeking a holistic and culturally responsive approach to trauma treatment. Through powerful metaphors like comparing the AIP system to a river cleared by EMDR, Jen demonstrates how nature can enhance therapeutic processes. The book's practical implementation guidance, offering specific methods for incorporating art, movement, and nature into each EMDR phase, combined with its emphasis on cultural humility, makes it a valuable resource for EMDR therapists ready to deepen their work with clients in meaningful and respectful ways."

—**Rotem Brayer,** certified EMDR therapist, EMDR consultant, advanced EMDR trainer, and founder of the EMDR Learning Community

"*Ecotherapy-Informed EMDR* is most certainly a book for our times. In an increasingly fragmented, polarized, and dangerous world that is reeling from one catastrophe to the next, Jennifer Marchand calmly leads us back to our grounding, soothing roots in healing cultural practices and the natural world. Her broad cultural experiences—both personal and professional—lend her an authentic authority to share the cultural humility that we all seek as therapists. Her experiences have vastly enriched her therapeutic approaches, which she generously shares with us in this book. She has seamlessly woven ecotherapy with EMDR in lovely iterations of connections among ourselves—our *whole* selves, the natural world, and ancient practices of art and healing. There were many moments while reading this book where I thought, 'Yes! Yes! This is how the healing journey can be expanded and supported!' I could not help but think that Marchand has not only given us powerful therapeutic tools. Far beyond that, she has offered an opportunity to immerse ourselves—both personally and professionally—in rich cultural vitality and in joyful reunion with the natural world, our true home. I enthusiastically recommend that therapists read this book and take to heart its grounding and healing practices."

—**Kathy Steele, MN, CS,** psychotherapist, consultant, trainer, and author

"Jennifer Marchand is one of the important voices challenging the status quo in the EMDR community. *Ecotherapy-Informed EMDR* is an important contribution to the EMDR world's body of knowledge, and I am particularly impressed with its attunement to cultural responsiveness and connection to the natural world. Marchand's depathologizing tone and voice throughout the book will be much appreciated by trauma survivors, especially those living with dissociative experiences. I truly enjoyed reading this book and learned a great deal from Marchand's lived experience with offering EMDR therapy globally."

—**Jamie Marich, PhD, LPCC-S, REAT,** founder, Institute for Creative Mindfulness, and author of *Dissociation Made Simple* and *EMDR Made Simple*

"This remarkable book, emerging from the author's work in diverse global cultures, provides a model for conducting local and global therapy that is centered on cultural humility and curiosity. Some of the most consistent points of tension in EMDR training communities relate to fidelity versus flexibility. As this book illustrates, therapies not grounded in relevant language, resources, materials, metaphors, and meaning-making are unlikely to be helpful. This book provides many examples of culturally relevant ways to engage in each of the phases of EMDR therapy. In this approach, what is helpful and powerful in EMDR therapy has the space and permission to metabolize into what is helpful and powerful in the client's internal and external worlds."

—**Thomas Zimmerman, MSEd, LPCC,** EMDR-approved consultant and trainer

"Jennifer Marchand's *Ecotherapy-Informed EMDR* is an inspiring and innovative guide for therapists seeking to integrate nature into their EMDR practice. With a blend of creativity and practicality, Marchand introduces readers to groundbreaking ways of using natural elements to enhance healing. Her approach enriches the therapeutic process and aligns with the growing recognition of nature's profound impact on mental health. The emphasis on cultural humility ensures that her methods are adaptable to diverse populations, fostering inclusivity in practice. In a time when therapy is evolving to embrace holistic methods, this book serves as a beacon for those looking to deepen their connection with clients through the healing power of nature."

—**Jocelyn Fitzgerald, LMFT,** art therapy and EMDR consultant

"A groundbreaking exploration of EMDR through an anti-oppressive and culturally responsive lens, this book is an essential resource for therapists trained in Western frameworks working in non-Western and Indigenous contexts. With deep respect for traditional healing practices and an understanding of colonial violence and its generational impacts, Jennifer offers an anti-oppressive lens to psychotherapy, making EMDR more accessible and adaptable for diverse communities. The nature-based framework integrates creative arts, ecotherapy, and embodied approaches to enhance trauma reprocessing, and the innovative visual mapping techniques make complex concepts accessible and applicable across diverse settings. A must-have for EMDR therapists seeking to expand their practice with cultural humility, creativity, and a decolonized approach to healing."

—**Olivia Scobie, MSW, RSW, MA, ACC, MSP,** founder, Canadian Perinatal Mental Health Trainings, and author of *Impossible Parenting: Creating a New Culture of Mental Health for Parents*

"Jennifer integrates EMDR with ecotherapy and creative arts to amplify trauma treatment across diverse cultural contexts. She makes a clarion call for therapists to consider generational trauma and to prioritize culturally responsive care. This thorough guide offers practical strategies that allow therapists to seamlessly integrate visual timelines, body-based techniques, nature-focused practices, and her transformative journey storytelling method into EMDR preparation. If you are invested in augmenting your work with practical approaches to make EMDR more accessible and effective for clients from diverse backgrounds, this book provides an abundance of valuable insights—gems, in fact—to support clients' healing journeys and increase your confidence."

—**Oraine Ramoo,** EMDRIA-approved consultant

"Although Marchand's approach is rooted in neuroscience and the adaptive information processing (AIP) theory, she outlines for EMDR therapists a needed perspective that is most often missing in the Western clinical psychotherapy environment. Using nature-based metaphors and expressive and embodied practices, Marchand extends the reach of the EMDR eight-phase model, infusing it with an awareness of sociopolitical, cultural, environmental, and historical understandings while recognizing the wisdom of ancient healing practices. Her experience and knowledge as an EMDR consultant and practitioner who has worked internationally for decades provides a needed fresh voice for trauma treatment approaches that uphold the client's dignity and respects the relationship of nature and healing."

—**Elizabeth Davis,** editor and coauthor of *EMDR and Creative Arts Therapies*

"Trauma therapy is not easy, and we can no longer expect clients to sit on the couch and be able to tolerate challenging moments from their life. Jennifer's book outlines the tools on how to be a different kind of therapist. She artfully uses playful approaches, creativity, and the natural environment to titrate the hardest moments in someone's past. Jennifer's approaches on how to be an EMDR therapist provide every therapist the solution to be successful with any culture, any setting, and any age. Thank you, Jennifer, for the artistry, innovation, and inspiration!"

—**Annie Monaco, LCSW, RPT-S**

Ecotherapy-Informed EMDR

A Holistic and Creative Approach to Providing Culturally Responsive Trauma Treatment

Jennifer Marchand,
MA, CCC, CCTP-II, RCAT

Foreword by David Archer, author of *Anti-Racist Psychotherapy*

Ecotherapy-Informed EMDR

Published by
PESI Publishing, Inc.
3839 White Ave
Eau Claire, WI 54703

Cover and interior design by Michelle Lee Lagerroos
Editing by Jenessa Jackson, PhD

ISBN: 9781683738084 (print)
ISBN: 9781683738091 (ePUB)
ISBN: 9781683738107 (ePDF)

Printed in the United States of America.

Table of Contents

FOREWORD

We need a revolution in psychotherapy. Today, the challenges of our world are vastly different from those of the past. The worries that our clients bring into our offices now—war, climate change, social media, and even the West's growing acceptance of fascism—demand new solutions. You don't need me to tell you this; turn on the news and you'll see it. Suffering isn't that hard to find. As therapists, we lend an ear to the stories of trauma survivors, and we have a responsibility to tend to the woundings of their darkest secrets.

However, those of us who think deeply about our field inevitably turn our attention inward. When we hold a mirror up to ourselves, we must ask: Do our clients genuinely feel understood? Are we meeting their needs with our approaches? Instead of molding people to fit our therapy, is it possible to craft a therapy together with them? These questions need innovative solutions, and Jennifer Marchand's groundbreaking approach places us in the right direction.

When Jen asked me to write this foreword, I was honored. From the moment I picked up this book, I couldn't put it down. Perhaps it was our similarities. Perhaps it was our differences. I am a Black Jamaican Canadian of African descent living in Montreal; she is a white Canadian of Acadian descent living in Addis Ababa. We have both developed therapeutic approaches that use creative arts, memory reconsolidation, and Africentric principles for transformative change.

We are both EMDRIA-approved EMDR consultants who spent our formative clinical years working with Indigenous communities in Canada—Jennifer with the Wit'suwit'en in the West, and I with the Kanien'kehá:ka in the East. We worked with survivors of state-sanctioned genocide and witnessed the devastating multigenerational impacts of colonialism, residential schools, addiction, and sexual violence. This work has been a calling for us. To respond to the call, we both trained in EMDR therapy and were drawn to the concepts of antiracist psychotherapy to provide culturally attuned ways of healing.

Jennifer Marchand is a revolutionary therapist. In this book, you will see how she masterfully weaves together EMDR therapy, ecotherapy, and the creative arts into a culturally responsive framework. This ability isn't just rooted in her therapeutic expertise but in who she is as an educator, a mother, and an ecocentric global citizen. Storytelling is deeply rooted in Acadian culture, and for Jennifer, metaphors come second nature to her. She shared that her knack for storytelling may trace back to her childhood in Cape Breton, when she would listen to the gripping tales told by her father about the mystical Lake Lakabouba. Her deep connection to regional identity, culture, and community also shaped her understanding of our interdependence with each other and the natural world. Her influences shine through in her work, where narrative, nature, and art serve as mediums for mental health recovery.

This book invites all of us—regardless of our backgrounds—to reflect on our practices. Trying new things can be intimidating, but art therapy isn't new. Healing through natural elements predates Western psychotherapy and even the concept of the West itself. Yet, art therapists still don't get the recognition they deserve. Jennifer's work challenges the status quo by demonstrating the transformative power of creativity and its rightful place within modern psychotherapy. Integrating sensory and body-based elements, traditional arts, and natural materials into our interventions can enhance our therapy, humanize our clinical work, and contribute to the infinite creativity of our clients. Therapy *must* evolve into a unique cocreation that honors the individuality of each client if it is to remain relevant for diverse cultural groups and future generations.

Jennifer's integrative ecotherapeutic approach is the answer we need. Each clinical hour brings a new experience. Her unique approach to EMDR honors the client's individuality by creating space for expression, such as the stones they choose, the colors and shapes they use, and even the "Zentangle patterns" they draw. The client's perspectives are mobilized to disconfirm the limiting beliefs of their oppressive pasts. Because many trauma survivors were traumatized without their consent, having choices both inside and outside of therapy is essential for recovery. Jennifer's integrative ecotherapeutic approach illustrates how art and nature can empower survivors to reclaim agency, cultivate playfulness, and experience joy.

Embodying cultural humility and anti-racist perspectives, Jennifer's work has taken her across continents, yet she remains grounded in her mission. Now residing in Ethiopia, she continues to teach, support, and advocate for global mental health. Her approach has made EMDR accessible in cultural contexts where traditional clinical language falls short. She humanizes trauma therapy in conflict-ridden areas. Her approach makes psychotherapy less about what's in our heads and more about what's in our hearts. In a world struggling with collective crises, Jennifer's approach to well-being cocreates solutions that are fresh, inspiring, and intuitive. By turning our attention to nature—to sticks, stones, and the wisdom of the earth—we reconnect with traditions that existed long before lines divided our nations and people. Her writings evoke an ancestral form of healing that has the potential to transform our future.

No matter your skill level, this book will resonate with you. If you are trained in EMDR, this book will offer refreshing perspectives and novel ways to guide your clients through the phases of trauma recovery. If you studied to be a creative arts therapist, this book will challenge you to think beyond a Eurocentric paradigm. And if you are neither an EMDR clinician nor a creative arts therapist, the pages that follow might just inspire you to sign up for your next training. We hope this book challenges your preconceptions, expands what you thought was possible, and moves you to not just read about revolutionary change, but to *be* about it.

Blessings and strength,

David Archer, PSW, MFT, MSW
Professional social worker, marriage and family therapist
Specialist in complex PTSD and racial trauma treatment
Author of *Anti-Racist Psychotherapy*
EMDRIA-approved consultant
Developer of Rhythm and Processing (RAP) strategies
Recipient of EMDRIA's 2024 Emerging Leader Award
https://archertherapy.com

PREFACE

My nature-based approach to **eye movement desensitization and reprocessing (EMDR)** has been shaped by over a decade of work in non-Western contexts and with Indigenous communities as a trauma therapist and trainer. I began my career in 2011 in Northwest British Columbia, Canada, on the unceded traditional territory of the Wit'suwit'en people. As a new practitioner working with Indigenous clients affected by sexual abuse and complex trauma, including the direct and generational impacts of colonial violence, I felt ill equipped to effectively respond to the profound need for healing I encountered. I quickly sought out training in EMDR as an evidence-based trauma treatment modality to bolster my work as an art therapist, but I struggled to find the language, metaphors, and tools that allowed me to bring EMDR into the communities I served in a culturally relevant and responsive way.

It wasn't until I received training in Indigenous psychotherapy and traditional healing practices—namely, **Indigenous focusing-oriented therapy (IFOT)**, developed by Shirley Turcotte, a Métis Knowledge Keeper and registered clinical counselor—that I was able to take a new perspective on EMDR as a healing modality and better understand how it intersects with traditional practices. This laid the groundwork for how I approach trauma therapy, guiding me to draw on the natural world to help EMDR resonate with clients across a range of settings and contexts.

In 2016, I moved to Vietnam and began supporting a team of psychologists working with survivors of human trafficking, a project founded by Chau Dinh, the head psychologist at Blue Dragon Children's Foundation. I recommended EMDR as a modality to reduce symptoms of acute distress, intrusive memories, and reexperiencing that resulted from the harrowing experiences that survivors were forced to endure, often for years or decades. I held a small introductory workshop on EMDR, but after sharing more about this treatment modality, it became clear that the terms used to describe EMDR's core concepts—such as adaptive information processing, three-pronged protocol, node, channel, and dysfunctionally stored material (to name a few)—were so complicated that practitioners could not grasp this powerful trauma treatment approach or see its appropriateness to their context. Not only did EMDR appear too complicated in its number of steps, but the terms lost context and meaning when translated into Vietnamese.

It was by drawing on the natural world and nature-based metaphors—which I learned in IFOT to be a fundamental component of trauma healing—that I was able to explain the core concepts of EMDR in familiar and more accessible ways. This allowed the team to grasp the concepts and find the appropriate words in their own language that conveyed the same meaning. Their motivation to learn EMDR increased, and we successfully organized the first-ever EMDR training in Vietnam with the support of EMDR Asia and Trauma Recovery/Humanitarian Assistance Programs (HAP). Blue Dragon Children's Foundation now uses EMDR as an integral part of its comprehensive and holistic services for survivors, and they continue to develop a sense of ownership over the scripts and practices within their context. Chau Dinh is also now a consultant-in-training with Trauma Recovery/HAP and is in the process of founding EMDR Vietnam.

I have since worked in a diverse range of settings and cultural contexts as a clinician, consultant, and trainer, which has allowed me to continue to build on these foundational experiences. In 2019, I began working with Medica Mondiale, an international women's rights organization, training health professionals in conflict-affected regions on the implementation of trauma-sensitive health care for survivors of sexual and gender-based violence. Alongside my work with Medica Mondiale, I have maintained a private practice focused on providing specialized online trauma treatment to people living in underserved settings, primarily in the Global South. I am also involved in various projects in Ethiopia, where I have been based since 2021, providing trauma therapy to Ethiopian frontline workers who are supporting survivors of sexual violence. In addition, I work very closely with a team of Ethiopian EMDR therapists to whom I offer consultation as well as monthly training sessions on specialized topics, including burnout prevention and self-care.

Combining EMDR with ecotherapy and the creative arts has allowed me to enhance cultural responsiveness in my approach to trauma recovery as a therapist and trainer. In this book, I hope to expand the work that I have been doing by providing EMDR therapists everywhere with a fresh reconceptualization of EMDR that breaks free from the Western and patriarchal ways of viewing healing and trauma recovery. I hope to offer clinicians from a diversity of backgrounds a novel way to connect with EMDR and to present it to their clients and communities in a way that supports their healing and transformation. With this possibility in mind, I invite you to continue reading and find out how this novel framework can be a welcoming and refreshing way to include more diverse perspectives and practices into the field of EMDR.

INTRODUCTION

There is a heightened awareness of the need for cultural humility, cultural competence, and cultural responsiveness in the field of trauma, especially since the COVID-19 pandemic exposed—and also exacerbated—many deep-seated social inequalities that have existed in our society for decades. The increased exposure to these inequalities brought powerful momentum to long-standing social justice movements in North America and globally, such as #BlackLivesMatter, #MeToo, and #FridaysForFuture, which have highlighted the importance of understanding trauma within a sociopolitical, cultural, environmental, and historical context, especially when working with clients who identify as Black, Indigenous, and People of Color (BIPOC).

In addition, large-scale migration and displacement events are increasing globally due to conflict, extreme violence, severe economic and political instability, and the impacts of environmental and climate change. There are currently more refugees in the world than ever before, driving the need for more culturally responsive trauma therapies that meet the needs of clients from diverse cultural backgrounds, especially as the prevalence of **posttraumatic stress disorder (PTSD)** among refugee and migrant populations is particularly high.

One revolutionary treatment approach that has shown promise in the treatment of trauma is EMDR, which is an evidence-based treatment that unblocks and accelerates the body's natural and innate healing capacities (Shapiro, 2018). Despite being a well-established treatment approach, the language used to describe the phases, working mechanisms, and treatment effects of EMDR can feel overly clinical, making it difficult to introduce this approach to clients in accessible and culturally responsive ways. Current conceptualizations of EMDR also obscure how this treatment approach is resonant across cultures and how it overlaps with traditional healing practices that have existed since before the advent of the biomedical model.

That is where this book can help. Based on my experiences working with clients of diverse backgrounds and in non-Western and Indigenous settings, I have found that connecting the core concepts of EMDR to the natural world provides an intuitive and universally understood reference point for effective intercultural practice. With that in mind, this book introduces a fresh, ecological consciousness into EMDR through nature-based language, metaphors, and materials that are presented in a comprehensive yet easily understandable way. In particular, this book aims to shift the field of trauma recovery from a Eurocentric to an **ecocentric** perspective to foster more profound healing for all clients. Whereas a Eurocentric understanding of the mind disconnects it from the body, relationships, and nature, an ecocentric perspective recognizes the interdependent and interconnected relationship of the mind to the body, to social support systems, and to the natural world (Summers & Vivian, 2018).

From this ecocentric lens, the comprehensive framework presented in this book ties the eight phases of EMDR together through nature-based metaphors, making it easier to learn and apply to clinical practice. These metaphors are important ingredients of ecotherapy and provide a powerful way to enhance healing in trauma recovery. For example, the **three-pronged protocol** used in EMDR (past, present, future) can be explained as the three strands of a braid or the branches of a river that flow and weave into each other. Since they are interconnected, we have to work with the material held in each strand or branch to provide the most thorough healing.

Another metaphor involves reconceptualizing the **adaptive information processing (AIP) system** as the innate system of integration and healing that flows within each of us like an internal river. The flow of the river breaks down our experiences and carries them toward wholeness and resolution. However, when an experience is too big, it cannot move with the river or get broken down; it stays stuck in that place, causing debris to pile up around it, burying it and blocking the flow of the water. This blockage can lead to flooding or even drought over time. The internal river metaphor reinforces that we are the source of our own healing and offers hope that we naturally have the capacity to move toward healing so long as we can unblock the flow of our internal river.

By connecting the core concepts of EMDR to metaphors from the natural world, the healing components of EMDR become more accessible and visible, allowing it to feel familiar and resonate with clients in diverse settings. Nature-based and creative approaches also lay the foundation for therapists to integrate more culturally relevant practices into their work and strengthen the client's connection to their cultural identity, such as through the use of certain materials, music and rhythm, or movement practices. Indeed, reclaiming culture is central to many social justice movements, including within the field of mental health. However, it is important to recognize that these body- and nature-based elements are not new. We must honor that these practices have roots in ancient traditions that are still a living part of many Indigenous and non-Western cultures and also acknowledge the communities that are reclaiming their practices in the face of colonization and oppression.

Chapter Overview

The overall structure of this book is organized by the eight phases of the EMDR standard protocol. Chapters 1 through 4 lay the theoretical foundation for integrating art- and nature-based strategies into EMDR and the treatment of complex trauma across various cultural contexts. Chapters 5 to 10 focus on the practical application of these strategies across all eight phases of the EMDR protocol, with accompanying infographics, scripts, and case examples.

Chapter 1 expands our understanding of trauma by discussing the trauma-informed model of care and describing diverse cultural perspectives on trauma, including various forms of psychological wounding like race-based trauma and generational wounding. Chapter 2 presents research demonstrating how the creative arts can enhance trauma work in intercultural contexts, especially with refugee populations. The eight core benefits of integrating the creative arts into EMDR are outlined, as well as how the arts can enhance cultural humility among therapists.

Chapter 3 discusses ecocentric versus Eurocentric perspectives and practices, highlighting the therapeutic benefits of embedding EMDR into an ecocentric model of healing. The field of eco-art therapy is presented as an approach to creatively integrate nature-based materials and metaphors into trauma work, specifically EMDR, to enhance healing and cultural connection. Chapter 4 provides a comprehensive ecocentric framework for understanding the eight phases of the EMDR standard protocol, including nature-based metaphors to describe the AIP model, memory reconsolidation theory, reprocessing, and the three-pronged protocol.

Chapter 5 moves into phase 1 of EMDR—history taking and treatment planning—and describes a trauma-sensitive and culturally responsive approach for gathering histories and mapping out treatment through the use of visual timelines. Chapters 6 and 7 both focus on phase 2: preparation. In particular, chapter 6 presents two art-based strategies to enhance stabilization (the Zentangle drawing method and the transformative journey storytelling method), while chapter 7 presents body- and nature-based approaches that increase stabilization and enhance readiness for reprocessing. This ensures that the process is predictable and the client feels like an active participant in each phase of EMDR.

Chapter 8 breaks down the phases of assessment (phase 3) and desensitization and reprocessing (phase 4) using a mountain metaphor. A thorough description of this metaphor is provided alongside illustrations, scripts, and procedural steps. A containment script is also provided for incomplete reprocessing. Chapter 9 walks you through the steps of phases 5 through 8. It first focuses on how to help clients reclaim and restore beliefs about the self via positive installation (phase 5), followed by nature-based techniques to clear out any residual somatic material after reprocessing (phase 6). It then discusses how to complete processing and "come off the mountain" (phase 7) and how to "revisit the mountain" to check progress and emotional charge (phase 8). Finally, chapter 10 focuses on working with clusters, including attachment trauma, and presents a nature-based approach for processing preverbal trauma.

Ultimately, it is my hope that this book illustrates how the mind-body connection, breathwork, movement, rhythm, connection to nature, and creativity are central to how we treat trauma. Not only do these approaches have the potential to enhance intercultural effectiveness, but they invite the client to engage in the therapeutic process in a more restorative and relational way. Although Western psychology is finally starting to acknowledge these other ways of knowing and exploring the full potential of these healing practices, the full benefits of EMDR can only be realized when it incorporates the wisdom of other cultural perspectives—wisdom that is rooted in ancient and traditional healing practices.

Indeed, many of our ancestors had a sacred, interdependent relationship with nature, a connection that has been lost through modernization and industrialization in many societies. It is imperative that we restore this connection with nature in order for healing and transformation to occur. Nature provides hope and comfort that intrinsically supports healing, which is why we have a natural impulse to connect with nature during hardship, adversity, and loss. Within these pages, let me show you how nature-based metaphors can carve a pathway for clinicians to expand approaches to healing and increase cultural responsiveness within the field of EMDR.

CHAPTER 1

Theoretical Foundations of Trauma

This chapter on trauma lays the foundation for the subsequent chapters on creative and nature-based approaches to healing trauma with clients across diverse cultural contexts. It makes sense to begin with what we are working with before we move into *how* to work with it. Therefore, this chapter explores the evolution of the field of trauma and makes the case that continuing to expand the definition and diagnostic criteria of trauma is necessary for culturally responsive care.

Recognizing the Prevalence of Trauma

Our understanding of trauma has evolved and broadened over the past few decades. We have moved beyond a narrow definition of **trauma** as extreme events that are outside the realm of normal human experience, such as armed conflict, and have begun to encompass a wider range of events that are or can be perceived as threatening, including those that are cumulative, complex, and even covert in nature. The high prevalence of trauma in our society is now well established by several groundbreaking studies, such as the Adverse Childhood Experiences (ACE) Study (Felitti et al., 1998) and the Women, Co-Occurring Disorders, and Violence Study (McHugo et al., 2005). These studies created the impetus to recognize exposure to trauma as the norm rather than the exception and have since fueled the movement of trauma-informed care across mental health, primary care, education, and other sectors, where responding to the needs of survivors is crucial to the safe provision of services and the prevention of retraumatization (Classen & Clark, 2017).

Judith Herman's (1992) seminal book *Trauma and Recovery* helped place trauma, as well as healing, in a relational context and increased our understanding of the complexities of interpersonal trauma and violence. She highlighted the role that power and oppressive systems play in trauma. In turn, we have come to recognize that at the core of trauma is often an imbalance of power where one person, group, or system exerts power over another, rendering an individual or group powerless. The harm caused by this abuse of power is the very definition of violence, which is why the **trauma- and violence-informed care (TVIC)** model introduced in Canada highlights the importance of keeping power dynamics at the forefront of trauma-informed care (Wathen et al., 2021). This model helps us understand the connection between trauma and forms of interpersonal and systemic violence—including the impacts of gender inequality, racism, heterosexism, ableism, ageism, and all forms of oppression and discrimination—and draws attention to the need for systems and providers to ensure culturally safe and equity-oriented services.

The demand for TVIC practices across an increasing number of sectors is encouraging. For example, I was invited to present at the Berlin Human Rights Film Festival in 2020 to speak to filmmakers and journalists on the needs of trauma survivors so that their stories could be documented and shared in ways that are safe, empowering, and uphold their dignity. I described the importance of offering trauma survivors increased choice and control over the process, teaching them stabilization skills that they can practice throughout storytelling sessions. In addition, a large part of my work over the past five years with Medica Mondiale has involved supporting trauma-sensitivity training for health professionals who work with survivors of sexual and gender-based violence in conflict-affected settings. In these contexts, self-care and staff care must be at the core of trauma-sensitivity training, given that health-care staff (and their families) are subjected to the same conflict conditions as their patients.

The Three *E*'s of Trauma

The word *trauma* is often charged and laden with multiple meanings, associations, and even stigma. One way to unpack some of the meaning the term carries is to use the three *e*'s of trauma, in which we refer not only to the traumatic **event** itself but also to the **experience** and the **effects** of trauma (Substance Abuse and Mental Health Services Administration, 2014). This more comprehensive understanding shifts the emphasis from a specific incident that is objectively defined as traumatic (the event) and incorporates the subjective experiences of survivors, their perception of the event, and the worldview through which they make sense of and ascribe meaning to the event (the experience). The three *e*'s also acknowledge the short- and long-term impacts of events, including how intersecting sociopolitical factors shape people's exposure and response to events (e.g., level of access to resources, protection, support), the aftermath of events, and potential vulnerabilities that may lead to further retraumatization (the effects).

Validating a client's subjective experiences of distress, as well as the personal and external circumstances that influenced the impact of events, can also help equalize the power dynamics within the therapeutic relationship. It underlines that the therapist's role is not to determine what is traumatic or not based on diagnosis or expertise but to appropriately respect and respond to the client's need for healing from experiences that caused harm, whatever the source. As Rebecca Kase (2023) states in her book *Polyvagal-Informed EMDR*, the field of trauma has focused on the event as an indicator of trauma for too long, as opposed to centering the client's experience. Limiting the definition of trauma can perpetuate suffering and shame because it fails to recognize and name certain experiences that cause harm, dismisses the impacts of certain experiences, reinforces the isolation and invisibility of the client's experience, and reenacts power differentials.

Continuing to broaden our understanding of trauma to encompass multiple perspectives and lived experiences also allows for more effective and culturally responsive trauma treatment. When working with individuals who have experienced collective and historical oppression and adversity, such as members of the BIPOC community, LGBTQ2S+

individuals, and other minoritized groups, it is essential not to limit trauma to the individual level. For example, David Archer (2024) expands the definition of racial trauma to include three interconnected aspects: the multigenerational legacy of trauma, present-day oppression, and the social acceptance of suffering.

As EMDR therapists, we need a broader understanding of trauma to be able to recognize, access, and process a diversity of experiences that impact clients' well-being, including any form of abuse, violation, betrayal, discrimination, marginalization, exclusion, chronic stress, gender-based violence, mass violence, race-based trauma, vicarious trauma, preverbal trauma, attachment trauma, medical trauma, reproductive trauma, ecological grief, natural disasters and climate breakdown, moral injuries, spiritual trauma, chronic stress, conflict, and displacement. We also need the awareness and skills to open up space and allow clients to access distress rooted in collective trauma so that they can process the multigenerational impacts of colonization, war, genocide, and oppression and situate suffering and harm in a sociopolitical and historical context as appropriate. As Sandra Grossman and colleagues (2021) point out, "A collective approach to understanding trauma gives the ability to look upstream at the root causes of ACEs, to see trauma as embedded in collective and structural elements of history, systemic oppressions, and racism" (p. 1).

Defining Traumatic Events

A simple way to speak with clients about events that may cause trauma is any experience that is "too much, too fast, or too soon." This definition is increasingly used in the field, including by Resmaa Menakem (2017) in *My Grandmother's Hands*. The phrase "not enough for too long" has also been used to describe the harm caused by more covert experiences of neglect during the developmental years. It can also encompass chronic poverty, deprivation, or the impact of resources being withheld or unavailable, such as in low-resource and conflict-affected settings. I would also add "too heavy, too ongoing" to capture the cumulative quality of experiences of suffering and hardship that are endured over time, such as discrimination and displacement as well as the weight of emotional burdens like complicated grief and loss.

Combining these phrases can encompass a broad range of personal and collective experiences in a way that supports therapeutic work with clients from diverse backgrounds and identities. Presenting trauma as "experiences and circumstances that are too much, too fast; not enough for too long; or too heavy, too ongoing" resonates for many clients. It makes sense that such experiences can cause distress and impact various dimensions of health and well-being. I sometimes add that "these experiences can simply be too much for our brains to make sense of, too much for our bodies to hold, and too much for our souls to heal." This approach helps explain how experiences can overwhelm the mind and body's ability to cope with and process through events. As a result, we may struggle to return to a state of safety and equilibrium.

Having such a relatable and accessible definition of trauma reduces defensive and reflexive responses such as "I have never experienced trauma." It creates space for clients to reflect on and recognize experiences that may have impacted them throughout their lifespan or their lineage, laying the foundation for thorough and effective information gathering in phase 1 of EMDR.

Defining Experiences of Trauma

Medical terminology is largely derived from classical languages such as Latin or Greek. For example, *trauma* is the Greek word for *wound* and has been used in the medical field since the 17th century to describe severe or critical physical injury resulting from an external source. In the mid to late 1900s, it was expanded to refer to psychological and emotional injuries caused by extreme or catastrophic events (Figley et al., 2017). Despite psychological trauma being a relatively new Western medical concept, there is some evidence that knowledge of psychological trauma has existed throughout human history, such as through ancient medical manuscripts, writing, and mythology, including old Greek epics like *The Iliad* and *The Odyssey* (Figley et al., 2017).

The oldest evidence dates back to the ancient writings of the Sumerians in southern Mesopotamia (modern-day Iraq and Kuwait) from around 1900 BCE, when the reactions of citizens akin to posttraumatic stress were recorded on cuneiform stones following the destruction of the city of Ur, referred to as "The Lamentation Over the Destruction of Ur" (Ben-Ezra, 2004). Such depictions are important as they show early understandings of psychological distress and disturbance (such as sleeplessness, anxiety, and flashbacks) in direct response to external events rather than due to supernatural powers (Figley et al., 2017).

Returning to the original Greek meaning of trauma as a wound often resonates with clients and carries over well into different contexts and work with diverse communities. The term *wound* is not only nonpathologizing—as it speaks to the impact or injury that results from something external rather than internal—but it also seems to intuitively speak to the experience of being psychologically or emotionally harmed by an event. For example, during my recent work in Ethiopia with humanitarian aid organizations, a staff member living and working in Tigray (where there had been a recent civil war) stated, "We have wounded minds." This powerful statement expressed the deep and lasting imprint of what they experienced as a community and how loss and suffering continue despite the end of active conflict. Similarly, in Eduardo Duran's (2019) book *Healing the Soul Wound*, the term *soul wound* was identified as a term used by Indigenous communities to speak to the deep impact that historical trauma has had on their people, such as the carrying of deep ancestral trauma.

Trauma as a wound is also a helpful metaphor because it carries a certain hope that we can heal with the right conditions for stabilization and support. As with physical wounds, we also have innate mechanisms that help us move through and recover from psychological injury. A metaphor proposed by Babette Rothschild (2017) in *The Body Remembers* is of the broken bone: When a bone breaks, we stabilize it with a cast or brace; while this does not heal the broken bone on its own, it holds the bone in place so that it can begin to regenerate new tissue and repair itself spontaneously. We do not have to tell our bodies how to heal; we naturally and gradually heal when the conditions are right.

Although some individuals may recover from experiences of trauma and adversity on their own or within their existing social supports, the responsibility should never be placed on individuals to repair their traumas in isolation. It is our work as trauma therapists to help create the conditions for healing for our clients and our collective responsibility as a society to create the right conditions for healing through TVIC, social support, solidarity, justice, and reconciliation.

Defining Effects of Trauma

Some wounds heal with time, especially when there is a supportive and safe environment in which to move through the psychological, emotional, and physiological reactions to a traumatic event. But when a wound cannot heal, the pain and distress of the event continue to impact the individual. The continued pain—alongside the behaviors the person engages in to avoid and cope with the pain—can be understood as posttraumatic stress. While it is not always necessary to diagnose traumatic stress as a disorder (although it can certainly be helpful and validating in some cases), it is important to recognize the profound and ongoing effects of unresolved traumatic wounds and to help clients make sense of how they contribute to the reactions, behaviors, and patterns that get in the way of their well-being.

It is important to remember that these behavioral patterns are adaptive and protective. You can think of them as attempts to put bandages and layers of protection around the wound to prevent it from being touched, exposed, and reexperienced. Although this provides short-term relief and allows the individual to function and move forward following a distressing event, all the layers of protection and avoidance prevent the wound from getting fully attended to and healed. So long as the wound stays under the surface, the original pain persists in the mind and body on some level, and the threat of reexperiencing that pain remains. Internal and external reminders of the event can unexpectedly break through and get under the bandages, touching the wound and causing its original pain to be felt. As reminders continue to break through, the wound can deepen or even become infected, metaphorically speaking, as the distress becomes generalized to other associated stimuli and the pain of the wound increases. This pattern heightens the fear of the original wound, leading to more bandages and protective strategies for the individual to cope and adjust.

Diverse Understandings of the Effects of Trauma

Research from the field of transcultural psychiatry suggests that although there are some consistent patterns in how humans respond to psychological trauma, such as nightmares and disrupted sleep (Kirmayer, 2019), cultural norms and scripts also play a significant role in the ways that people cope with and adjust to trauma (Chentsova-Dutton & Maercker, 2019). Therefore, when working with clients in diverse cultural contexts, it is important to acknowledge that posttraumatic stress can manifest in ways that do not easily fit into the core DSM-5 and ICD-11 categories of PTSD or **complex posttraumatic stress disorder (C-PTSD)**. For example, among many cultural groups, there is more emphasis on physical symptoms (e.g., headaches, digestive issues, feeling cold), grief and mourning, disrupted relationships, and spirituality (e.g., supernatural experiences with ghosts and visitations). For some clients, it is not even as relevant whether or not they meet any specific diagnostic criteria; instead, their overall experience of disharmony and imbalance is more important, as Eduardo Duran (2019) speaks to in his work with Indigenous populations.

Understanding how different cultural groups express their experiences of distress—called **idioms of distress**—is an important area of inquiry in the field of transcultural psychiatry. Laurence Kirmayer and colleagues (1998) state that although distress resulting from traumatic events can be observed across many cultures, there are often local idioms used to express experiences of distress. One example is from Rwanda, where one of the few psychiatrists practicing at the time of the 1994 genocide spoke of "lungs without breath" (Chentsova-Dutton & Maercker, 2019). This idiom may overlap with the Western concept of a panic attack, but it is always important to listen for idioms of distress and cultural expressions of distress in order to center the client's experience.

In my experiences working in countries such as Vietnam and Ethiopia as well as in Indigenous communities in northern Canada, leaving out the spiritual effects of trauma dismisses a primary dimension of experience. It is crucial that EMDR therapists listen to their clients' experiences and presenting concerns with curiosity and openness, creating space to validate and respond to their experiences of distress from the client's worldview—rather than trying to fit the client's experiences into a Western model that may not feel entirely resonant or helpful to their healing journey.

I often present an overview of eight domains of distress that can be helpful in explaining the effects of trauma to clients. The aim is to normalize and help clients make sense of their experiences of distress to reduce feelings of shame. These eight domains are adapted from the core PTSD and C-PTSD symptoms as presented in the DSM-5 and ICD-11, respectively, and are expanded to include areas that have felt helpful and relevant to the communities I have worked with. These adaptations echo the work of Chentsova-Dutton and Maercker (2019), which demonstrates the need for further emphasis on physical symptoms, grief and mourning, disrupted relationships, and spirituality to provide more culturally responsive understandings of trauma.

The Eight Domains of Distress

1. **Imbalance of energy:** Upsetting experiences can leave us with too much energy, called *hyperarousal*, or too little energy, called *hypoarousal*. In a state of hyperarousal, the body can feel unsettled, like it is always on alert, always ready to react. It is like there is excess energy that can lead to anxiety, irritability, jumpiness, and restlessness. It can feel difficult to experience a sense of safety or calm in the present moment, as if the threat were still present. This can lead to fear, terror, or panic, like fast breathing and elevated heart rate. The excess energy in our bodies can also cause poor sleep, changes in appetite, attention difficulties, and a feeling of being distracted or disconnected from daily life. In a state of hypoarousal, we may feel like our energy has been drained, like there is a heaviness or exhaustion; this can make it difficult to react to things in the ways we would like to be able to.
2. **Reexperiencing/reliving:** When we reexperience the past, it can suddenly feel as though the event is happening all over again, as if we are back in that time. We can reexperience any element of the past in our minds (e.g., thoughts and images) as well as in our bodies (e.g., emotions, sensations, physical pain, discomfort, loss of feeling, numbness, tension, digestive issues). We may also experience urges to move, fight, run, or hide, like our bodies are still responding to the event. Sensory cues from the environment can remind us of the event, causing the memory to come back into our present awareness. We may also have frightening or upsetting dreams that might even repeat specific moments from the event.

3. **Avoidance:** There is often an effort (consciously or unconsciously) to avoid thinking or feeling anything about the upsetting event and to stay away from any reminders of it. The need to avoid distressing thoughts, feelings, or sensations may lead to behaviors that help us push the event out of our minds, such as distraction, overworking, self-harm, numbing out, behavioral addiction, substance use, or dissociation. We may change our routines to reduce or remove any reminders of the event, including avoiding people, places, and things that cause distress, even if they used to create happiness before the upsetting event happened.
4. **Changes in mood and thought patterns:** After upsetting events, we may lack interest in things that used to bring us joy and find it difficult to laugh or feel happy. We may even feel detached from our lives or have a sense that things are not real. Often, we may feel a sense of responsibility for what happened, accompanied by a sense of shame and guilt, which can create feelings of heaviness or powerlessness in our bodies. In our thoughts, we may have a hard time remembering aspects of the events—they may feel fragmented or hard to piece together—making it hard to make sense of the event or why or how it happened. We can experience low mood, sadness, grief, and a loss of hope for the future.
5. **Changes in beliefs about ourselves:** Upsetting events can change how we feel about ourselves, such as our worth, lovability, and sense of belonging. We may notice more negative thinking about ourselves, like *There is something wrong with me*, *I am a failure*, or *There is nothing worth believing in*. In some cases, we may feel like we've lost our sense of identity or a part of ourselves, like we're changed or damaged in a way that cannot be repaired. These changes in self-concept not only decrease our self-esteem, but they can reduce the sense of agency we have over our lives, rendering us unable to make decisions or act in ways to take care of ourselves and assert our needs.

6. **Imbalance of emotions:** Upsetting events can make our emotions feel imbalanced: they may feel too big, too little, or out of control. It may feel harder to calm down or hard to feel anything at all. We may react more to things around us and may feel more upset by the things people say or do. We may feel overwhelmed by the sensations and emotions that come up in our internal world and need to disconnect from them in order to cope. This can lead to numbing-out behaviors that help push feelings away or shut them down so that we feel more in control. We may also feel exhausted, like our emotions are just too much or too heavy.
7. **Loss of trust and social well-being:** It can feel more difficult to trust others and experience a sense of meaningful connection in relationships after an upsetting event. It is as if a trust has been broken. We may react differently to people and notice ourselves withdrawing from those close to us. We may avoid social gatherings, even if attending those social events felt good and enjoyable before. Sometimes we might feel like we cannot share our story or feelings with others, making it difficult to feel real or genuine with others, like there is distance or detachment. We may even fear relationships or any amount of closeness or intimacy.
8. **Changes in spiritual well-being:** Upsetting events can sometimes change our sense of connection with the spiritual world and cause us to question our beliefs, such as the purpose and meaning in life. We may even feel a loss of trust in God or our belief systems, asking ourselves, *How could this happen?* We may experience a sense of disconnection or imbalance with the spiritual world or shifts in our connection with God, spirits, or ancestors. At the same time, we may also seek a deeper connection with our spiritual beliefs for understanding, comfort, and healing.

The Memory as the Wound

As discussed earlier, traumatic memories are like wounds under the bandages. These unresolved memories are not stored in the same way as normal memories because they are not integrated into long-term memory, as part of one's past or as part of a coherent life narrative. Instead, **unresolved memories** are often stored as fragmented experiences without a clear sense of time. These memories are stored differently because traumatic stress overwhelms the brain regions that allow events to be recorded as verbal, declarative memories (Bremner, 2006). As a result, traumatic memories can be relived as if they are happening in the present. It is as if the wound remains open and unhealed, making it susceptible to being touched—that is, triggered—in its unprocessed state.

Indeed, unresolved traumatic memories often carry a very vivid and powerful emotional charge that can be easily triggered by sensory cues from the environment. However, these traumatic memories are not always consciously remembered when someone is triggered. Rather, they are often reexperienced or relived in the form of sensations, images, beliefs, feelings, or even actions that are connected to the traumatic event (Levine, 2008). As such, it can be difficult for the person reliving a traumatic memory to know that what they are experiencing is a body-based memory. To them, it feels like the event is happening in the present, and the brain lacks a coherent story to make it clear that this experience is from the past (Fisher, 2017). Nontraumatic memories, on the other hand, tend to lose their vividness and emotional charge with time, and they can be recalled without feeling like it is happening again and without losing orientation to the present moment.

To further this metaphor, you can think of healed traumatic memories like scar tissue. Sue Genest, a Canadian EMDR trainer, drew this analogy in a training I took with her in 2014. She stated that although memories can leave a lasting mark, they are no longer an open wound; the person can remember what happened, and it might feel sensitive or uncomfortable to the touch, but they do not experience the original pain as if it is happening again. Understanding the reliving quality of unprocessed traumatic memories can help clients make sense of their present distress. It can also help them understand why accessing the unresolved material under the bandages is often necessary for sustainable healing, with scar tissue being the goal of treatment, rather than additional layers of bandages.

Generational Wounds as Presenting Memories

When pain is too unbearable for one generation to heal, or the environment is not safe enough for the pain to be resolved, then it can get passed on from one generation to the next. When this occurs, the distressing material that clients access in sessions may be rooted in **collective and generational trauma.** This is like peeling back the layers of bandages and finding that the wound underneath is older than the client, and was passed on to them from a previous generation.

Trauma can be transferred directly from one generation to the next through patterns of coping within a family lineage, which can include emotion dysregulation, dissociation, and addictions. These coping mechanisms can interfere with a child's ability to form healthy attachments, especially if the caregiver is dealing with their own unresolved trauma, which is a strong predictor of attachment trauma (Siegel, 1999). Trauma can also be transferred more indirectly through caregiver-child interactions that lack family cohesion and connectedness or that are devoid of warmth and parental involvement (Sangalang et al., 2017). Maternal stress can also lead to intergenerational trauma by impacting fetal development (Kinsella & Monk, 2009). In particular, when there are excess stress hormones in the mother's body, it can increase stress in the developing fetus, reducing the infant's ability to tolerate stress or experience a sense of calm and safety throughout their lifespan.

There is also emerging research in the field of epigenetics showing that traumatic wounds can be passed from one generation to the next (Jawaid et al., 2018). This research shows that our genes are turned "on" and "off" by certain environmental or psychosocial stressors, which can impact how we cope with adversity and can even influence what personality traits we develop. When certain genes are turned on in caregivers—for example, genes associated with higher stress sensitivity—these can be passed down to the next generation, while genes that are turned off or suppressed are not carried forward. In other words, the genes that helped our ancestors survive and adapt to their environment (e.g., genes associated with a heightened fight, flight, freeze response) are the ones that are passed on, even if they no longer serve us now.

The carrying forward of trauma can also be facilitated by society through ongoing discrimination, oppression, and stigmatization—both overt and covert (Gump, 2010). The ongoing stressors of racial trauma, for example, can result in epigenetic changes in one generation that influence the physiological and psychological vulnerabilities of subsequent generations (Archer, 2021). In this case, it can be adaptive and protective to pass on patterns of protection and coping to the next generation because the environment may continue to be unsafe, oppressive, and threatening from one generation to the next.

Healing Psychological Wounds with EMDR

EMDR uses Francine Shapiro's (2018) AIP model as a theoretical framework to explain trauma and conceptualize treatment. The AIP system is our innate system of integration and healing that moves our experiences toward resolution. The advantage of the AIP model is that it allows you to work with memory-based distress, with material from experiences in the past that did not get fully integrated, resolved, and healed. You can work with the wound under the bandages, sometimes without even knowing what explicit event caused the wound. Memories can be reprocessed so long as you can locate the wound and access the unresolved material held in it. The wound may be generational, implicit, collective, or personal.

In EMDR, you are not working with the actual event that happened in the past, but with what the client carries with them from the event today, the imprint of the experience that remains, like the wound. You are changing how the memory is stored and the client's relationship to it, without needing to determine whether the client meets criteria for PTSD—because, as Francine Shapiro (2018) states, "Any event that has a lasting negative effect on the self or psyche is by its nature 'traumatic'" (p. 39). The AIP model will be discussed in more depth in chapter 4, along with visual and nature-based metaphors that can help clients understand the healing process used in EMDR in ways that feel resonant and restorative.

CHAPTER 2

The Creative Arts in Intercultural Practice

This chapter provides you with a theoretical framework for integrating the creative arts into your work with complex trauma. The first half of this chapter provides an overview of the primary benefits of integrating the creative arts into EMDR, drawing on research from the fields of trauma, neuroscience, and the creative arts, as well as research with refugee populations and clients of diverse cultural backgrounds.

The second half of this chapter discusses the importance of cultural humility and presents guidelines for integrating creative arts into EMDR in diverse settings. It also outlines ways that the creative arts can enhance cultural humility and responsiveness. This information will allow you to begin intentionally using creative, art-based techniques that make trauma reprocessing more responsive and effective for clients from a diversity of backgrounds and identities. You do not need to be an art therapist or trained artist to integrate these approaches into your work. You just need to know when and how to use creativity with therapeutic intention.

Creative Interventions with Diverse Populations

An alarming uptick in migration and forced displacement worldwide—due to conflict, economic instability, and climate change—has increased the need for **culturally responsive trauma interventions** that effectively reach and support diverse populations. There is growing evidence that the use of creative interventions can meet this need and support increased cultural responsiveness in the field of trauma as a whole. Creative interventions can also enhance the efficacy of evidence-based treatment modalities, such as EMDR, when working with severe and complex trauma. For example, Schouten and colleagues (2019) found that art therapy combined with trauma-focused psychotherapy was more effective in reducing symptoms than trauma-focused psychotherapy alone.

Creative interventions can also support refugee populations as they navigate adversity and loss by providing them with a safe space to work through their trauma, to engage in self-expression, to rebuild social connection, and to retell their stories (Zadeh & Jogia, 2023).* Importantly, creative interventions allow clients to move implicit, sensory-based material (such as images, feelings, and sensations) into the verbal realm so they can safely reflect on and share about their lived experiences, such as through the retelling of their story. The process of reflection also allows clients to develop new insights and perspectives on what they have witnessed or experienced, which can transform their relationship with those experiences in ways that support integration and resolution.

Creative and visual forms of expression can also be an effective way to circumvent language barriers that may exist when you are not working in a client's native language, as is often the case with refugee and migrant populations (Kolah, 2023). Language barriers aside, trauma creates its own language barrier, given that areas of the brain associated with verbal communication, namely Broca's area, shut down during overwhelming

* Kalmanowitz and Ho (2016) rightly point out that *refugee* is not synonymous with *trauma*, given that not all refugees, asylum seekers, and internally displaced people are traumatized. However, this population typically experiences a higher prevalence of posttraumatic stress, complex trauma, and other related mental health issues compared with the general population (Blackmore et al., 2020), providing new directions for how to work with complex and ongoing trauma.

and traumatic experiences (van der Kolk, 2014). Creative expression facilitates the processing of sensory material that cannot be put into words, strengthening the efficacy of trauma treatment when words are not enough to capture the complexity, depth, and sometimes horror of a client's lived experiences. Creative and expressive interventions actively engage both the body and mind, which allows this implicitly held material to reconnect with areas of the brain that are responsible for higher cognitive functions. This helps bridge the implicit somatic material to words, language, narrative, and meaning-making processes (Malchiodi, 2003).

Once you have a framework through which to understand the concrete benefits of integrating the creative arts into your work with complex trauma, you can begin to intentionally weave it into your practice to strengthen resources and skill building and make trauma reprocessing more tolerable for clients from a diversity of backgrounds and identities.

Eight Core Benefits of Integrating Creative Interventions with EMDR

Art therapy and EMDR are complementary modalities. In art therapy, the therapist embodies a **stance of not knowing**—a reverent witnessing as the client's process unfolds. They accompany the client by attuning to the material that arises from their internal world without interruption or intrusion. This is the stance EMDR therapists are encouraged to take during phase 4 of treatment (reprocessing and desensitization) as well. However, in my work as an EMDR consultant, I have observed that many EMDR therapists from various therapeutic backgrounds struggle with this nonverbal, process-oriented element of EMDR. In this respect, I believe there is a lot that the field of EMDR can learn from the creative arts, including how the arts help us curiously embrace the wisdom that arises from sitting with uncertainty.

Drawing on research, as well as my own experiences in cross-cultural settings, I have identified eight primary benefits of combining EMDR with the creative arts that are most relevant to expanding the reach of EMDR:

1. Physiological calm
2. Containment
3. Externalization

4. Embodiment
5. Accessing unprocessed material
6. Dual attention
7. Meaning making
8. Cultural connection

Many of these components are core concepts in art therapy and are foundational to our therapeutic goals as trauma therapists. Although these concepts are woven throughout the book to help you understand how the creative arts can support EMDR in each phase of treatment, I have provided a more detailed description of them here to facilitate your understanding as you read on.

Physiological Calm

The use of various materials in the creative process provides a sensory experience that is soothing, nurturing, and grounding. It slows clients down and helps them regulate physiologically and emotionally by downregulating the brain's emotional center (the **amygdala**) while keeping the brain's cognitive center (the **prefrontal cortex**) active (Kaimal et al., 2017; Magsamen & Ross, 2023). This is key since emotion regulation is vital to building stabilization and restoring a sense of safety, which is the first step of trauma treatment (Herman, 1992). This first step can be challenging with complex trauma, especially when the trauma is ongoing, as is often the case with refugees who face continued challenges and insecurities during transition and adjustment (Kalmanowitz & Ho, 2016). When this occurs, art making provides an external anchor for the client to focus on while beginning to notice their internal experiences, which increases safety while building up affect tolerance and somatic awareness. Through repeated experiences of emotion regulation and control through art making, the client can build a foundation of internal safety over time. This can connect the client to a place where the trauma itself is over and there is a restored or newly established stabilization, even if environmental stressors are ongoing.

Containment

Art can create a sense of containment in various ways. The use of structured materials such as pencils, colored pencils, and modeling clay (as opposed to more fluid materials such as watercolor paints or wet clay) can provide the client with a sense of control over the material, which helps contain and regulate the expressions of their emotions and sensation (Naff, 2014). The use of structured materials that allow for more controlled expression can prevent flooding and overwhelm during art making as well, further reinforcing an internal sense of control, containment, and regulation (Hinz, 2009). When a client can represent an internal thought, feeling, or sensation externally, it also provides containment through form and shape. For example, the edges of a piece of paper or the shape of a clay structure provide natural boundaries that contain the expression and delineate the space between the client and the distressing material.

Imaginal containment is a core skill taught to clients in phase 2 of EMDR (preparation) to help them put away distressing material and gain increased control over intrusive thoughts. Although containment is a fundamental skill to safely and effectively work with clients with complex trauma and dissociation, clients with C-PTSD often struggle with this skill. They may have difficulty storing distressing material in the container or be unable to store the material long enough for containment to be effective (Davis, 2022). You can use the creative arts to strengthen this skill by inviting the client to create a physical container (rather than an imaginary one) using a box, drawstring bag, basket, or other object—allowing the client to physically place distressing words, images, or other material into the container. This allows the client to experience a tangible sense of distance and containment that can scaffold the skills needed for imaginal containment.

Externalization

Externalization is the process of giving our internal experience an external representational form through expression—be it visually through images or symbols, clay or sculpture, movement, sound, or words. The distance created by externalization makes it more tolerable to face and work through our thoughts, emotions, and sensations rather than avoiding them or pushing them away, as is often the impulse that comes with trauma

(Greenwald, 2013). Through externalization, the expressed components of the internal world "can begin to take up physical space outside of the individual and can be seen, heard, and interacted with, potentially leading to change" (Kalmanowitz & Ho, 2016, p. 60). With increased distance and control, the client can more safely explore, work through, organize, transform, and integrate these experiences.

In addition, since clients with complex and intersecting trauma histories can have difficulty with imaginal exposure techniques, externalization can be a helpful strategy to make the exposure more tolerable, especially when there is a risk of destabilization in exploring a specific memory or component of a memory. For example, in phase 3 of EMDR (assessment), the use of art materials to represent the image (or other sensory component) that is the worst part of the experience can provide an element of distance from the memory, making it more manageable for the client to reflect on the negative belief that they internalized at that moment, as well as the associated feelings and sensations.

Externalization can also be used as an interweave when processing is blocked. For example, you can slow down the reprocessing work in phase 4 and invite the client to use pastels or markers to represent a distressing sensation that comes up—allowing them to externalize its size, color, texture, energy, emotional charge, and any other quality that the sensation holds. While holding or looking at the representation with some distance, the client can begin to get curious and ask themself: *What does that sensation want to do, say, or hear? What does it need? Where does it want to go?* From there, you can move back into reprocessing—"Go with that"—which often allows the material to move toward fulfillment and resolution (be it through validation, reassurance, expression, or release) and for the reprocessing work to continue.

Embodiment

Art making and creative expression are active experiences that take place in the present moment. The physical materials used to facilitate the creative process engage the senses and move the client into their body and more fully into the present. When a client can focus on a particular sensory experience—by feeling the texture of a material in their hand or watching color move onto a page—they can become more aware of internal sensations and their internal world (Hinz, 2009).

This is especially important in working with complex trauma, as many survivors are afraid of their internal sensations (Steele et al., 2017) and have learned to disconnect, numb out, and shut down connection with their bodies as a form of coping with unbearable pain and distress. Going inward too quickly can cause overwhelm. Using art making to increase sensory engagement and awareness can slowly expand their ability to mindfully notice their internal world at a more comfortable pace. For complex trauma survivors, this can help restore the connection between the mind and body and rebuild the interoceptive pathways that were compromised due to cumulative experiences of interpersonal trauma and threat (Emerson, 2015).

Accessing Unprocessed Material

One of the ways we understand the working mechanisms of EMDR is through **memory reconsolidation theory** (Gunter & Bodner, 2009), which I discuss more in depth in chapter 4. For memory reconsolidation to occur, you must first access and activate the distressing material (Ecker et al., 2024). In EMDR, you do so by guiding clients to identify the events in their past that were too painful, terrifying, or overwhelming to get fully processed and that contribute to their present distress, negative beliefs about the self, and unhealthy coping strategies. Identifying and organizing these memories provides you with a treatment map that you can use to access material from the past and reprocess it so clients can get the relief they need in the present.

However, there are many cases, especially with complex trauma, dissociation, and attachment trauma, where clients struggle to access explicit memories from their past, complicating the mapping of treatment. This is where the use of art can help access and unlock the implicit impressions of traumatic experiences. Art can allow implicit material to take form and act as a concrete reference point for memories that feel elusive or confusing. In fact, the visual images that a client creates can express their state of being more clearly than words (Talwar, 2007). The art can then be used as the target memory, even if no explicit memory has been identified, as it allows the client to retrieve and activate the unresolved material connected to the distress. When working with attachment trauma, using art can be particularly useful for eliciting implicit memories that became encoded before the brain developed the ability to process those experiences with language. I present a preverbal protocol more in depth in chapter 10.

Dual Attention

In EMDR, staying oriented to the present moment while mindfully tracking the internal experiences associated with the past is referred to as **dual awareness** or **dual attention**. It is a balancing act between the past and the present (Marchand & Simpson, 2022). The art-making process naturally allows for a state of dual awareness as the client is continually oriented to the present moment through mindful and intentional engagement with the art. As Kalmanowitz and Ho (2016) describe it, for the client to creatively explore the past, they must simultaneously engage in the act of art making in the present. While the client is pulled into the past through the reliving quality and emotional charge held by the memory, the creative process grounds and anchors the client into the present. Achieving present-moment orientation and helping the client become aware of the sensations and feelings in their body in the present moment are primary goals of trauma therapy (van der Kolk, 2014).

In addition to dual awareness, the creative process facilitates a process of bilateral activity in the brain. Although we used to think creativity was restricted to one hemisphere of the brain, this is an outdated concept, and we now recognize that the creative process engages multiple brain regions (Zaidel, 2005). For example, participating in art making requires not only sensory engagement but also cognitive engagement as the client makes conscious decisions about the material, color choices, composition, and so on, which engage in both hemispheres. Therefore, art making is not merely nonverbal but an integrative and complex process that promotes the sensory, affective, and cognitive reprocessing of traumatic material (Talwar, 2007).

Meaning Making

Trauma therapy is about learning new ways to think about and make sense of past experiences. Creativity supports this process by allowing clients to develop their own way of knowing and learning from a hands-on, experiential process that promotes exploration, investigation, and discovery. Francine Shapiro (2018) calls the insights and new perspectives that arise throughout reprocessing "spontaneous adaptive resolution." These moments of insight occur because our system naturally moves toward healing and integration when we are safe enough to process through distress. Through art making, clients actively generate adaptive information from within and develop new insights that allow them to update old trauma memories. This is the very core of memory reconsolidation theory and what we call introducing **corrective information**. This process of transformation and integration shifts clients' understanding of the past and decreases the distress associated with it.

Ultimately, art making allows clients to make sense of the world from their own perspective rather than being told the meaning or truth from an external source (Paton & Linnel, 2020). When clients can make sense of their experiences, they can adapt and move on. I often speak to my clients about a traumatic experience simply being something we cannot make sense of. The experience is so outside of our worldview—it is too senseless, too big, or too painful—that we cannot integrate it into our life narrative. Through art making, clients transform their experiences so that they make sense in a new way, working them through to a type of resolution.

Cultural Connection

Finally, the creative process can become a platform for cultural expression, especially when there is diversity and choice in the materials offered. A powerful example involves a recent art-therapy program for Syrian refugees, which integrated embroidery work into group therapy as a way to help clients connect with their cultural heritage in a strengths-based way (Hanania, 2020). Often, when people think about art, they imagine drawing and painting. However, in order to remain culturally sensitive, you must allow clients to choose culturally relevant, soothing, and empowering art materials that honor their unique preferences. Sandra Paulsen and Shelley Spear Chief (2024) assert that when building stabilization skills with Indigenous clients, using traditional arts and crafts such as beading or making moccasins can be more effective and grounding than verbal strategies. By offering a variety of different art forms, you ensure that the therapy is flexible enough to meet the needs of clients from various backgrounds and circumstances (Al-Hroub, 2023).

Cultural Humility in the Creative Arts and EMDR

Integrating art therapy into EMDR or any other type of therapy does not, by default, increase the cultural relevance or appropriateness of the modality. Although art therapy is often considered less culture-bound than traditional forms of psychotherapy, it is dangerous to assume that art therapy is "culture blind," because the field of art therapy is nonetheless Euro-American in origin (Hocoy, 2002; Jackson, 2020). Therefore, it is important to move beyond the assumption that art therapy is universally applicable and can be used indiscriminately across cultural contexts and populations. This assumption can render art therapy ineffective and can cause further harm because it ignores the sociocultural factors that influence a client's expressions, needs, and preferences.

This is where cultural humility becomes key, as it lays the foundation for integrating the arts and creative expression into trauma treatment across diverse contexts and worldviews. **Cultural humility** is distinct from cultural competence in that there is no end point; it is a lifelong process of reflection and learning (Tervalon & Murray-García, 1998). You can think of cultural competence as a "way of doing" while cultural humility is a "way of being" (Stepney, 2022). Cultural humility as a way of being helps you take a more open and curious stance toward your clients and yourself. It helps separate your responses and perspectives from those of your clients so you can better respond to their needs.

Guidelines for Practicing Cultural Humility

This section presents five core guidelines for practicing cultural humility that will guide your therapeutic work with clients from diverse cultural backgrounds and identities:

1. Self-awareness
2. Intersectional understanding of culture and identity
3. Balancing power dynamics
4. Stance of not knowing
5. Offering choice

Self-Awareness

Self-awareness is essential to the development of cultural humility. You need to learn not only about other cultures but also about who you are and your own cultural identity, values, beliefs, practices, and histories

(Tervalon & Murray-García, 1998). Recognizing culture as an essential part of all of us—not just people who are "racialized" or through your perception of them as "having" culture (Kirmayer et al., 2014)—highlights the need for all therapists to develop awareness of their personal, social, and cultural identities. Resmaa Menakem's (2017) groundbreaking book *My Grandmother's Hands* is a resource that can help therapists from all backgrounds explore their own cultural identities and generational legacies of trauma, loss, and resilience.

As you develop greater self-awareness, you can become more aware of the cultural lens through which you filter, make sense of, and respond to your clients' expressions (Hocoy, 2002). For example, while a client's use of color, symbols, words, or movements may create an emotional response within you, you cannot assume that it carries the same emotion or meaning for the client. Observing and challenging these assumptions allows you to remain curious and open to discovering the client's perspective and process of meaning making. This ability to simultaneously discern between "the self" and "the other" is an essential part of cultural humility that helps you move between both worlds (Soulé et al., 2022, p. 2).

For white therapists, it is especially important to become aware of the impacts that being socialized in a white supremacist society can have on self-awareness. White people are often shielded from race-based distress, creating a sense of "white fragility" that can make having constructive and critical conversations about race emotionally distressing (DiAngelo, 2018). In order to work effectively across cultures, white therapists need to become aware of their white racial identity and understand what it means to be white in the therapeutic space. This process of white racial identity development involves seven phases (Stepney, 2022; Sue et al., 2022):

1. **Naivete:** You maintain a neutral stance toward race.
2. **Conformity:** You believe that white culture is superior to other cultures and worldviews and internalize this perspective.
3. **Dissonance:** You are exposed to a particular experience or encounter new information that forces you to acknowledge your whiteness. This is where real change begins.
4. **Resistance and immersion:** You begin to question and challenge the racism within yourself and in society, and whiteness begins to lose its neutrality.

5. **Introspection:** You question what it means to be white and develop the sense of having a cultural self: *Who am I as a racial and cultural being?*

6. **Integrative awareness:** You become aware of yourself as a racial and cultural being, and you both appreciate and respect racial and cultural diversity.

7. **Commitment to antiracist action:** You use your privilege to work against systems of oppression, taking direct action to combat racial issues in everyday life.

Living and working in cross-cultural contexts for most of my adult life has provided ideal settings for me to confront my whiteness and my own cultural identities. I belong to a minority group in eastern Canada called the Acadians, who experienced ethnic cleansing in the mid-1700s by British loyalists. My ancestors were displaced across the Americas, the Caribbean, and France. Of the approximate 11,000 Acadians deported, nearly half died of disease and starvation. The families that managed to escape to remote locations experienced loss of resources, loss of their way of life, and marginalization under British rule. Belonging to a minority group that has fought for cultural preservation and representation prevented me from fully recognizing the ways that I benefited from the privilege of whiteness, being largely of European descent. It was not until my undergraduate years—when I left Canada to do an exchange program in Ghana on sub-Saharan African art history—that I shifted my social positioning and entered my own phase of dissonance and journey of white racial identity.

One afternoon, we were discussing the transatlantic slave trade and the art of the African diaspora. At this point, everyone in the class directed their attention toward me—the only white woman in the room. I asked, bewildered, "Why are you all looking at me?" I was genuinely naive that my white skin inherently connected me to the slave trade and the acts of oppression and colonization committed in Africa by white people since the 15th century. This was a moment of dissonance. I was pushed out of a sense of naivete and had to confront what I represented.

I have since gone through my own journey of acknowledging how my skin has afforded me unearned privileges and power throughout my life. It has been a process to acknowledge my heritage with "historical honesty," a term used by Eduardo Duran (2019) in his work with Cree communities, where he highlights how important it is for white therapists to increase their comfort with discussing issues of historical trauma and acknowledge their complicity in being part of the historical perpetrator. Living in cross-cultural contexts has challenged me to learn who I am and what I represent, to recognize my own racial biases and assumptions, and to acknowledge the unearned power, privilege, and resources I have been afforded at the expense of others, including the Mi'kmaq People, who welcomed my ancestors as uninvited guests to their land, Mi'kma'ki (Nova Scotia), centuries ago. This has motivated me to actively listen to, learn from, and lift up historically underrepresented voices when and where possible in my work and in my life.

Ultimately, I believe that the more we know about who we are and what we represent as individuals, the more effectively we can broach issues of race, ethnicity, and power with clients and display historical honesty about the legacies of our ancestors. When we enter relationships with clients and communities from a place of self-awareness and humility—knowing who we are, our lineage, our customs, and our cultural lens—we are better able to listen from a stance of curiosity, nondefensiveness, and deep respect while supporting clients' needs for validation and solidarity as they heal from race-based trauma and other forms of oppression and discrimination.

Intersectional Understanding of Culture and Identity

It is important to remember that clients can have multiple intersecting identities influenced by various cultural, social, economic, structural, and historical factors. This includes factors such as race, ethnicity, gender, socioeconomic status, religion, sexual orientation, gender identity, and ability—though additional factors such as language, geographical location, values, worldviews, traditions, gender roles, education, immigration, and migration can further influence and shape a client's identity (Stepney, 2022). **Intersectionality** is a framework for understanding how these various dimensions of identity interact to create combinations of oppression or privilege (Crenshaw, 1991). Honoring the complexity of each client helps you maintain humility, curiosity, and openness and allows you to explore and validate experiences of trauma, adversity, and oppression and—in turn—meet their needs for healing more effectively.

Balancing Power Dynamics

Cultural humility also requires that you maintain an awareness of the inherent power imbalance in the therapeutic relationship and that you recognize the client as the expert on their identity, cultural perspectives, and ways of knowing (Africa & Endres, 2009). This is especially the case if you are a therapist working with trauma, as power imbalances in the therapeutic relationship can reenact the very same trauma dynamics that rendered (or continue to render) the client powerless. Taking a stance of cultural humility in this case can prevent you from assuming a position of power and privileging your own perspectives and worldviews over the client's. The ultimate goal of cultural humility is to join with the client to explore their perspectives and worldviews (Hook & Davis, 2019).

One way to address this power imbalance is to interchange the teacher-learner role. You must allow the client to become the teacher by treating them as the expert on their own experiences, and you must become the learner by listening to the client's stories, not only with your ears and eyes but also with your heart (Jackson, 2020). In this learning role, you are more open to new perspectives, ways of knowing, and thinking, and you are able to join with the client from a place of compassion, honesty, integrity, and respect. Empathy is also essential to this process, including what Stepney (2022) has called "culturally sensitive empathy." Whereas cultural humility can be understood as a way of being, culturally sensitive empathy is a way of seeing. It allows you to bridge the gap between the client and yourself, allowing you to see deeper into another's experience.

Stance of Not Knowing

To be truly process oriented, you must take a stance of not knowing. With EMDR and the creative arts, you accompany the client as they access their internal resources and move toward their own healing. It is through the client's process of discovery that the unknown becomes known. One way to facilitate this process is through the creative arts, as the client's creative expressions can hold a complexity that cannot always be expressed in words, allowing meaning to change and develop on a nonverbal level without defining it too soon. It is important that you do not interfere with this process by prematurely requiring your client to explain or justify their perspective; you must instead learn to sit in the unknown while accompanying the client on their journey. From this humble stance of not knowing, you refrain from interjecting your own assumptions or ideas about the direction the client should take based on your own needs or cultural lens.

Offering Choice

Another key element of cultural humility involves offering choice and control around the materials and creative modalities offered. You must prioritize the client's choices and preferences over any predetermined notions of what might be most theoretically beneficial. This is especially important when it comes to culturally meaningful materials. For example, the **EMDR integrative group treatment protocol (EMDR-IGTP)**, developed by Ignacio Jarero and Lucina Artigas (2009), invites clients to use paper, colored pencils, or crayons to represent elements of their traumatic experience. The EMDR therapists I work with in Ethiopia have shared with me the importance of offering clay as a medium when doing an adapted version of EMDR-IGTP, as it allows clients to engage in the process more effectively by providing a familiar and culturally meaningful material that connects them to their childhoods of playing with clay and mud (A. Tibebe & M. Mekonnen, personal communication, April 21, 2024). In addition, colored pencils and crayons risk provoking shame and feelings of inadequacy due to high illiteracy rates and lack of familiarity with mark-making materials.

Offering choice not only ensures that clients are working with materials that are comfortable and hold meaning for them, but it also gives power back to the client, which is essential to restoring safety and resisting the reenactment of trauma dynamics.

How the Arts Promote Cultural Humility

Art making can promote cultural humility because it allows you to recognize the limits of your own worldview and to see beyond yourself by imagining into the world of another. The art-making process can also help you critically reflect on how you respond to a client, and it provides a safe space to express and explore challenging issues around power dynamics, privilege, race, and identity. For example, the creation of **response art**, defined as art created after a session in response to a client or topics that emerged in the session, has long been used in art-therapy supervision to help supervisees gain insight into their responses, both implicit and explicit, so that they can be further explored with the guidance of their supervisor (Nash, 2019). Response art can also be a medium for therapists to explore discomfort with cultural differences or issues around power, privilege, oppression, or identity with supervisors. By expressing and externalizing the thoughts, feelings, and urges that get stirred up during a session, therapists can find the reflective distance they need to thoughtfully examine the origin of these responses and actively engage in a lifelong journey of learning, critical reflection, and self-discovery.

In my own practice as an art therapist working with Indigenous children who experienced sexual abuse, I was able to use response art to express a fantasy about adopting one of my clients and essentially "rescuing" her. By processing this art expression with my supervisor, I was able to deconstruct the protective urges I felt toward her as paternalistic, which is a violation of one of the basic tenets of cultural humility: developing nonpaternalistic and mutual partnerships with individuals and communities (Tervalon & Murray-García, 1998). While it was a relief to give expression to this fantasy through the art-making process, it also made it possible to challenge the emergent "white savior" fantasy by honoring the resilience of her community, exploring the cultural resources she had available to her, and acknowledging that my role was to support her recovery by fostering a meaningful connection to her resources.

In addition, body- and nature-based approaches can enhance cultural humility by increasing self-awareness. For example, Isabelle Soulé and colleagues (2022) have found that the use of yoga and forest therapy can help health professionals become more embodied—in other words, more physically aware and present within themselves—which can increase empathy and attunement with others and enhance a willingness to learn from diverse lived experiences. Yoga and forest therapy can also promote a calm, mindful state, which is vital to reducing the cumulative stressors and anxieties that interfere with interpersonal connection, curiosity, and compassion.

In the next chapter, you'll learn more about creative and nature-based approaches to EMDR that increase cultural humility and responsiveness in cross-cultural settings. You'll learn how elements from the natural world as well as embodiment practices can facilitate a culturally responsive practice in trauma healing.

CHAPTER 3

Ecotherapy and EMDR in Cross-Cultural Settings

This chapter presents an overview of the emerging field of ecotherapy to support the view that bringing natural objects, materials, and nature-based metaphors into EMDR can provide a deeper healing experience. Bringing nature into the therapeutic work can not only enhance trauma recovery but also promote culturally responsive therapy by providing a deeper connection to ourselves, each other, our cultures, and our evolutionary roots.

Ecotherapy

The term **ecotherapy** was coined by Howard Clinebell (1996) in his book *Ecotherapy: Healing Ourselves, Healing the Earth.* Since that time, ecotherapy has become an umbrella term for therapeutic approaches that invite active engagement with the natural world and recognize its vital role in health and healing (Buzzell & Chalquist, 2010). Ecotherapy operates from the paradigm that humans are inseparable from nature and embedded in the web of life and that reconnecting with nature is innately restorative.

Ecotherapy also addresses the impact that highly destructive human behavior has had on the environment, especially the exploitation of natural resources in pursuit of industrial growth and profit. Ecotherapy seeks to repair this rupture in the human-nature relationship by increasing ecological consciousness and restoring a sense of reverence for the natural world. This can motivate people to take meaningful action against the ecological crises we find ourselves facing, such as climate breakdown, loss of biodiversity, and an increase in natural disasters, and help us cope with our corresponding ecopsychological anxiety, fear, hopelessness, loss, anger, guilt, and uncertainty, which has been referred to as "ecological grief" (Comtesse et al., 2021).

Arne Næss's (1973) influential writing on deep ecology has also contributed to the theoretical foundation of ecotherapy. **Deep ecology** can be defined as the restoration of a deep respect for nature and the richness of diversity in all life forms. This is not just a theoretical concept but an experience of deep, mindful, and embodied interconnectedness with nature and a sense of belonging within the larger ecosphere. This is in contrast to **anthropocentrism**—the root of our current climate crisis—which is the belief that human beings are the most significant life forms and are separate from and superior to nature. This is a worldview that is embedded in Western religions and philosophy (Tokay, 2023). Deep ecology facilitates a philosophical and embodied shift from anthropocentrism to **ecocentrism**, where the intrinsic worth of every living entity is valued beyond its usefulness for human purposes and where we have an ethical and moral obligation to protect the climate and all living entities (Næss, 1973).

Disconnection and Disharmony

Ecotherapy maintains that our psychological suffering is the result of our split from the natural world (Atkins & Snyder, 2017). Our mutually interdependent relationship with the earth has been lost in many cultures through Eurocentric worldviews that prioritize individualism, dominance, and industrial growth. This disconnection from nature, and from the practices and rituals that have kept us aligned with the natural world for millennia, has led to imbalance and disharmony that impacts the human psyche in ways we are only beginning to understand. From an ecocentric perspective, living in harmony with the natural world creates a deep sense of well-being, whereas living in disharmony creates distress and illness.

This ecocentric perspective of illness and distress aligns with the understanding of suffering in many Indigenous and non-Western cultures. For example, balance and harmony are essential elements of the Africentric worldview described in David Archer's (2022) *Racial Trauma Recovery*, in which he writes that "life is made meaningful by finding one's place in nature, not trying to master it. Spiritual imbalances are responsible for most of our physical, emotional, and mental challenges" (p. 22). Similarly, many Indigenous communities believe that we can restore balance through rituals that foster healthy relationships with self, others, Mother Earth, the Cosmos, and the Creator (Linklater, 2014). These ecocentric approaches to healing view repairing our connection with nature as integral to restoring balance and harmony in our lives.

However, because the Eurocentric worldview is so embedded within many Western societies, we often address psychological distress from a biomedical model, using reductionist cognitive models that separate healing from other traditional practices and belief systems. In contrast, ecocentric approaches to healing have a holistic quality and are based on the belief that wellness comes from balance, interconnectedness, and embeddedness within systems of life.

Modernization and Lost Knowledge

Many of our ancestors had a deep and respectful relationship with nature that honored our connection with the land and placed us as humans within the web of life. For example, early agriculturalists in old European societies carried Shamanistic ideologies over from the hunter-gatherer world, which often looked to animal spirits and earth-based rituals to help procure food and get through difficult winters. They also practiced complex winter fertility rituals in various regions across Europe to ensure good harvests (Kezich, 2014).

However, these ancient religious and spiritual traditions began to change around the 17th century, a period marked by the transition from the magical to the scientific (Yates, 1964). It was during this time that René Descartes, a French mathematician and philosopher, created a distinction between the human psyche and the physical world, thus separating humans from nature (Blum, 2018). Descartes's theory rejected the worldview held by many of our ancestors that the natural world has inherent worth and a sacred core that must be respected. Instead, he believed that humans should seek to master nature through the "superiority" of rational thought and reason.

Descartes came to this conclusion because he viewed the mind and body as distinct entities made from separate substances, with the mind being immaterial and the physical body being material. Often called the **Cartesian split**, this mind-body dualism viewed the human mind as able to control the physical body, in much the same way that Descartes believed the mind could control and dominate nature—literally, mind over matter. This perspective is now deeply entrenched in the Eurocentric understanding of the mind, which views it as separate from and superior to the body, nature, and the more-than-human world.

As a result, traditional medicinal practices, such as the use of herbal medicines and rituals that kept life in balance with the rhythms and seasons of the earth, became regarded as "primitive" and backward by the scientific community. The practices of traditional healers were deemed as witchcraft or heresy and were increasingly devalued, suppressed, and made illegal. In fact, Europe went through multiple outbreaks of witch hunts, with a peak between 1600 and 1650, when mostly women who were highly knowledgeable in the healing power of plants and herbs were targeted (Ben-Yehuda, 1980). Some believed that these women were practicing magic due to their ability to use herbal remedies to successfully alleviate or cure ailments, alongside other healing rituals and ceremonies they performed. As a result, women in colonial North America lost the cultural knowledge that they carried with them from Europe and suffered countless acts of violence to suppress their knowledge, such as the Salem witch trials in the 1690s (Karlsen, 1987).

Essentially, the development of modern science in 17th-century Europe brought with it an intolerance for other ways of knowing. Knowledge was reduced to empirical inquiry, and different traditions of knowing and healing were banned by colonial powers and acts of cultural genocide in other parts of the world. Indigenous peoples in Canada and the United States were persecuted for engaging in traditional practices. Traditional African medicine was undervalued or banned under colonization (Chaitanya et al., 2021). As a result, many old ways of being were lost or suppressed.

Reviving Traditional and Holistic Healing Practices

Although the scientific movement caused the Western biomedical model to become predominant, many individuals believe the biomedical model is lacking when it comes to healing from trauma, as it ignores our connection with the world beyond us, be it with the earth, our ancestors, or the spiritual world (Linklater, 2014; Mehl-Madrona, 1997). Leaving these elements out entirely disregards a fundamental level of healing, especially when working with clients of diverse backgrounds. It is for this reason that many Indigenous and traditional communities around the globe have reclaimed their ancient ways of healing.

For example, in my own history, Acadian folk medicine has been adapted through our relations with the Indigenous Mi'kmaq in eastern Canada. It is acknowledged that without the Mi'kmaq—who shared with my ancestors how to use spruce tips for vitamin C, thereby preventing scurvy, and how to bring down a fever with yarrow root—my ancestors would not have made it through their first winters. In addition, many of the clients I worked with during my time in Vietnam would light incense and pray to their ancestors to achieve balance and support from the spiritual world. In Ethiopia, where I currently live and work, traditional medicine is highly practiced and follows a holistic approach that mixes both herbalism and spiritualism. Many Ethiopians believe that holy water, called *tesbel* in Amharic, is an elixir that heals and soothes most illnesses (Chaitanya et al., 2021). Holy water is drunk or bathed in, which provides a meaningful connection not only to specific spiritual places—such as the Blue Nile in Ethiopia, where some holy water is sourced—but to spiritual beliefs and opportunities for reflection and prayer.

To allow for true healing and transformation, we must revive our deeply human practices that connect us to each other and to the natural world. We must honor the Indigenous communities, Knowledge Keepers, and activists who continue to fight to protect, reclaim, and pass down a sacred relationship with the land in the face of colonization, industrialization, and oppression across the globe. We must respect their traditional ways of knowing and their continued stewardship of the land. For example, the Innus of Ekuanitshit in Canada fought for the Magpie River in Quebec to be granted legal personhood. It is now recognized as a living entity and protected under nine rights by Canadian law, including the right to flow and the right to be free from pollution. Its protection acknowledges Indigenous rights to traditional healing and land-based practices tied to the river and the ecosystem it supports, the very rights that were denied through acts of colonial violence (Lowrie, 2021).

Healing the Cartesian Split Through Embodied Practices

As you've learned, the separation of the mind from the body—the Cartesian split—is woven throughout medicine in the Western world. Treatment has become a largely disembodied practice that relies on information gathered from cognitive observations rather than embodied experience (Bennett & Castiglioni, 2004). However, cognitive approaches are limited in that they exclude or devalue the important information that the body holds, including perceptions, feelings, emotions, and visceral responses.

As therapists, healing the Cartesian split requires that we learn to listen to and work with the body. We must learn to value once again the vital information the body brings to healing work, as discussed by Babette Rothschild (2017) in *The Body Remembers* and Bessel van der Kolk (2014) in *The Body Keeps the Score*. Their work has demonstrated how embodiment practices, such as movement, yoga, rhythm, mindfulness, and the creative arts, provide access to trauma and healing on a deeper level than cognitive-based treatments. Healing the Cartesian split is also essential to build a therapeutic relationship characterized by attunement and connection. By bringing the body into treatment, you can provide clients with coregulation and safety as you remain grounded in your own body, and you can also better use movements, gestures, posture, tone of voice, and proximity to respond nonverbally to cultural cues. This can all enhance trust and feelings of safety in the relationship.

Eco-Art Therapy and Nature-Based Practices

The creative arts are a powerful way to integrate both the body and nature-based materials into healing modalities such as EMDR, while also providing a deeper connection to our evolutionary roots and a sense of belonging in the world. In a way, all creative arts are nature based: natural pigments, clay, fibers, and the sensory experience of our bodies—it all comes from the earth (Atkins & Snyder, 2017).

Eco-art therapy is an emerging field that aims to actively reunite art making with the natural world, seeing the split from nature as more recent than the use of nature in art itself, which is part of our ancient human story (Speert, 2016). Eco-art therapy involves the use of nature-based materials in the art-making processes, viewing these materials as a source of healing, strength, comfort, nurturance, and groundedness. Having worked in low-resource settings where costly art materials are often inaccessible, eco-art therapy is also a way of working with what is available in a specific setting or place. For example, when I interned at a psychiatric hospital in Accra, Ghana—a very low-resource setting with few fine arts materials available at the time—we used colorful flowers, petals, leaves, sticks, and upcycled materials for art making. This was a soothing and satisfying process for the individuals I worked with. Engaging with the sensory elements of the materials and arranging them into complex designs provided a sense of groundedness, resilience, and beauty in the face of marginalization and ostracization, as mental health issues were highly stigmatized at the time.

Art making has been a part of human societies throughout history, fulfilling a biological need to make meaning of our existence (Dissanayake, 2015). This is different from Western concepts of art, where art is disconnected from its functions in daily life. In contrast, traditional societies view the arts as an integral part of social life. The arts become a way to demonstrate belonging and place in society, a way to mark time and milestones, a way to experience synchronicity with the seasons, a way to tell cultural stories and teach lessons, a way to connect with the earth and one's sense of place and home, and of course, a way to heal.

In Ghana, while studying sub-Saharan African art history, I began to understand art as a ritual, art as a ceremony, and art as a craft—not art as removed from daily life on gallery walls. For example, the intricate kente cloth from the Akan people in Ghana tells the cultural story of how their ancestors learned how to weave by observing a spider weaving its complex web. The spider—named Ananse, a clever trickster figure in West African mythology—taught them how to weave in exchange for favors (Lloyd, 2016). The intricate basket-like patterns were initially woven in black and white to resemble the play of light off the spider's web and later integrated the use of dyed cotton or silk, where each color has a meaning and purpose (Micots, 2024). In addition, kente cloth has various social functions, as it is used to denote status or royalty, during weddings and ceremonies, and for shrines to honor deities. Kente cloth also carries meaning in the African diaspora, as African American students who wear kente stoles during graduation do so as a way to celebrate their ethnic heritage.

Nature-Based Materials

As discussed in chapter 2, when doing eco-art therapy, it is important to offer a variety of nature-based materials so clients can choose materials that connect them to their cultural traditions, crafts, ceremonies, and a sense of place or home. Creative expression takes on different forms and functions in different cultures, so you want to avoid confining a client's creative and cultural expressions to any one medium or approach. By being open to different art mediums, such as writing, movement, dance, craft, and expressive arts, you create the space for clients to connect with and tell their cultural stories. This helps you maintain a culturally responsive approach.

For example, in 2006, I was living in Aotearoa (the Māori-language name for New Zealand) while gaining experience to prepare me for my master's studies in creative arts therapies. I began working with an organization called Arts Access Aotearoa as part of their Arts in Corrections program, which advocates for the use of arts in prisons to support rehabilitation and reintegration. The majority of the men in my art groups were Māori, the Indigenous people of New Zealand who arrived from the Pacific islands in the early 1300s. We referenced traditional tattooing, called *tāmoko*, as a culturally meaningful form of art to express their heritage and identity. Designing and drawing tattoos using simple pen and paper was therapeutic in that it provided a way for the men to think about their future and about the tattoos they might get after being released, or even to represent tattoos of loved ones whom they missed. This process was also powerful in that they were reclaiming their culture through an art form that was suppressed and disrupted during colonization in the mid-19th century (Te Papa Tongarewa, 2024). Connecting with culture was especially important in supporting successful reintegration after release from prison.

As you'll learn in chapters 6 and 7, it is also possible to use various nature-based materials during EMDR to facilitate dual attention and enhance present-moment orientation during reprocessing. Some examples of nature-based materials you can bring into the therapeutic process may include seeds, nuts, seashells, stones, petals, wood, branches, bark, cotton, silk, yarn, string, natural pigments, clay, hide, bone, soil, clay, sand, herbs, essential oils, drums, minerals, gems, different types of paper, water, incense, gourds, musical instruments (such as drums, chimes, bells, tuning forks), depictions of animals, and actual animals (as is the case with animal-assisted therapy).

Nature-Based Metaphors

Nature-based metaphors are another important ingredient of eco-art therapy and ecotherapy more broadly. When used as part of treatment, metaphors can deepen the meaning and associations you bring to an idea, image, or object—which opens up new possibilities for understanding and interpretation (Stepney, 2022). When used with EMDR specifically, metaphors provide new ways for therapists and clients alike to connect to various components of the modality. For therapists, it makes it easier to learn and apply the core concepts of EMDR to clinical practice. For clients, it allows the EMDR model to resonate on a deeper level, making it accessible and easier to participate in the process.

There are several nature-based metaphors you will find presented throughout this book. For example, in chapter 4, I discuss how you can think of the AIP system as an internal river that flows within each of us, giving us the natural capacity for healing so long as the river remains unblocked. Also in chapter 4, I describe several different metaphors that can be used to conceptualize EMDR's three-pronged protocol, including the three strands of a braid or the three interlocking loops of a Celtic knot. Similarly, in chapter 7, I discuss the importance of uprooting the weeds or invasive plants that have taken over a client's soil bed (negative cognitions) to create space for new plants (positive cognitions) to grow and take root. These are only some of the many metaphors that I share within this book.

Nature-based metaphors are inherently strengths based and provide clients with new ways of understanding themselves and the healing process. That's because nature provides a profound source of strength, resilience, and hope through its myriad examples of adaptation, recovery, and transformation. Clients can lean into the solace, hope, protection, and soothing properties of nature that restore their sense of connection and harmony with the natural world.

Connecting to Culture Through Nature-Based Materials and Metaphors

Since it is not always easy for clients to communicate their culture on a verbal level, integrating nature-based materials and metaphors into treatment is a powerful way for them to share their stories both verbally and nonverbally. As the client shares their creative process, a powerful interpersonal exchange occurs between you and the client as they symbolically communicate their experiences, worldviews, values, needs, roles, and challenges. This can help lay the foundation for treatment that feels relevant, respectful, and responsive across contexts and settings. Above all, remember to offer choice and to collaboratively adapt treatment to flexibly respond to the diverse needs of each client. In the following chapters, you'll learn more about specific creative and nature-based approaches you can use throughout the eight phases of the standard protocol to enhance your clinical practice across cultures.

CHAPTER 4

A Nature-Based Framework for EMDR

This chapter presents a nature-based framework for the eight phases of EMDR, including the AIP model, memory reconsolidation theory, and the three-pronged protocol. Although EMDR is a holistic, embodied, and integrative approach to healing, the language and concepts used within this approach can be difficult to understand. The nature-based framework presented here provides accessible language that can help you deepen your understanding of these concepts and connect with the phases, processes, and steps of EMDR in a more intuitive way. It also allows you to more easily carry over EMDR into different contexts and into work with diverse populations.

The Adaptive Information Processing System

Francine Shapiro (2018), the founder of EMDR, proposed AIP theory as a neurophysiological hypothesis of how we process experiences and heal from trauma and adversity.

According to the theory, pathologies occur when our innate information-processing system gets blocked by overwhelming events and the memory is unable to be adequately processed and integrated with other memories. Therefore, the goal of EMDR is to unblock the body's innate self-healing capacities so that memories that are stuck and inadequately stored in isolated neural networks can be accessed, reprocessed, integrated, and moved toward adaptive resolution.

Part of preparing clients for EMDR involves explaining the AIP model, but using neurophysiological terms to explain this model may not always be useful. One way to explain the AIP model in a culturally comprehensible manner is to draw on a client's existing knowledge and to use accessible metaphors that allow the client to connect to the model in meaningful ways (Nickerson, 2016). I have seen some powerful and effective ways in which this has been done. For example, when I was helping organize the first-ever EMDR training in Vietnam, one of the trainers from Indonesia, Tri Hadi, who is now the president of EMDR Indonesia, ingeniously placed a banana in his armpit to demonstrate how trauma memories are inadequately stored when the AIP system becomes blocked at the time of the event. These memories cannot be broken down as long as they remain stored in this state-dependent way, which is why we have to access these memories (i.e., the banana in the armpit) and activate them so they can move into a place where they can be digested. (At this point, he removed the banana from his armpit, peeled it, and began to eat it.) Tri explained that with EMDR, the body and mind can then store what is useful from that experience (e.g., the banana's nutrients) and discard what is no longer adaptive, such as the emotional charge and negative beliefs (e.g., the banana's peel).

The process of digestion is a widely used metaphor to understand the AIP system. As with digestion, clients move through and break down their experiences in stages, taking in what is adaptive and letting go of what they no longer need. Through digestion, they integrate these experiences with the rest of their stories and their history, where they can bring their psychological resources to help them integrate and heal from the experience. They break down and move blocked or isolated trauma memories to long-term memory storage, where they become part of the past and no longer have the same emotional impact.

A Nature-Based Metaphor for the AIP System: The Internal River

As I mentioned in the introduction, another metaphor for understanding the AIP system is to describe it as an internal river that flows within each of us, breaking down our experiences and carrying them toward wholeness and resolution. The internal river metaphor can enhance the explanation of the AIP model through nature-based language that resonates with clients across cultural and geographical contexts. This metaphor reinforces that we are the source of our own healing. In exchanging with Lacey Poltorasky, an Indigenous Canadian therapist and EMDR International Association (EMDRIA)-approved consultant, she shared the perspective and lived experience that too many clients, especially those from oppressed and minoritized groups, have the experience of being told explicitly or implicitly, over and over, that the answers are outside of them, which erodes trust in the knowledge and wisdom that they carry within (L. Poltorasky, personal communication, November 4, 2023).

Describing the AIP system as an internal river that runs through us, guiding our capacity to process and integrate experiences into our life narrative, can be a soothing and empowering idea for clients to hear. The internal river also provides a profound metaphor for healing, since rivers are often places of cleansing rituals and are viewed as sources of energy, vitality, and continuity (Buettner, 2023). This helps clients take comfort from the healing properties of water and connects them to their internal strengths and resources.

In addition, a river is a processing system in its own right: It moves, breaks down, and transforms what it carries, depositing what it no longer needs and moving the rest forward. Just as a river flows toward the open sea, we too have a natural direction, carrying our life experiences toward integration, wholeness, and resolution. The continuous movement of our internal river reshapes memories as they are carried along, broken down, and rolled alongside other memories. Difficult experiences are like hard and heavy rocks that fall into the river's flow. They may temporarily disrupt or block the flow, but eventually, they get pushed along and broken down. Their sharp, painful edges get smoothed over and transformed, and they become integrated into the river, just as difficult and painful experiences become part of our life narrative.

However, when an experience is too big and heavy, it cannot move with the river. It gets stuck, blocking the flow of the water. As with an unprocessed memory, it remains stuck back at the time and place of the trauma, not moving or changing. It maintains its original state—the same shape, size, heaviness, and texture—just as the memory holds the images, sounds, sensations, beliefs, and emotional charge from the original experience. It cannot be transformed and integrated into the client's life narrative. Things begin to pile up around it, creating problems in their present life, like pools of water that suddenly flood into the present, or drought and decreased vitality. It can be hard for clients to see that those buried memories in the past are contributing to the issues they experience today. Your aim is to get the water flowing again by clearing the blockages.

In EMDR treatment, you travel upstream to uncover the memories that block the flow of the water. By identifying and accessing the memories in the past that were too big and heavy to integrate, you can gently free them and let the river break them down. The movement of the water carries them into the present, where they can mix with the positive experiences, wisdom, resources, and updated perspectives that the client holds within.

The movement of the water is the client's self-healing process, which is stimulated by the use of **dual attention bilateral stimulation (BLS)**, like eye movements and tapping, which allows the transformation and integration to occur. The memories get broken down into smaller pieces and reshaped as they tumble, collide, and integrate with other material held in the river. The sharp, painful edges break off and get smoothed and polished, eroding and washing away the emotional charge—the minerals, quartz, and gems held inside become visible and available to the system. The client's internal river can begin to flow smoothly again, giving them access to all their life energy, well-being, and wholeness.

The Movement of the Internal River

First and foremost, EMDR is about restoring movement when things get stuck or blocked. You use a combination of dual attention BLS and free association to accelerate the movement of the internal processing system, as if you are creating rapids and currents that unblock and move material along. The EMDR protocol itself is like a riverbed, holding and containing the flow of the client's free associations. You follow the flow and direction of the client's river as it moves and meanders, trusting that it carries and moves unprocessed material toward the knowledge and wisdom needed to heal. The movement of the water creates new pathways so the material can flow into the branches of the river that hold the associative material and internal resources needed for integration. You follow the flow of the client's mind until the memory is worked through to completion and resolution, cleaning and clearing out the blockages so the water can move freely.

Internal River and Dissociation

When clients dissociate in the wake of trauma, their memories can become disconnected and held in isolated neural networks, much like branches or tributaries of a river that get carved out and cut off from other waterways. Essentially, a blockage forms to disconnect them from material that is too painful and unbearable to integrate. Since rivers operate as a system of waterways that flow together and interconnect, when a blockage forms, the waterways are not able to flow together and intersect. In turn, the material held in disconnected or blocked-off branches cannot flow into the main stem of the river—as in, the neural integration of memory is prevented from occurring. In EMDR, you clear these blockages, bit by bit, using dual attention BLS to encourage information to flow together so that memories are no longer held in isolation.

The goal is for healing to be felt within the entire river system by restoring the flow of information—not by removing any parts or tributaries of the river system (i.e., any parts or self-states in the system that hold the memory of the event). When working with clients who experience dissociation and different self-states, treatment has historically been focused on integrating all self-states into one cohesive self-identity. This internal river metaphor emphasizes that the goal is, instead, to honor and respect how a client's system has formed and developed as an adaptive and protective response to trauma and to simply restore the flow between the parts of the system (i.e., foster co-consciousness and collaboration between self-states). This can help therapists and clients conceptualize the treatment of dissociation in a more restorative and nonpathologizing way.

Memory Reconsolidation

Memory reconsolidation is one of the predominant theories explaining the working mechanisms of EMDR (Ecker & Bridges, 2020). According to the theory, when clients access and activate a memory by bringing it into working memory, it is in a labile form—meaning it can be updated and transformed through the introduction of contradictory information and new learning, such as an adult perspective or a restored sense of safety. It is also difficult for clients to hold a distressing event in working memory while simultaneously performing a demanding task, such as tracking a hand with their eyes or engaging in self-tapping, which is one reason bilateral movements play such a prominent role in EMDR.

However, many therapists struggle to present memory reconsolidation theory to their clients in a way that is not overly complicated and that increases trust and willingness to try dual attention BLS. I have found that this is especially the case in certain cultures where there is skepticism that the therapist is doing something *to* the client through eye movements, like a form of hypnotism or voodoo. (This is an issue that many of the Ethiopian EMDR therapists I consult with face with their clients.) Walking clients through the process of memory reconsolidation with the internal river metaphor can reinforce that the healing process occurs within them, while also clarifying the role of eye movements, tapping, or other forms of dual attention BLS.

The Five *S*'s of Memory Reconsolidation

I have developed a framework to explain the steps of memory reconsolidation to clients called the five *s*'s: stuck, stir, sets of movement, shift, settle. I walk them through each *s* to explain how EMDR works:

1. **Stuck:** Stuck memories or material are stored in a state-dependent way, as if they are locked in the past with the raw, unprocessed emotional charge from that time. You have to go back and access the memory at the place where it got stuck or buried.

2. **Stir:** When you find the stuck memory, you stir it up to activate it. Activating it is the second step of healing a memory. This means you bring it into awareness in a safe and supportive setting. You stir up the images, thoughts, feelings, sensations, and anything else that got stuck back at that time, while staying connected to the present moment, observing from a place of curiosity and distance.
3. **Sets of movement:** Once you stir the memory up, you introduce sets of dual attention BLS, such as eye movements or tapping, to stimulate reprocessing. This gets the material moving again. You follow the flow of the client's mind, watching what emerges into awareness—any thoughts, beliefs, emotions, sensations, or urges—letting whatever surfaces, surface. Again, you observe what arises with curiosity, letting it move and mix with other thoughts and experiences in the client's mind, like everything mixing and rolling together in a river's current.
4. **Shifts:** Spontaneous changes and shifts happen as you follow the flow of the mind. The memory gets broken down into smaller pieces as it tumbles and collides with other experiences and perspectives held in the mind. It gets transformed and reshaped, just like how a river's current can break down big rocks into smooth stones and pebbles over time. The original state of the memory changes and the emotional charge begins to wash away, helping it move toward integration and resolution.
5. **Settle:** When the memory is resolved and the emotional charge is washed away, it can settle and sink back down in a new state, in a new form. It is no longer stuck. It can be accessed and recalled without distress. It has been integrated into the river of the client's life story.

When clients can draw on the five *s*'s of memory consolidation during phases 3 (assessment) and 4 (desensitization and reprocessing), it helps them maintain a stance of mindful noticing and curiosity when distressing material arises.

Mountains of Reprocessing

Another metaphor that I have used to help therapists and clients grasp the steps and phases of EMDR reprocessing is the visual metaphor of climbing and journeying through a mountain. Mountains form when something big happens, when there is so much pressure and intensity that the earth folds, buckles, or erupts. For this reason, mountains have historically been used as metaphors for challenges that seem almost too insurmountable to overcome, especially when standing at the base of the mountain (Wiest, 2020). They feel too big, too difficult to move through—blocking us from what is on the other side.

In the same way, trauma memories can feel intimidating and overpowering when clients look at them from the bottom, which is why in EMDR, you help clients face and overcome these memories. When there is enough readiness, you accompany the client to the peak of the mountain—to the worst part of the memory—so they can get the clearest view from the top. It is here that they can examine the beliefs they hold as a result of this experience and determine what they would rather believe about themself. They can also identify any associated emotions and sensations. Then you follow the client through the pathways down the mountain, trusting that the direction the client chooses will lead them to healing and resolution.

This mountain metaphor of reprocessing, which I expand upon in chapter 8, can help you navigate the phases of reprocessing, all the way from assessment (phase 3) to body scan (phase 6).

Overview of the Nature-Based Framework for the Eight Phases of the Standard Protocol

As you've learned so far in this chapter, my nature-based framework for EMDR uses the metaphor of a river to represent how the AIP system flows throughout treatment, while the metaphor of a mountain is used to visually outline the phases in which reprocessing work occurs. In phases 1 and 2, you lay the groundwork for trauma reprocessing by gathering information about the client's presenting issues and past experiences to map out treatment (phase 1) and build the skills and resources needed to reprocess memories (phase 2). In the assessment phase, you leave the flat, stable ground and accompany the client to the top of the mountain—the worst part of the memory (phase 3)—and then begin journeying up and down the mountain to find and reprocess any material that needs healing (phase 4), including the beliefs the client holds about themself (phase 5) and the emotions and sensations they hold in their body (phase 6).

At any point during these phases, the client can step off the mountain to take a break and stabilize and contain the memory (closure and containment). When all aspects of the memory are reprocessed, the client moves off the mountain to close and reflect on their journey (phase 7). They may return to the mountain to reassess whether more material needs healing and, if so, follow any new pathways until healing and resolution is complete (phase 8). From stable ground, you once again consult the treatment map and decide what mountain (i.e., memory or material that needs reprocessing) to go to next—be it in the past, present, or future—and what resources and skills are needed to make that journey (returning to phase 2 and moving through phases 3–7 again). The ability to journey to any point along the timeline is at the core of the three-pronged protocol that characterizes EMDR.

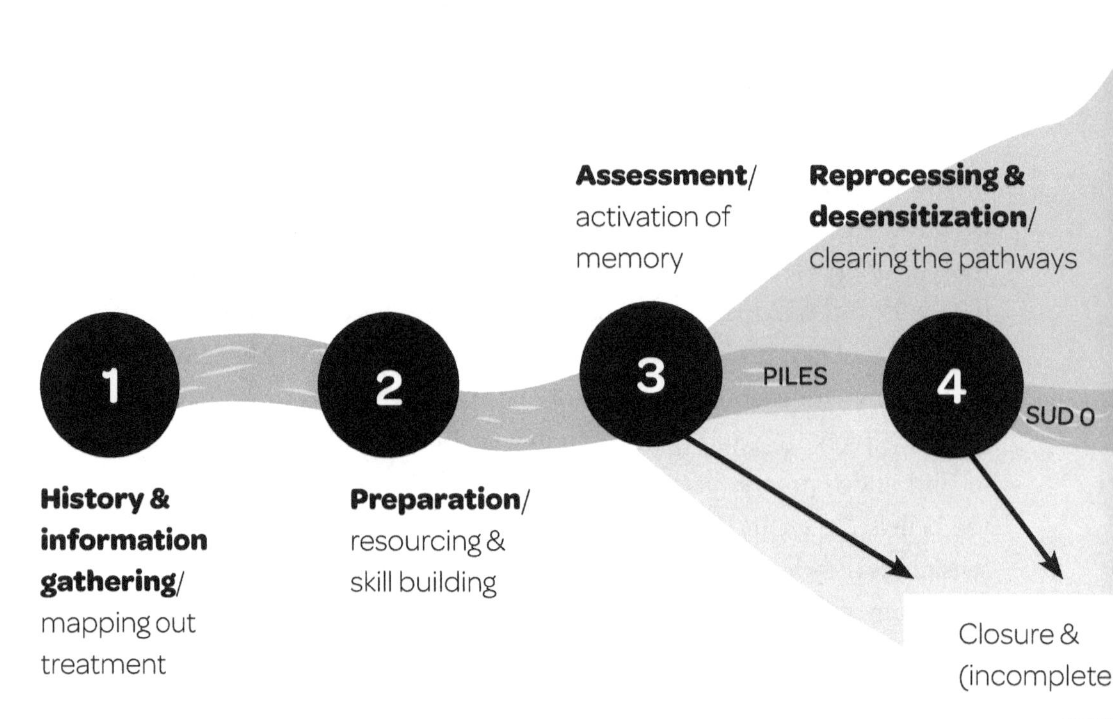

Metaphors and the Three-Pronged Protocol

According to Shapiro (2018), you must access and work with the past, present, and future for trauma treatment to be effective. However, the term *three-pronged protocol* does not well capture the fluidity of time since it brings to mind the metallic tines of a fork or the prongs of a plug that are

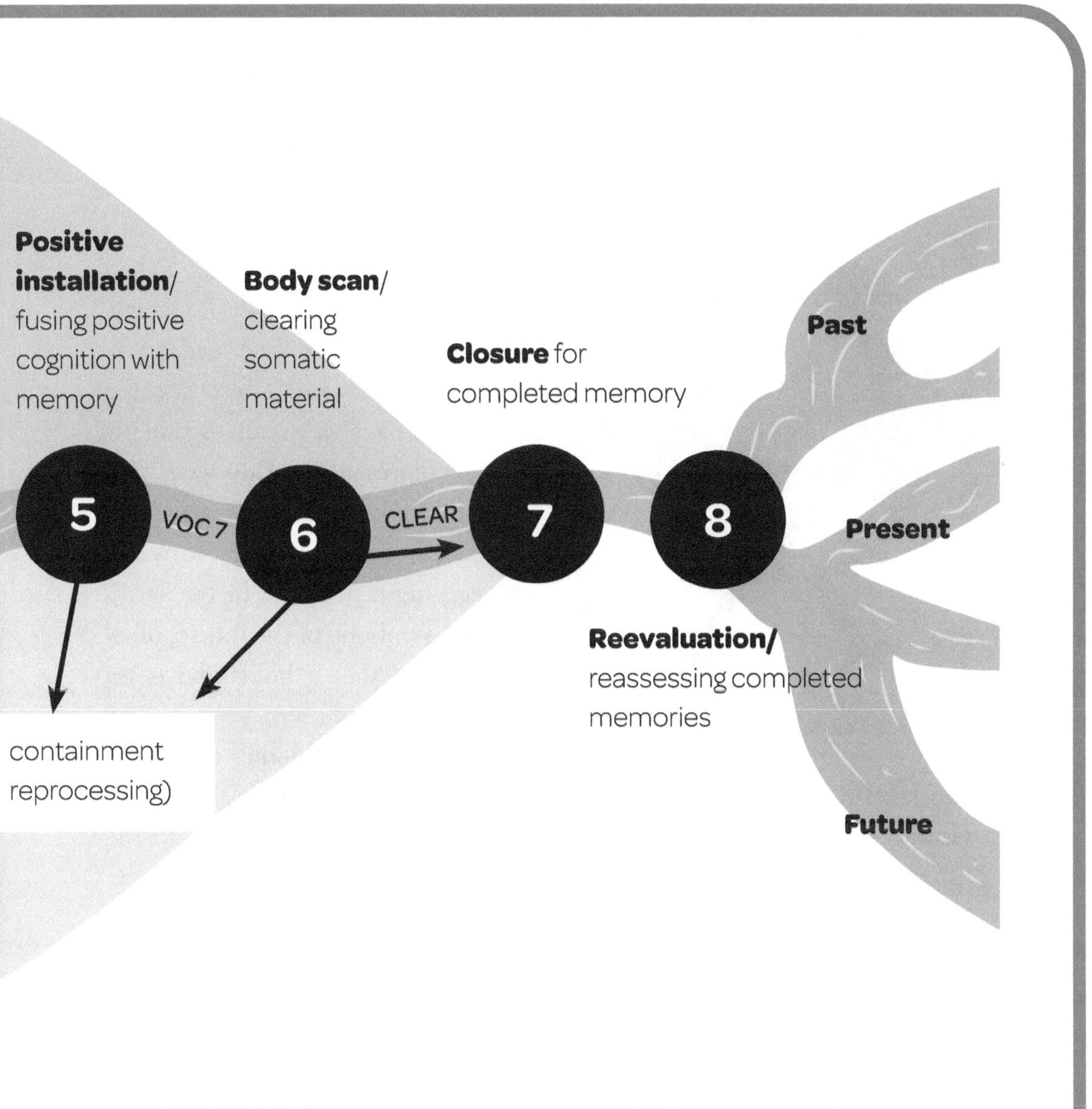

separate and unmoving. Prongs do not fluidly flow together and intersect as the concept of time does in many cultures. Instead, I have found that using the metaphor of a river is more effective in describing the three-pronged protocol, as rivers are fluid and not fixed. You can access any part of the river, upstream or downstream, from the present and go where we need to go to find healing.

This metaphor has resonated with the diverse communities I have worked with, as many cultures understand time as a nonlinear concept where the past and future are accessible at any moment and the past, present, and future all hold equal importance (Archer, 2022). In Ghana, the Akan people developed the **sankofa** symbol to represent this nonlinear nature of time. When translated from the Twi language, *sankofa* means to *go back and get it.* It is a symbol with a bird turning toward its back with an egg in its mouth, representing the idea that we must look back and learn from our past before we move forward. The egg often depicted in the bird's mouth is symbolic of the future, of all the potential that it holds and is yet to be hatched and seen.

Sankofa also embodies the stance you take in EMDR therapy: standing in the present and going back and visiting the past in the service of the future. You don't venture into the future without acknowledging and attending to the past first; you are always connecting the past to the present experience. In doing so, you also help the client bring old knowledge, traditions, ancestors, and resources into the present and with them into the future.

In addition to the sankofa, another cultural symbol of time is the **triquetra Celtic knot**, widely believed to symbolize the past, present, and future and all time with no beginning or end. The interlocking loops can be traced back to at least the 5th century BCE, which may also symbolize the interconnectedness of the earth, sea, and sky, as well as the harmony and balance between the mind,

body, and spirit. Just like with the triquetra knot, in EMDR, we honor the connectedness of time and the ability to move into the past, present, and future to create harmony and balance in our lives.

Finally, another useful and culturally meaningful way to present the three-pronged protocol is through the concept of braiding threads of time. **Braids** have many different meanings and functions across cultural settings. Still, almost every culture has a connection to a braid in some way, whether through hair designs, jewelry, textiles, bread, or the braiding of natural fibers (such as the braiding of sweetgrass in Indigenous communities in North America). Braids have three primary strands that are woven together, like the three arms of the river intersect, to represent the past, present, and future.

EMDR is truly a three-stranded process, making the braid a useful and culturally adaptive visual metaphor where the past, present, and future are interwoven and interconnected. In the process, you first work with the strands of the past, then the strands of the present, and then the strands of the future (or in the order that is most helpful to the client), weaving in resources throughout and allowing the client to go where they need to go to find healing.

CHAPTER 5

Mapping Out Treatment with Visual Timelines in Phase 1

As Francine Shapiro (2018), says, "Effective EMDR processing depends on effective targeting" (p. 53). Therefore, the first phase of EMDR (history taking and treatment planning) involves gathering the information needed to create a clear and comprehensive treatment plan, primarily by identifying the experiences in the client's past that contribute to their current distress. You must survey the whole landscape of the client's past to understand their presenting issues and develop a map of experiences to target for reprocessing.

In this chapter, you'll find a creative approach to history taking that involves the use of visual timelines to promote present-moment orientation and stabilization. The first half of this chapter describes the benefits and main elements of creating visual timelines, while the second half walks you through the steps of creating visual timelines using various nature-based materials for additional grounding. Your ability to ensure that the client feels in control and supported during this first phase of work builds trust in the therapeutic relationship and lays the groundwork for the rest of treatment.

Therapeutic Benefits of Visual Timelines in History Taking

There is a lot of therapeutic value in isolating and organizing memories visually and collaboratively with the client. The past, present, and future orientation of the visual timeline creates a clear, overall picture of the client's distress, resources, and goals. It becomes the map that you and the client can refer to throughout treatment to create a target sequence plan and track progress.

However, it is vital to make the process of history gathering as tolerable and collaborative as possible, especially when working with clients who have complex trauma histories and who are from diverse cultural backgrounds. History taking comes with inherent risks of destabilization and overwhelm since most clients have covered their wounds with layers of bandages, leaving the memories unhealed and unprocessed under the surface. As you gather history with clients, you are beginning to turn toward, rather than away from, these experiences by looking under the surface. In doing so, you must make adaptations as needed to ensure the client feels safe, in control, and supported. Otherwise, you run the risk of increasing their fear of the past and breaking therapeutic trust.

History taking should not only be a means to an end but also viewed as a process that has therapeutic benefits in its own right. Slower is faster when it comes to complex trauma treatment, and it is worth taking the time to fully engage the client in this process rather than moving through history taking too quickly. In the following section, I outline the many therapeutic benefits of using visual timelines to facilitate the history-taking process, which include:

- Providing psychological distance
- Locating memories in the past
- Integrating experiences into a life narrative
- Creating space for self-compassion
- Facilitating dual attention
- Giving memories shape and form

Providing Psychological Distance

When working with clients, I often describe the first phase of EMDR as taking a "bird's-eye view" of their past in order to gain an overview of the whole landscape of their experiences. This phrasing is inspired by the lifeline activity in **narrative exposure therapy (NET)**, where the client is invited to reflect on their positive and negative experiences before identifying any specific traumatic or overwhelming events. Taking this whole-life perspective is a form of titration, as it creates distance from traumatic events. You want your client to have some psychological distance from their memories so you can gather the information you need without opening up these memories too soon.

Creating visual timelines is one way to help clients maintain this reflective distance and stay oriented to the present while exploring their past. This is especially the case for unprocessed memories, which often hold a heightened emotional charge that makes it challenging and even confusing for some clients to sort through and organize them. By visually representing their memories and physically marking them on a timeline, you support the process of organizing the past, making it easier for clients to differentiate between events and periods of time. Clients can use colors, symbols, or objects like buttons or stones to organize their experiences, creating enough psychological distance and containment to gather the information needed for treatment planning without destabilizing them. Creating visual timelines is a safe and collaborative approach to helping clients organize and map out memories for reprocessing.

Locating Memories in the Past

The concrete nature of a timeline supports clients in marking and anchoring memories to a specific location on the timeline, such as to an age or a time period. Locating where memories fall on the timeline is immensely therapeutic when working with trauma, as it can visually emphasize to the client that those memories are fixed in the past. From where the client stands in the present, they can take in the information that (1) they are no longer that age, (2) the time period or phase is no longer happening, and (3) they are no longer back in that place where the memory occurred. The memory can take its place in the past.

The concept of **place** is central to Indigenous focusing-oriented therapy (IFOT), which is a culturally specific and body-based approach to working with complex and generational trauma in Indigenous communities. Indigenous communities often have a profound sense of connection to place through reciprocal and respectful relationships with the land. The language used in IFOT revolves around place (Turcotte & Schiffer, 2014, p. 58), specifically the place where the trauma occurred, which allows clients to go to that time *there*, that place *there*. This language continually differentiates between present and past, between here and there, so that the client can experience enough distance to become curious about the memory back in that time. In addition, the place where the trauma happened may have healing elements—such as supports, lessons, or land-based helpers—that can bring resolution to that time. Differentiating between *here* and *there* also supports dual awareness by allowing clients to stay present in the moment and in their bodies while "visiting" and bringing healing to, or receiving healing from, the memory located in the past. Visiting the past differs from reliving a memory (such as when a memory intrudes into the present), as the client is in control and does not lose orientation to the here and now.

Integrating Experiences into a Life Narrative

Trauma interferes with the brain's ability to organize information in a coherent, chronological narrative. As a result, traumatic memories do not receive the "time stamp" needed to give them their proper place in the past and in the client's life narrative. By creating visual timelines, you can support the integration of these traumatic experiences into the client's life narrative. When a client places a memory on their timeline, it physically and concretely takes its place in the past, like a time stamp, and the client can begin to see their life story take shape in front of them. They can see how the pieces of their story fit together and overlap. New insights can begin to emerge, such as "Wow, it makes sense why I was so numb and shut down. Look at all the things that were happening at that age." The client can also see how their experiences link up to the present moment—a place where those past events are no longer happening, a place where they are over.

Creating Space for Self-Compassion

As the timeline unfolds through the creative process, the themes associated with the client's experience become externally represented. This allows the client to reflect on how their past experiences interconnect with their present distress and how these experiences have led them to adapt certain coping styles. When the client sees all of this laid out, they can begin to feel compassion toward themself and toward all that they have been through. Their present distress begins to make sense in the context of their lived experiences. It also allows the client to recognize the strengths, skills, and strategies they used to navigate adversity and make it to the present, where they stand now. This, in turn, builds hope that they can continue moving forward toward the changes they hope to make for their future.

Facilitating Dual Attention

When you and the client collaboratively map out their past, present, and future through the use of visual timelines, it also facilitates a form of dual attention. That's because as the client engages in the creative and sensory components of creating their timeline—while also scanning internally for memories or distressing material—they are simultaneously focusing their attention on two different tasks. As discussed earlier, the use of dual attention BLS increases safety because it continually orients the client to the present and taxes their working memory resources, which prevents upsetting material from flooding in. It also allows you to more easily redirect the client to the task at hand if a particular memory starts to get activated.

Curiosity and collaboration are both vital to the safe exploration of the past. According to Shapiro (2018), you want to encourage your client to examine their life with an "attitude of exploratory interest" while you serve as their "reinforcing partner" in this process (p. 99). By maintaining a shared focus on the external task of creating the visual timeline, the client can remain grounded in the present. They can better differentiate between the past and the present, which is crucial to decreasing overwhelm and destabilization during history taking.

Giving Memories Shape and Form

When helping your client create a visual timeline, the use of lines, colors, and words can sometimes provide enough psychological distance from their memories, but when possible, I prefer to use physical objects to represent memories. Objects can provide an additional level of externalization from the client's memories, giving them shape, form, texture, and even weight. The experience of seeking and finding the right object to represent a memory is a form of dual-tasking that is orienting and grounding on its own. As the client feels the object's shape, texture, and weight in their hand and places it down at just the right place on the timeline, it can also provide a physical sense of space and distance. Some clients express a sense of relief, almost like they are putting down the weight of that experience when they place the object on the timeline. In addition, using nature-based materials as objects provides an additional dimension of grounding that supports healing and restoration.

Key Elements to Creating Visual Timelines

When working with your client to create a visual timeline, there are several key elements you must keep in mind in order to safely and effectively guide this process. These include:

- Finding representative moments
- Determining age anchors
- Leaving certain memories undisclosed
- Assessing attachment trauma
- Identifying clusters
- Finding resources
- Continuing into the future

Finding Representative Moments

For treatment mapping to be effective, you must delineate between memories with as much specificity as possible. Since clients do not always identify specific memories when creating a timeline—they may first identify general or even elusive themes—you can further delineate these experiences by looking for key representative moments. These moments provide a specific entry point into the distressing material that needs reprocessing. To uncover these moments, you can ask questions such as:

- "What memory or experience could represent that for you? That feeling of _______ [*e.g., being lonely in childhood*] . . . that experience of _______ [*e.g., doing bad in school*] . . . that belief of _______ [*e.g., I always mess up*]?"

Identifying and reprocessing representative moments can also allow for generalization to occur such that healing can spread across associated experiences. Not every upsetting memory in the client's past needs to be processed, as healing can naturally generalize to other associated experiences. Creating a visual timeline allows you and the client to identify the representative memories that enable the most expansive level of healing to occur. The visual and chronological layout of the timeline also makes it easy to locate the earliest material, and the client can begin to see how unprocessed earlier memories act as an underlying source of distress to later experiences. The visual map increases the client's understanding of why we would want to work with these earlier experiences first and how resolving the underlying source of distress can allow healing to generalize to later experiences.

Determining Age Anchors

When a client identifies a memory or representative event, the next step is to ask, "How old would you have been then?" If the client does not know, you can ask, "What's your felt sense as to how old you were then?" This allows the client to know where to visually mark or place the memory on their timeline. The age anchors the memory on the timeline and creates a reference point, a neutral way to refer to memories in any phase of treatment, especially when memories are too overwhelming to name. I might refer back only to the age, such as "Would it be okay to work on that six-year-old time?"

Age is also a component of the memory that does not change. The client's relationship to the experience changes (including the words they use to describe the event, images, cognitions, emotions, and sensations) but not the age at which it was experienced. I think of age as a neutral reference point that can also be a helpful way to reorient the client in the reprocessing phases (e.g., "Go back to that six-year-old time"), especially if the process of free association brought them to various memories of different times or ages.

Leaving Certain Memories Undisclosed

Sometimes during history taking, clients simply do not wish to name certain events. Privacy is very important in many cultures, and it is a relief for them to know that, as their therapist, you do not need to know what the memory is. Respecting a client's need for privacy can also build therapeutic trust and create the feeling that you are holding and guiding the process by helping them stay within a tolerable zone of arousal. This method of undisclosed or symbolic memories can also be used when the client has a sense that something happened at a certain point in their past, but they do not have an explicit memory of it or can access only fragments of the experience. The client can visually mark or represent such memories on their timeline without needing to know exactly what the memory is. This creates space on the timeline for implicit memories, generational material, dreams, and other experiences that can open up meaningful pathways to unresolved distress and healing.

Assessing Attachment Trauma

Clients do not often come into therapy with the skills to name their experiences of attachment trauma. While overt traumatic experiences, such as physical or sexual abuse, may be evident, it is the more covert experiences—such as absence and neglect, misaligned attachment, invalidation, violation, pressure to achieve, criticism, and shaming behaviors, to name a few—that are challenging for clients to recognize as having had an impact. In addition, clients often have defenses built up around these experiences that allow them to dismiss, normalize, or minimize their impact. As a result, clients may not initially identify these experiences during history taking, and there is a risk that this dimension of their experience will be missing from the overall clinical picture and treatment map.

Integrating specific questions from the Adult Attachment Interview (AAI) while creating the timeline can help you locate those attachment experiences in the client's past. The AAI is a semistructured interview developed by Mary Main and colleagues (George et al., 1985; Main & Hesse, 1990) that assesses a client's state of mind concerning their relationship with their attachment figures. The interview contains 20 open-ended questions inviting the client to recollect their childhood. The main goal of the questions is to "surprise the unconscious" so that the unconscious reveals itself through the personal narratives the client uses to answer the questions (George et al., 1985).

Although learning to score the AAI requires training, leaders in the field, such as Dan Siegel (2012), have noted that there is a benefit to using the measure to gain more insight into the quality of the client's attachment relationships without needing to be trained to score the interview. Learning to listen to *how* the client answers the questions is particularly important to using the AAI in a clinical context, including whether they (1) answer with coherent responses versus confused or confusing responses, (2) answer with short, dismissive, or defensive responses, or (3) become absorbed in the retelling of an event and lose orientation to the present moment and to the question you asked. Often, with secure attachment, clients are able to maintain orientation to the present and meaningfully reflect on their attachment relationships with fresh insight, integrating new perspectives and staying engaged with you as a conversation partner (Siegel, 2012; Steele & Steele, 2008). You'll learn more about this adapted approach to using the AAI later in this chapter, under the **Steps for Creating a Visual Timeline**.

As a note, the adaptation of the AAI that I use here does not require the client to share a story about the representative moment; they merely need to identify and mark it on the timeline. This can provide insight into the quality of the attachment relationship and guide the treatment plan, such as whether attachment resourcing is necessary in phase 2 (preparation). It may also point to the need for preverbal reprocessing when there is enough readiness to move into memory reprocessing. Chapter 10 provides an art-based preverbal reprocessing protocol called the **Resource Place**, which you can use whenever attachment trauma is identified.

Identifying Clusters

Sometimes the memories that clients identify are not single incidents but experiences that span across a range of time or across multiple events that are thematically or meaningfully connected. Grouping and clustering these events together can maximize treatment by enhancing the generalization effect across associated memories during reprocessing (Shapiro, 2018). According to Shapiro, **clusters** are experiences that are associated, connected, and stored together. These can be:

- Relational experiences, such as intimate partner violence, childhood sexual abuse, ongoing abuse by one perpetrator, or bullying
- Specific experiences that occurred multiple separate times, like medical traumas or sexual assault by different perpetrators
- Ongoing experiences with multiple components, such as poverty, displacement, conflict, chronic health conditions, discrimination, or race-based trauma
- Experiences associated with a predominant negative belief about the self, such as *I am a failure*
- Experiences associated with a primary sensory cue, like loud noises or yelling
- Experiences associated with a predominant physical sensation, such as choking, difficulty breathing, panic, the feeling of being enclosed or tied down, pressure or pain in a certain part of the body, or hunger due to restricted eating or deprivation
- Experiences associated with predominant emotions, such as loneliness, shame, or fear

You need to be skilled in listening for material that has a cluster quality to properly group and cluster events on the timeline during history taking. If the client identifies a moment or memory with a cluster quality (e.g., "My uncle touched me when I was a child"), you then inquire whether it was a single event or something that was ongoing. If the client states that it occurred multiple times or over a period of time (e.g., "Yeah, that happened a lot, I don't really remember how many times"), then you want to map out the cluster on the timeline by identifying the beginning point and the end point. If a cluster is ongoing and does not have an end point, the client can mark the end point in the present (as the cluster is continuing to this present time) or at some point in the future—wherever it feels right to them. The specific steps for identifying clusters are described under the **Steps of Creating a Visual Timeline** later in this chapter.

Note that inviting the client to identify multiple memories that fall within a cluster is often unhelpful and unnecessary in this phase of treatment, as it risks destabilization. However, when the client is ready for reprocessing, it is useful to start gathering more information about the cluster and work through it one step at a time. You can find more information on working with clusters in chapter 10.

Finding Resources

Once the client has identified and represented the events in their past that have impacted them in some way, the focus shifts to finding resources. Deb Dana (2018), who has been instrumental in bringing polyvagal theory into clinical practice, has introduced **glimmers** as the antidote or remedy to triggers. Glimmers are the memories, skills, supports, routines, rituals, resources, and practices that help people return to a place of safety and regulation in the face of distress. This might include:

- Experiences of mastery or success
- Positive attachment figures or role models
- Experiences of being nurtured and nurturing
- Relationships with pets or other animals
- Experiences of empowerment, agency, or control
- Spiritual practices
- Connection with nature or a particular place in nature
- Activities or hobbies that the client enjoys or is proud of
- Experiences where the client learned something new
- Personal qualities or personality traits
- Moments of feeling calm, contented, or relaxed
- Experiences associated with a sense of belonging or connection
- Experiences associated with a sense of awe or wonderment
- Experiences associated with a sense of meaning or purpose

It is always important to locate these experiences in time and place by identifying a representative moment or event. For example, "What moment or event could represent [*e.g., that sense of success*] for you?" or "What moment or event could represent [*e.g., being proud of that hobby*]?" Identifying glimmers helps bring balance to the negative memories on the timeline and encourages the client to recognize the various ways that they have navigated challenges and adversity.

Continuing into the Future

Since a client's life does not end in the present, it is essential to lay out the timeline in a way that extends into the future to make space for future goals. Therefore, after mapping out impactful experiences and positive resources, you want to invite clients to imagine a future where they can develop new ways of thinking, feeling, and being that move them closer to their goals. Since clients often present their goals in the negative—as in, what they would no longer be doing (e.g., "I wouldn't be numbing out all evening" or "I wouldn't be yelling at my kids")—your role is to help clients flip their negative goals into positive ones: "If you weren't doing that, what would you be doing instead?" This is a cognitive-behavioral and solution-focused strategy also used by AJ Popky (2005) in his DeTUR (Desensitization of Triggers and Urge Reprocessing) protocol for addictions.

Helping clients connect with a positive goal not only creates hope but also builds motivation to overcome strong urges to avoid upsetting memories or engage in trauma healing, even though it is challenging. Essentially, goals make trauma work worth it for the client.

The following is an example of a visual timeline created collaboratively with a client during a telehealth session. (Note that some information has been crossed out or removed to protect identity. The client's original timeline also had lines and events drawn in different colors based on the client's choices.) The client was a white, European humanitarian aid worker living and working in various African countries. She was high functioning and well resourced but struggled with feelings of inadequacy, anxiety, and isolation. In mapping out her timeline, she identified single incidents, such as "ballet" at age 8, as well as clustered experiences, such as "restrictive eating" that began at age 17 and continued until age 30.

Memories from her attachment relationships were gathered using questions from the AAI. We drew a line for her relationship with her mother above the timeline and an additional line for her relationship with her father below the timeline, both of which started at conception and continued into the future. She shared that she often felt triggered in her relationships with her parents and wanted to develop a calm yet boundaried relationship with them, with the specific goal of being able to speak with her mother one time per week without tension or conflict, and without feeling activated or overwhelmed after ending the call. Although she used positive words to describe her relationship with her mother (such as *security* and *warmth*), some representative experiences that she provided had to do with being protected from or escaping the father.

She also provided positive descriptive words for her relationship with her father, such as "playful" (with a representative experience of helping him in the garden), but only until age four, which she marked on the timeline with a vertical line and the words "stress increased" due to financial stressors, her parents having a third child, and needing to build a larger home. After this point, her father's behavior became abusive and violent, and words like "not fair" and "ticking time bomb" were used to describe their relationship. This process helped her recognize the connection between her father's demanding and abusive behavior and her fear of making mistakes, which also led to increased control over her eating as a form of coping and as a way to signal to the adults in her life that she needed help.

She was also able to recognize the positive and grounding role her husband and children had in the second half of her life, including in changing her relationship with food and her body. (You can see that the cluster of restrictive eating continues until her first pregnancy.) In our following session, we focused more on resources and supports, which included traveling, her faith, her relationship with her grandmother, and her tenacity.

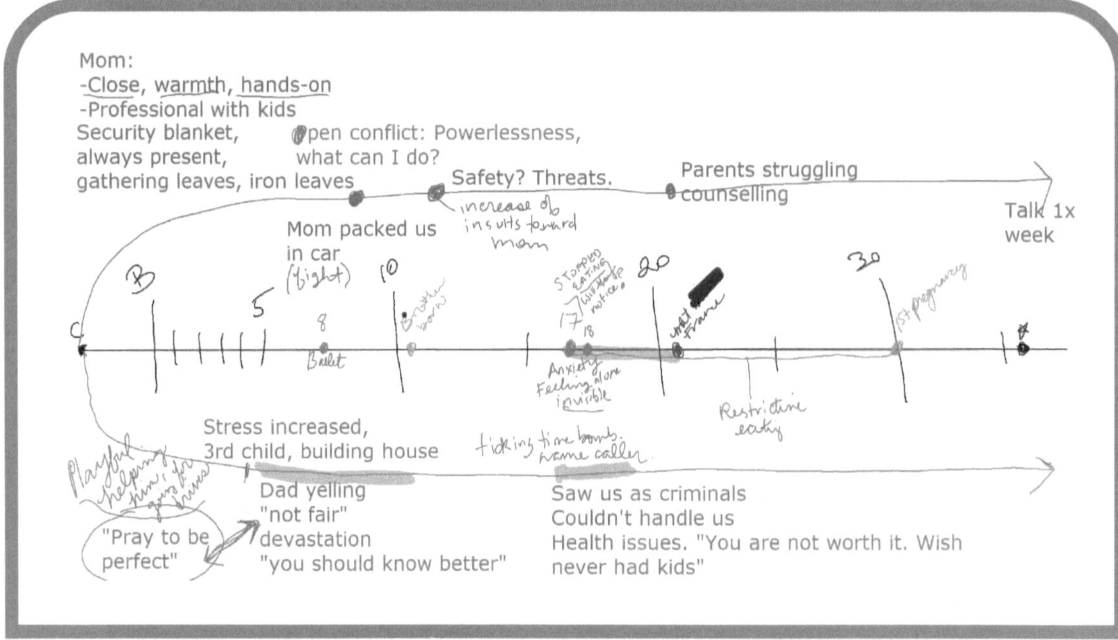

Steps for Creating a Visual Timeline

The following section guides you through a 10-step process for helping clients organize their experiences on a visual timeline. This entire process can require one to two sessions, or longer if you need to practice grounding and stabilization strategies in between. Steps 1 through 6 focus on identifying upsetting or traumatic material from the client's past, while steps 7 through 10 are focused on finding positive resources and future goals.

It is important to maintain attunement with the client throughout this process, regularly assessing their level of presence and activation so you reduce the risk of destabilization. If at any point you notice your client becoming activated, you can do a containment or grounding activity to help them regulate. If the timeline is incomplete before the end of the session, it is advisable to document and contain the timeline until the following session (e.g., by placing it in a folder or box) and then participate in a movement, breathing, progressive muscle relaxation, or other regulating activity before closing the session. (See chapters 6 and 7 for stabilizing activities.)

Step 1: Psychoeducation

Begin the process by explaining to the client that sometimes memories don't get a chance to heal at the time that they were experienced because they are too painful, upsetting, and confusing. We often cope by covering them up as best as we can and moving on, trying our best not to think about them or feel them. These unhealed wounds often get touched by things that happen in our lives, causing us to reexperience the pain from the past as if it's happening again, and we end up having bigger responses to people or situations in the present than is helpful. When we go back and find these memories and bring them some healing, we often start to get some relief from the present distress too, and we are better able to manage current situations because we aren't reacting to the past and the present all at once. In making a visual timeline, we can start to map out some of those experiences so that we know where to go in our work together.

Step 2: Laying Out the Visual Timeline

Draw a line across a large piece of paper (or multiple pieces of paper taped together horizontally). Mark conception, birth, the first five years, every ten years thereafter, the present (i.e., the client's current age), and a line extending into the future with an arrow on the end. The example below is for a 33-year-old client.

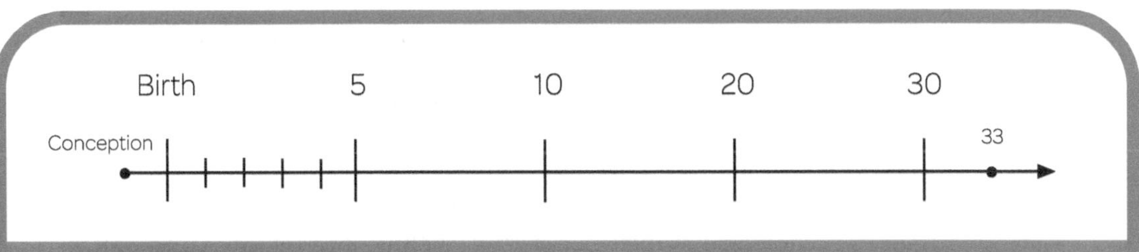

Step 3: Starting with Presenting Issues

The primary goal of the timeline is to gather the information needed for phase 1 with as little activation as possible. For this reason, I often begin with direct questioning while doing the timeline to help the client maintain a bird's-eye view. To do so, you ask the client to first identify present distress:

- "Let's start with what is happening for you in the present. What behaviors, patterns, emotions, or beliefs cause distress or interfere with your well-being and functioning?"
    - **Representative moment:** "What recent experience could represent that [*behavior, pattern, emotion, or belief*] for you?"
    - **External representation:** "Choose a color for that experience."
    - **Location:** "Go ahead and mark it there on your timeline, in the present."
    - **Label:** "What word would you use to label that [*current issue*]? Write that on the timeline."

You then use direct questioning to connect it to the past:

- "How far back does this go? When was the first time you remember acting, feeling, or thinking this way?"
    - **Representative moment:** "What specific moment or event could represent that [*behavior, pattern, emotion, or belief*] for you?"
    - **External representation:** "Choose a color for that memory."
    - **Age:** "How old would you have been then?"
    - **Location:** "Go ahead and mark it there on your timeline."
    - **Label:** "What word could you use to label that point in time? Write that on the timeline."
    - **Associated events:** "Are there other moments or events when you remember acting, feeling, or thinking this way? Mark those on the timeline."

You then repeat this process with any other presenting issues. However, if the client struggles to access earlier material or past memories, you can use the **floatback script** to increase the client's felt connection with the past, making earlier events more accessible. Since this can also increase the risk of destabilization, it is important to help the client maintain present-moment orientation and grounding during the process and to keep momentum by inviting the client to mark it on the timeline using color and a label and moving to the next memory:

- **Representative moment:** "Think of that recent situation that made you act, think, or feel in that way [*in reference to the presenting issue*]."
- **Float back:** "As you think of that moment, notice the thoughts coming to mind, as well as the feelings and sensations in your body, and let your mind float back to an earlier time that felt anything like this. Just trusting that any moment or memory that comes up is important in some way. When you land on something, let me know."
- **Age:** "How old were you then?"
- **Location:** "Go ahead and mark that on the timeline."
- **Label:** "What word (or symbol) could you use to label that point in time? Write that on the timeline."
- **Continue to float back:** "When you think of *that* experience, notice the thoughts, feelings, and sensations coming up for you, and let your mind float back to an even earlier time that felt anything like this one . . . When you land on something, let me know."
- **Age:** "How old were you then?"
- **Location:** "Go ahead and mark that on the timeline."
- **Label:** "What word (or symbol) could you use to label that point in time? Write that on the timeline."

Continue floating back and marking the memories on the timeline until no earlier memories come up.

Step 4: Open Questions and Free Association

You then ask your client about other experiences in their past that were hard or impactful in some way. They do not need to identify memories in any specific order. Whatever memory the client identifies as being impactful in their life, they can mark that event on their timeline—without opening up or recounting it—and then move to the next.

If they identify a single incident:

- **Representative moment:** "What specific moment or event could represent that [*experience*] for you?"
- **External representation:** "Choose a color for that memory."
- **Age:** "How old would you have been then?"
- **Location:** "Go ahead and mark that on your timeline."
- **Label:** "What word could you use to label that point in time? Write that on the timeline."

If they identify a cluster of incidents:

- **Verify it is a cluster:** "Is that something that happened once, or was it the kind of thing that happened more than once or continued over a period of time?"
- **Identify the beginning point:** "How old would you say you were the first time you experienced anything having to do with [*the clustered material*]? When did that first start?"
- **Location:** "Mark that point on the timeline."
- **Identify the end point:** "And how old would you say you were when that experience was over?"
- **Location:** "Mark that point on the timeline." [*If the cluster is not over yet, invite the client to mark the end point in the future when they can imagine it being over, or as over as it could possibly be.*]
- **Delineate the cluster:** "Now draw a line connecting those two points using any color you would like. This line is like a thread, stringing together all those experiences from the beginning to the end so that we know they're there. But we don't have to open them all up today, we're just mapping it all out."
- **Label:** "What label or name would you give that period of time? Go ahead and write that down on the timeline."

If the client cannot access an explicit memory, they can identify a sensation, symbol, or imagined event to represent the implicit material:

- **Symbolic representation:** "What could symbolize that [*implicit material*] for you, even if it is something you imagine now or a story you heard about that time?"

- **External representation:** "Choose a color for that symbol."
- **Age:** "What's your best guess at how old you would have been then?"
- **Location:** "Go ahead and mark it there on your timeline."
- **Label:** "What word could you use to label that symbol? Write that on the timeline."

Step 5: Assess for Undisclosed Memories

As you continue gathering information, give the client an opportunity to mark any undisclosed memories on their timeline:

- **Undisclosed representative moment:** "If there are any memories that impacted you in some way and that you think are an important part of your past—but that you don't want to talk about right now—you can represent them in some way on your timeline. For example, with a color, word, or symbol. You do not have to share what it is; we can just know that it's there."
- **External representation:** "Choose a color for that memory."
- **Age:** "How old would you have been then?"
- **Location:** "Go ahead and mark it there on your timeline."
- **Label:** "Would you like to label that experience in some way? Write that on the timeline."

Step 6: Attachment Relationships

To assess for the quality of the client's attachment relationships, begin by identifying the primary caregiver(s) involved in the client's upbringing:

- "Which adults were influential in your life? Who raised you?"

Then ask the client to think of five words to describe each caregiver using this question from the AAI:

- "Think of five words that describe your relationship with your [*e.g., mother/father/aunt/uncle/grandparent*], starting from as far back as you can remember."

Write down the five words the client uses to describe their relationship with that caregiver and then ask the same question for the next primary caregiver, if applicable. After identifying these adjectives, the next step is to ask the client to recount a memory or event that best represents each word they used to describe the relationship. The goal is for the client to scan through their memories to find the one that best matches each descriptor:

- **Representative moment:** "What moment or event would represent [*e.g., your mother being protective*], going as far back as you can remember?"
- **External representation:** "Choose a color for that memory."
- **Age:** "How old would you have been then?"
- **Location:** "Go ahead and mark it there on your timeline."
- **Label:** "What word could you use to label that memory? Write that on the timeline."

Asking these questions can also help identify positive attachment experiences that can be marked on the timeline as resources, such as experiences of being loved, supported, nurtured, or validated.

Step 7: Finding Resources

Once the client has identified and represented the events in their past that have impacted them in some way, the focus shifts to finding resources:

- "What are some positive memories or experiences from your past that feel good to think about today?"
- "What strengths, skills, supports, and resources would you say have helped you navigate the difficult experiences in your life?"

Then find the representative memories that go with each resource:

- **Representative moment:** "What moment or event could represent that [*skill/strength/support/resource*] for you?"
- **External representation:** "Choose a color for that resource."
- **Age:** "How old would you have been then?"
- **Location:** "Go ahead and mark it on your timeline."
- **Label:** "What word could you use to label that resource? Write that on the timeline."

Step 8: Future Goals

Once you've finished mapping out the client's past and identified positive resources, invite them to imagine what they'd like their future to be like:

- "Let's say our work together is successful, and we can process through these experiences so that they're not getting in your way. What would change in your life?"
- "What would it mean to heal from these experiences?"
- "How would you prefer to act and feel? What would you prefer to believe about yourself?"

Then find a representative memory that goes with each future goal:

- **Representative moment:** "What future moment or event could represent achieving that for you?"
- **External representation:** "Choose a color for that goal."
- **Age:** "How old would you hope to be by then?"
- **Location:** "Go ahead and mark it there on your timeline."
- **Label:** "What word could you use to label that goal? Write that on the timeline."

Step 9: Documentation and Containment

To document the client's work, you or the client can take photos of the entire timeline as well as certain time periods in the client's life, such as each decade. The photos can be used as a reference point throughout treatment. Putting the timeline away and storing it is also an act of physical containment that clients often find therapeutically beneficial. There is often a sense of relief that the memories have been given a place until the client is ready to work on them.

Step 10: Reflection and Closure

In closing the session, it is important to encourage a more reflective stance to help the client gain distance from the material, such as by asking whether they gained any new or helpful insights from the activity. Reflection is a cognitive task that can help the client return fully to the present moment and support emotion regulation. In asking the client what they need to close the session, you assess whether they require any additional regulation or grounding, such as a breathing or movement exercise, and create the space to engage in that activity together if so. It is also helpful in some cases to make a plan with the client to engage in self-care after the session, such as taking a walk, talking to a friend or loved one, or simply being reminded to be gentle and compassionate with themself as they stirred up old memories and material during the session and it can take time for it to settle back down:

- "We can use this timeline as a map to guide our work together. It's like a reference point to track your progress. Was there anything new, surprising, or helpful? What do you need to be able to close this session?"

Using Art- and Nature-Based Materials to Enhance Visual Timelines

When working with clients to create visual timelines, the introduction of art- and nature-based materials can deeply enhance the process, as they provide clients with a tangible and concrete way to represent their experiences. In this section, I discuss how you can use rocks and gems, as well as buttons, to facilitate this process.

Rocks and Gems

In chapter 4, you learned about the internal river as a metaphor for understanding the AIP system. In much the same way, you can introduce visual timelines as a way to explore the river of a client's life journey. Like rivers, the journey of life is also filled with twists, turns, challenges, and changes.

To create a visual timeline using this metaphor, you simply ask the client to map out their memories along a line or rope that symbolizes the river of life, using rocks to represent experiences of trauma and adversity, and gems, crystals, and other stones to represent resources and positive experiences.* River rocks are my preferred rocks to use to represent experiences of trauma and hardship. These are often drab gray stones with lines of quartz or calcite

* This approach has been adapted from the river of life history-taking approach in NET.

running through them. The minerals running through the river rocks are harder and more robust than the rock itself. I talk to clients about how the mineral stripes on the rocks are like resources held within the memory—they represent the strengths, knowledge, and wisdom the client accessed to get through that experience. As part of the healing, I explain that we want to wear away and break down that heavy rock into pebbles or sand so the client can more easily see and access the resources inside. However, if you don't have river rocks, any collection of rocks will work for the client to choose from to represent their traumatic experiences.

In addition to rocks, you will want to have a basket of gems of various colors and shapes available to represent the client's resources (e.g., skills, support, strengths). This might include granite, basalt, agates, jasper, quartz, obsidian, petrified wood, and others. Rocks and gems are very grounding materials to work with, and clients often enjoy holding them, feeling the weight in their hands, placing them down, and arranging them on the timeline. My collection of rocks and gems is pictured here.

You will also need either a roll of paper or multiple pieces of paper taped together horizontally, with each piece of paper representing a certain period of time (e.g., five years). The length of the line or string used to depict the client's life—from birth to present and into the future—will depend on the client's age and how much space is used. I prefer to draw a line across the paper, as this allows the client to mark out clusters, add labels, and write additional information.

To introduce this river-and-rock metaphor to your client, you can say:

- "This line is like the river of your life. [*Draw a line horizontally across the paper or, ideally, across multiple pieces of paper taped together or a long piece of paper.*] Every river has a source, known as its headwaters or beginnings. That is like the very beginning of your life, like conception. [*Mark a beginning point where the line starts.*] Since then, your life has continued to move forward, like a river moving toward the sea, all the way to the present [*mark a point on the timeline to represent the present*] and into the future." [*Draw an arrow where the line ends to show that time continues.*]

Once the whole timeline is drawn, mark key ages on the timeline—birth, the first five years of the client's life, and every decade thereafter until the client's current age. Then give directives for completing the timeline:

- "These rocks represent different events in your life that have impacted you—the hard things, like painful or heavy experiences, even experiences of loss—while the minerals and gemstones represent the resources, skills, and supports that are part of your life too."
- "This timeline will help us map out our work together so that we can help your mind break down the hard and heavy experiences into pebbles or sand so they're not as sharp, jagged, and painful to carry. This frees up the minerals held inside the rocks so they are available to you as strengths and resources. Memories, like rocks, can be reshaped and polished by our work together so that the beautiful lines and patterns running through them will become more visible (like these river stones). You can see things about that experience and about yourself that were perhaps not evident before—things that were hidden by the size and weight of the experience."

Once you introduce the materials and directives, guide the client through the remaining steps of the visual timeline presented earlier, beginning with step 3 (**Starting with Presenting Issues**). Whenever the client is invited to represent a distressing memory by choosing a color, they can choose a stone instead. Whenever the client is invited to represent a resource by choosing a color, they can choose a gem instead.

The following is an image from a workshop I facilitated in Ethiopia to teach EMDR therapists this technique for history taking. In the photo, Tigist Waltenigus (pictured on the left) is guiding her colleague through the process using both buttons and stones. Tigist is an EMDR therapist and cofounder of the Erq Me'ad Counselling Center in Addis Ababa. She recently published the first book written in Amharic on the topic of trauma, called *What Is Wrong with Me?*, meant to be accessible to the general public to increase understanding of the impacts of trauma on social well-being and attachment relationships within Ethiopian culture.

Buttons

Buttons are an additional material that can enhance the process of creating visual timelines. Not only can buttons be aesthetically pleasing, but the highly tactile process can support present-moment orientation as the client scans internally for memories—making this a form of dual-tasking. In addition, just as buttons can hold together pieces of fabric, the buttons on the client's timeline can hold together pieces of the client's story, stringing together experiences and themes in their past.

Buttons are also an ancient part of our human story and quite possibly one of our earliest art objects. For example, shell disks with holes drilled through them were found at a Neolithic burial site in present-day Pakistan dating back to 7000 BCE (Stone, 2020). It is perhaps for this reason that sifting through a bowl of buttons often brings clients into a state of curiosity as they look for the right button to represent a particular memory, relationship, resource, or period of time. Clients can feel or look at each button's shape, color, and texture as it sits in their hands, creating a sense of closeness and connection while they freely associate about their past.

I recommend including buttons of various sizes, shapes, and materials, especially natural materials like shell, clay, antler, bone, metal, leather, wood, glass, amber, cotton, silk, and stone. It is especially important to have a variety of buttons available when working with clients from diverse cultural backgrounds, as it can increase connection with their cultural identity and roots. For example, when using this timeline approach with a Vietnamese client, colorful silk buttons elicited associations with traditional clothing and female figures in her life. Similarly, many Indigenous communities along the Pacific Northwest coast of Canada use mother-of-pearl buttons to create traditional button blankets, where the buttons are used to embroider and outline figures of clan animals and family crests. Button blankets are most often worn like capes during ceremonies or important social gatherings to demonstrate identity, family, and clan history. My collection of buttons is pictured here.

Similar to the river-and-rock timeline, you will also need either a roll of paper or multiple pieces of paper taped together horizontally for this activity. To introduce the button timeline to your client, you can say:

"This line is like a piece of thread that strings together the pieces of your life story. [*Draw a line horizontally across the paper or, ideally, across multiple pieces of paper taped together or a long piece of paper.*] From the very beginning of your life [*mark the beginning point where the line starts*], all the way to the present [*mark a point on the timeline to represent the present*], and into the future." [*Draw an arrow where the line ends to show that time continues.*]

Once the whole timeline is drawn, mark key ages on the timeline—birth, the first five years of the client's life, and every decade thereafter until the client's current age. Then give directives for completing the timeline:

- "These buttons represent different experiences in your life that have impacted you, like upsetting or painful experiences—things that were too much. You don't need to tell the whole story of those experiences, you can just use the buttons to represent them so we can map it all out and create a plan for our work together. You can also use the buttons to represent the positive experiences and resources that are part of your life too."

Once you introduce the materials and directives, guide the client through the remaining steps of the visual timeline presented earlier, beginning with step 3 (**Starting with Presenting Issues**). Whenever the client is invited to represent the memory or resource by choosing a color, they can choose a button instead.

Documentation and Closure

Whether you are creating a river-and-rock timeline or a button timeline, I recommend taking photos of the timeline for documentation. When this step is complete, clients often enjoy the tactile experience of returning the rocks, gems, or buttons to the baskets, which can provide a sense of closure and completion. The paper can then be folded up and safely stored in a folder or box. Any additional memories or notes can also be added to the timeline in later sessions.

Using the Visual Timeline to Map Treatment

Once you and your client have created a timeline, you can see where present distress is rooted and collaboratively discuss where to start treatment. When there is readiness, you ideally want to work with the earliest material in the client's life first, as these experiences can act as feeder memories that drive current distress. However, the specific plan will depend on your case conceptualization and collaborative understanding of what will bring the most sustainable relief and move the client toward their goals, alongside considerations of time, needs, readiness, level of distress tolerance, and external circumstances. With EMDR's three-stranded process, you can move around all points on the timeline—like the river, sankofa, Celtic knot, and braid—to follow where the client needs to go to find healing, relief, and movement toward their goals.

CHAPTER 6

Enhancing Phase 2 with the Creative Arts

This chapter focuses on phase 2 of EMDR: preparation. In this phase, the primary goal is to build readiness for reprocessing by helping the client develop skills, internal resources, and stabilization strategies. You prepare the client to handle upsetting material that may arise during reprocessing by building their capacity to observe their internal world from a mindful, present-oriented stance. During this phase, you also orient the client to the steps of the EMDR process so their expectations are clear and the process feels predictable.

To facilitate this process, this chapter presents two art-based activities that you can use during phase 2. The first is a mindfulness-based drawing activity that promotes nervous system regulation and a calm physiological state (the Zentangle drawing method), while the second is a six-part storytelling activity that helps clients identify their personal and cultural strengths and also introduces them to the steps of EMDR (the transformative journey storytelling method). These activities can also promote relational safety and the development of therapeutic trust.

Zentangle Drawing: An Art-Based Approach to Calm Place

The **calm place** (or **calm state**) is one of the first skills that you offer clients in the preparation phase. For this skill, you invite the client to think of a memory, place, or activity that feels good and calming when they bring it to mind. You then enhance the positive feelings associated with this memory, place, or activity by connecting to its sensory elements and adding slow, short sets of dual attention BLS. Once the calm place is established and enhanced as an internal resource, the client can use this skill to shift from a state of distress to a state of calm or neutrality. You can guide the client to practice shifting states by asking them to connect to their calm place, bring to mind a distressing event, and then shift their focus back to their calm place. As the client repeats this over time, including between sessions, they build their capacity for affect regulation and increase readiness for reprocessing.

However, many trauma survivors struggle to connect internally with a calming memory, place, or activity long enough to enhance it as a resource. Upsetting images, thoughts, feelings, or sensations associated with the memory can intrude on and taint the client's experience, creating dysregulation or even shame. For many clients who have experienced displacement, loss, or other significant life transitions, connecting with memories from the past can also bring up grief and longing, even when the memory itself is positive. Some clients do not know what it feels like to be calm, present, and grounded, or they struggle to connect with the neural networks that hold that information. Other clients may struggle to shift out of states of hypervigilance, believing that "letting their guard down" is unsafe or too vulnerable a state.

For these clients, it can be helpful to use the creative arts to provide an externally focused experience in the here and now, instead of requiring them to bring something from the past to mind. Many clients, especially with activated nervous systems, respond well to being in a state of *doing*, as opposed to a state of *being* that requires an inward focus. The embodied act of art making and the external focus on its sensory components can slow them down, regulating the nervous system and downregulating the amygdala. This can lead to an increased awareness of the internal world while staying anchored in the present moment. The sensations of calm that clients begin to notice in their bodies can then be enhanced and installed as a calm place resource using dual attention BLS.

One well-established method of using the creative arts to facilitate preparation is the **Zentangle** drawing activity. This method was developed by Maria Thomas, a professional calligraphy artist, and her partner, Rick Roberts, who saw the parallels between his own meditative practice and the calm, focused state brought about by the repetitive calligraphy strokes. The idea for the Zentangle drawing was born from these parallels and the bringing together of art, primarily calligraphy, with meditation through the creation of simple and structured nonrepresentational patterns. As clients intentionally focus on just the line they are drawing, one stroke at a time, it helps them orient to the present moment.

I have been integrating the Zentangle drawing method into trauma work since 2014, when Tina Daye, a colleague at Northern Society for Domestic Peace, introduced me to it as a creative way to engage youth. It has since become a standard stabilization strategy in my practice, and I have found it especially beneficial for clients who struggle with the calm place activity due to complex trauma symptoms. Not only is it effective, but it is accessible and easy to learn. It does not require technical ability, space, or lots of equipment, making it especially beneficial in low-resource settings. Although there are a lot of high-quality materials that you can purchase for Zentangle drawing, these materials are not necessary to reap its benefits. The only materials you need are paper, pencils, and pens. In 2022, I became a certified Zentangle teacher so I could teach EMDR therapists how to use it with their clients for stabilization. I also offer it for self-care and staff-care

workshops for therapists and frontline workers in conflict-affected settings, such as Ethiopia. The Zentangle drawing here was created by an EMDR therapist in Ethiopia who was learning the Zentangle method for the first time at a group workshop for self-care.

Connecting to Culture Through Zentangle Patterns

The Zentangle technique is a modern mindfulness practice that is secular in nature. Even though it has the word *zen* in it, it is not associated with Zen Buddhism or any religion. Rather, the goal of this art practice is to achieve calm by creating beautiful art with gratitude and appreciation. At the same time, it is important to acknowledge the indirect and direct cultural influences on the Zentangle method. For example, Chinese calligraphic handwriting is a traditional meditative art form that has demonstrated effectiveness as a stress-reduction strategy (Kao et al., 2014). Similarly, Zen art is a practice in Japan that is grounded in the philosophy of Zen Buddhism, in which the goal is to lose one's self (and sense of ego) through the creative act. Additionally, mandalas (Sanskrit for *circle*) are widely recognized as a meditative tool that promotes integration and wholeness with deep spiritual meaning in various religions.

In addition, the use of patterns (central to the Zentangle method) is ubiquitous in cultures around the world and throughout history, as evidenced in the patterns we find in textiles, quilts, art, pottery, and architecture, to name a few examples. We see patterns in Celtic knots and spirals, medieval church labyrinths, Indian *mehndi* tattoos, the geometric patterns of Moroccan architecture, and the flowers and animals of European folk art. Many Zentangle patterns mimic the natural world that exists all around us, such as blades of grass, ripples of water, lines of spider webs, rings of a tree, climbing vines and leaves, or spiraling ferns and shells. Although Zentangle patterns are nonrepresentative, clients may find their own meanings in the patterns you introduce. This may bring clients closer to the pattern as they engage with it, allowing positive personal or cultural associations to emerge that further enhance the resource. As clients become more familiar with the Zentangle patterns, they can choose patterns that resonate most deeply with them.

Components and Characteristics of Zentangle Patterns

To create a Zentangle drawing, you start by creating an outline (called a **border**), which can be done by making four dots on a page (like four corners of a square) and then connecting those dots. Your client may also enjoy tracing their hand as a border. The second step is to divide the border into different spaces with a single line or multiple lines (called a **string**). Then, different patterns, called **tangles**, are drawn within the spaces. Tangles have different visual characteristics that are made by combining **elemental strokes** like lines, curves, dots, and circles. Some are curvy, organic patterns that seem to grow on the page as the pattern unfolds, while others are more straight or geometric, with sharper corners or shapes. Some use grid-like patterns of intersecting lines and sections that can be filled in. Some are highly textured or take a high level of focus, while other patterns are more spontaneous and playful.

Zentangle patterns are fun and easy to learn, but delving into the world of Zentangle patterns can be overwhelming if you do not know where to look, especially as there are hundreds of patterns to choose from. For this reason, I have created an instructional booklet of 15 Zentangle patterns to help you learn Zentangle drawing. You can access the booklet with the QR code on this page.

The 15 tangles in the booklet are easy patterns that have a good balance between the visual characteristics and qualities of tangles. You do not need to learn all 15 tangles and can simply choose a few to become familiar with as you experiment with the sequence of steps involved in this process. The sequence of steps for a tangle can slowly be learned by heart, like song lyrics or a recipe. The more comfortable you get with tangles, the more you can start playing and experimenting with them, such as by mixing and combining patterns in new ways.

As you increase your familiarity with the Zentangle patterns, you can guide and draw alongside your client, even experimenting with new patterns, creating what is called a **shared authentic experience**, a concept from Trauma Center Trauma Sensitive Yoga, where the client and therapist move together to build relational safety and connection. Similar to movement practices, making art together is a shared, relational experience that keeps you and the client connected to each other in the present moment. For clients who have experienced interpersonal trauma and violation, the therapeutic power of this experience cannot be overstated, as it provides them with a nonthreatening space to engage in their own process. One of my clients once commented how new it felt for her to be aware of her own internal experience while in the presence of a care provider, as she typically focused externally on their nonverbal cues to assess for danger and threat.

It is also important for you to embody a healthy attitude toward your own drawing and to model being forgiving, curious, courageous, and not overly perfectionistic. There is always permission to make mistakes in Zentangle drawing. Drawing in pen, you may make a mistake, but you find the courage to work the mistake into the drawing by creatively problem-solving and trying something new. You move on, rather than discarding the drawing and starting again. For clients who struggle with shame and self-criticism, this creative process can be a gentle way of learning new and more compassionate ways of relating themselves. When you can laugh at your "mistakes" and be playful, the client learns to relax into their own process. I often say to clients, "No matter how many times I do a Zentangle pattern, they never look alike. It depends on my mood, energy, and tension in my muscles. Sometimes I have these tight perfect lines, sometimes my lines are shaky, and sometimes they are loose and playful." As my instructor in the Zentangle method training, Katharina Königsbauer, said, "Love your lines!"

Zentangle drawings are also a regular part of my own self-care routine. I created this Zentangle drawing using four different patterns called Crescent Moon, Printemps, Gneiss, and Bales. The steps to each of these tangles are included in the Zentangle workbook, as well as in the previous QR code, which contains a video showing the process of creating this Zentangle drawing from start to finish.

Steps for Using the Zentangle Drawing Method

The following section walks you through the steps for using the Zentangle drawing method with clients, along with suggested scripts to facilitate this process. This involves: (1) introducing the method to your client, (2) creating the border and the string, (3) introducing the steps to a specific Zentangle pattern or tangle, (4) using dual attention BLS to enhance the calm sensations that the client notices in their body, and (5) closing the activity by providing psychoeducation on how the client can use the drawing (or a cue word) to practice and enhance their calm place. A containment script is also provided in case any distress or negative self-talk arises during the process. Images from my instructional booklet are provided throughout as visual aids to the script.

Step 1: Present the Zentangle Drawing as a Stabilization Strategy

- "Let's find something that can feel calming and soothing to focus on, something to help us be here in the present moment."
- "What do you think about trying Zentangle drawing? It's a mindfulness-based art therapy technique where we create simple patterns using repetitive lines and strokes. It can really help people enter a state of flow and calm focus and let other thoughts fall into the background. Even if we only draw for a short period of time, it can give your mind some space to rest."

Step 2: Set Up the Zentangle Drawing

- **Border:** "Begin by making a border or outline with a pencil. There are different ways to do this. You could make four corner dots anywhere on the page, or at the corners of the paper, and connect them with loose, freestyle lines (not with a ruler). Or you can trace your hand."
- Demonstrate these different options to the client and guide them to choose what they would like to try.
- Here is an example of a border made by creating four corner dots and connecting them with loose lines.

- **String (optional):** "If you would like, you can draw some loose, light lines within your border, called a string. The string creates multiple spaces within the border so that you can fill each space with a different pattern and have multiple patterns within a border—it can be fun to experiment with how the patterns look next to each other. Or you may wish to keep the space inside the border open by not drawing a string and using the whole space for just one pattern. The string can also be done with a pencil and is really spontaneous and light, so try not to put a lot of thought into it. No two strings look the same! Strings can be straight, curvy, loopy, or jagged. You can make freestyle lines to divide the space, or you can make the string by . . .
    - drawing a line with one or two loops, beginning at one edge of the border and ending at another
    - drawing a diagonal Z shape within the border
    - drawing an X shape within the border
    - or you can keep the space inside the border open by not drawing a string."
- Demonstrate the different options and guide your client to choose what they would like to try. Here are some examples of strings.

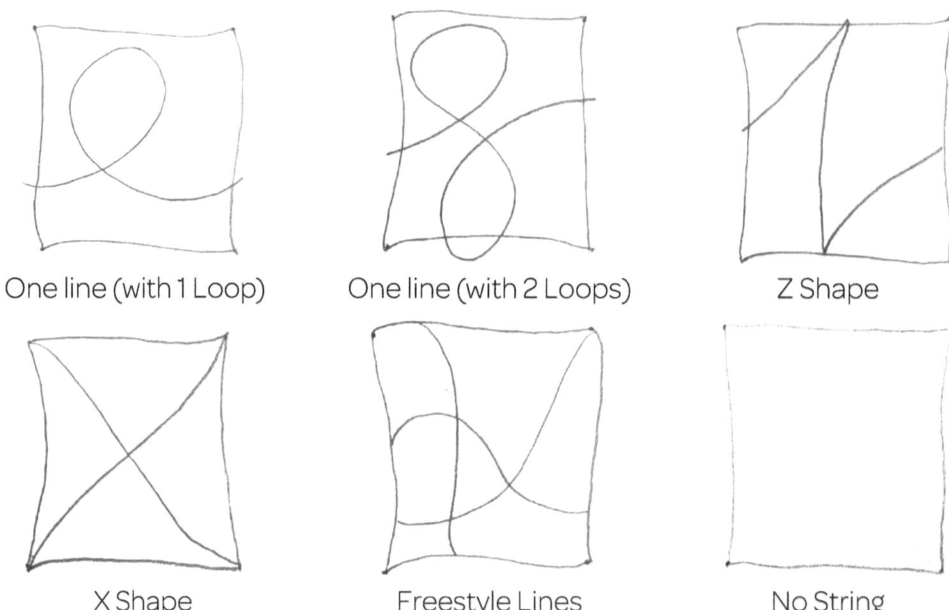

Step 3: Introduce a Zentangle Pattern (the Tangle)

- Introduce the client to one of the 15 Zentangle patterns in the workbook, where you will find the visual steps to creating each pattern. In this section, the steps to introducing a tangle are illustrated using a pattern called Crescent Moon, which is often the first tangle I share with clients as it is simple yet appealing, and it introduces clients to some of the basic Zentangle strokes and techniques:
    - "We will fill one whole space with a pattern, one step at a time. Choose a space created by your string to begin, or if you do not have a string, you can use the whole space within the border for this pattern. We can start with a pattern that's called ________ [*name the pattern*]."

    - Here is an example of a completed Crescent Moon tangle. Note that the square border is not divided by a string, so the pattern takes up the whole space within the border.

- Introduce the client to the first step of the pattern by demonstrating it on your own drawing. In the case of Crescent Moon, the first step is drawing semicircles or half-moon-like shapes along the contours of the border or string, leaving a bit of space between each one.
- Encourage your client to go with their own flow: "Take your time, drawing the lines at your own pace, focusing on just one line at a time."
- Encourage the client to rotate their paper as they draw—turning their paper 90 degrees, then 180 degrees as they work their way around the entire inside space, and eventually a full 360 degrees to complete the step. Rotating the paper as they draw can make it

easier to feel in control of their lines and to keep their hand in a comfortable position.

- Continue drawing with the client, making your own Zentangle drawing while staying aware of the client's process.

- When the client completes the first step, demonstrate the second step of the pattern. In the case of Crescent Moon, the second step is filling in the half-moon-like shapes around the contours of the border or string. Some clients may wish to use a thicker pen or marker for this, if available, and others enjoy just focusing on the process of filling it in with a fine pen. There is no rush with drawing Zentangle patterns.
- As the client draws, provide some relaxation prompts:
    - "Try to notice your breath as you draw, without needing to change anything about it, just noticing your breathing as it is now."
    - "Notice any tension in your muscles, perhaps in your shoulders, or in your hands. See whether you can relax them a little bit."

- When the client indicates that they have finished this step, move to the next step of the Zentangle pattern. In the case of Crescent Moon, the next step is drawing lines that trace around the semicircles while keeping the space between each line about as equal as possible. The technique of tracing around a shape with a line is called **aura-ing** in the Zentangle method.
- With Crescent Moon, you continue tracing around each individual semicircle until there is no more space for the lines to "land" between the shapes. At this point, you begin joining the semicircles

with your lines, tracing or aura-ing the shapes with about the same distance between each line. Eventually, one line will move around the entire inside space, joining all semicircles. You continue aura-ing and filling the space as you work your way into the middle.

- Once the space is full, the client may like to experiment with adding shading with a pencil to add some dimension and depth to the pattern, or they may enjoy adding color.

- When the client has completed their tangle, you and the client can collaboratively choose another tangle from the workbook of 15 Zentangle patterns to experiment with; often, clients enjoy looking at the different patterns and choosing one that appeals to them. The next pattern can be drawn in another space created by the string or within a new border.

Step 4: Enhance and Install Calm Place

- Help the client identify a positive feeling state by asking them to notice what they feel in their body as they draw. This can be done intermittently throughout the drawing process.
- If the client reports calm, positive, or neutral sensations in their body, invite them to take a break from their drawing and really tune into that sensation, letting it enhance and expand using the butterfly hug technique, in which they cross their arms in front of their body and tap back and forth on their chest or upper arms (Artigas et al., 2000):
    - "Would it be okay to take a pause from the drawing and focus on those sensations for a moment?"
    - "You could even try crossing your arms over your chest and tapping slowly, back and forth, on your chest or upper arms,

back and forth, like this. [*Demonstrate for the client.*] As you notice those sensations, maybe let them expand, strengthen, and settle in your body."

- Check in with the client to determine how the butterfly hug went: "What are you noticing now?" [*If the client reports calm or positive sensations, you can invite them to do the butterfly hug again. Then, return to the Zentangle drawing and continue as time allows.*]

Step 5: Psychoeducation and Closure

- Encourage the client to practice using this drawing method out of session whenever they want to return to the present moment and feel a sense of calm in their body:
    - "You can do these drawings and follow these steps any time you would like, such as when you are feeling stressed, overwhelmed, or disconnected from your body or the present moment. As you draw, if you begin to notice calm or positive sensations in your body, you can pause and let them enhance, strengthen, and settle, maybe even tapping slowly back and forth if that feels helpful."
- Invite the client to think of a cue word they can use to remember the positive feelings associated with this practice:
    - "You may want to remember how it feels in your body right now. Is there a cue word that you could use to remember this feeling?"
    - "You could try saying that word to yourself and tapping back and forth to help your body remember and return to this feeling you are noticing. Would you like to try that now?"
- Check in with the client to determine how using the butterfly hug to strengthen the cue word went: "What are you noticing now?" [*If the client reports calm, positive, or neutral sensations in their body, encourage them to do the butterfly hug again to strengthen the association with the cue word.*]

- Inform them about the benefits of using the cue word and butterfly tap out of session:
    - "Whenever you are feeling distressed, you can say that word to yourself and tap back and forth, as we did just now. This can help your body shift out of a state of stress and back to a state of calm, which is always available for your body to return to."

If distress or self-criticism arises for the client at any point during the Zentangle drawing activity and does not subside through continued focus and engagement in the drawing, it can be helpful to pause and guide them to contain the distressing material. To do so, you can use steps 3–6 of the **Grounding and Containment Script** provided at the end of chapter 8 and then invite the client to come back to the drawing when they are ready.

The Zentangle Drawing Approach to the Flash Technique

Another way to integrate Zentangle drawing into EMDR is by combining it with the **Flash technique**, which was developed by Philip Manfield (2017), a prominent EMDR trainer and innovator in the field of trauma. This technique prepares clients for reprocessing by providing them with microexposure to the target memory using a form of titration that decreases distress and enhances their capacity for processing. The Flash technique has been shown to significantly reduce the emotional intensity and distress associated with unprocessed memories (Brouwers et al., 2021), which can help stabilize the client for the trauma work to come. The Flash technique can be done on any memory before full EMDR reprocessing to make it safer and more tolerable for clients.

In using the Flash technique, the client is discouraged from thinking about the distressing memory (such as by containing it) and encouraged to focus on something positive that holds their attention, such as a pleasant memory. This is called a **positive engaging focus (PEF)**. The client is simultaneously invited to focus on a form of dual attention BLS, such as tapping, eye movements, or even the sound of the therapist counting, as is the case in the Counting Version of Flash developed by Ricky Greenwald (2017). You then periodically invite the client to blink their eyes as a form of subliminal exposure to the distressing memory, allowing the brain to lightly "touch" the distressing material without having to directly think about it, so that memory reconsolidation can occur without needing to consciously activate the memory (Wong, 2021). The client is periodically guided to turn their attention back to the distressing memory to check for any changes or reduction in distress. The client then returns their attention to the PEF and the process is repeated until the distress is reduced.

By combining the Zentangle drawing method with the Flash technique, the act of drawing Zentangle patterns becomes an alternative PEF, which I refer to as an "engaging present-moment experience," as the Zentangle drawing fully engages the client in a calming and absorbing present-moment activity, instead of mentally focusing on a memory from the past. I began using Zentangle drawing as an alternative PEF because many of my clients with complex trauma and dissociation struggled to identify a positive memory. Others could identify a positive memory, but they struggled to hold on to the positive elements of the memory throughout the process as upsetting associations came to mind.

Using Zentangle drawing has allowed me to circumvent these challenges as well as other challenges that I encounter in my work, such as navigating language barriers and working with clients with complex trauma and dissociation. The mindful focus of Zentangle drawing seems to create a physiological state of calm by anchoring the client in the present moment, which is essential when doing the Flash technique with clients who experience dissociation (Shebini, 2019). The art making in itself acts as a form of dual attention BLS as the client balances external and internal awareness. Throughout the process of creating Zentangle drawings together, I invite the client to blink periodically, using the word *flutter* as a prompt (as an alternative to the word *flash*). I introduce the act of blinking with the directive "When I say flutter, you can just let your eyelids flutter like this. [*Demonstrate three quick blinks.*] When you blink, don't think about the memory that's held in the __________ [*name the container the client created for the distressing memory*]. Just stay focused on your drawing, like you're taking little snapshots of your drawing and how it changes as you work on it."

I had the honor of presenting the Zentangle approach to the Flash technique at the Second Annual International Flash Conference hosted by Philip Manfield and Lewis Engel in June 2024. Feedback from participants was overwhelmingly positive, as many found this approach helpful, interesting, and new.

Transformative Journey Storytelling Method

At the beginning of treatment, it is often challenging for clients to believe that they can overcome the challenges they have faced and experience relief from the pain and patterns they feel stuck in. One way to help clients connect with a sense of hope is to use the transformative journey storytelling method, which is a form of embodied storytelling that uses the hero's journey metaphor. This technique is inspired by the Six Part Storymaking Method (6PSM), a therapeutic approach to storytelling developed by Mooli Lahad (1992) and Alida Gersie (1997). The hero's journey is a common narrative arc that appears in stories across time and cultures, in which a character transforms into a hero by facing and overcoming adversity (Campbell, 1949). Similarly, the transformative journey storytelling method provides a way to for you and the client to collaboratively discuss how trauma and adversity are obstacles that can be overcome with EMDR treatment.

This storytelling method has three parts. In the first part, you invite the client to imagine a character and to draw (or write) their character moving through the stages of the hero quest sequence. You then invite the client to tell their story from beginning to end. During this process, you take on an active listening role and do not interrupt the story. In the second part, you guide the client through a series of reflection questions to enhance the positive cognitions, sensations, and strengths elicited in the story. The questions are then further installed to transform the client's attitude toward the obstacle and to increase their courage, motivation, and readiness to face obstacles in their own life. In the third and final part of this method, you relate the client's story to trauma treatment by using the metaphor of a journey. Using the metaphor of EMDR as a transformative journey, you play the role of a guide, mapping out the journey and accompanying the client to ensure they do not get lost or stuck. You trust the client to lead the way, following them as they go where they need to go to find healing and resolution along the pathways of healing.

The Hero's Journey in Trauma Treatment

Using the hero's journey to enhance approaches to trauma therapy is not new, as the use of story and metaphor can prepare clients to confront trauma memories rather than remain stuck in avoidance patterns. The hero's journey is also strengths based and emphasizes that preparing for the journey—that is, building the skills needed to endure the challenges presented in trauma treatment—will lead to rewards, growth, and personal transformation (Williams, 2019). Importantly, the hero's journey narrative does not require clients to imagine themselves as heroes for this intervention to be helpful, as people's everyday lives have the same elements of a hero's journey. This is one of the reasons I use the language "transformative journey" for this approach, as transformation is the most important aspect of the hero's journey.

The hero's journey has also been used in the field of EMDR. Ricky Greenwald (2015) created a fairy-tale story based on the hero's journey to train therapists in the steps of trauma-informed treatment. Andrew Dobo (2023) then aligned the steps of EMDR with the hero's journey, beginning in phase 1 (history taking), where the client is brought out of the "ordinary world" and into the hero's adventure. The journey continues through the trials and transformations that occur during reprocessing and the "rebirth" of the client's sense of self—all the way to phase 8, where the client assimilates into their new way of being. As they move through the stages of the hero's journey, it is important to trust that "the needed thing will show up at the right moment" (Dobo, 2023, p. 12), which reflects spontaneous adaptive resolution.

Presenting the hero's journey framework to your client can shift their perspective and encourage them to reconsider the stories they tell themself about who they are, taking a new outlook that may better align with their goals and values (Rogers et al., 2023). It also connects you and the client to the sense of resolution at the end of the story, increasing the belief that recovery and posttraumatic growth are possible. When life experiences are organized to follow this arc of the hero's journey, clients are more likely to find meaning as a source of posttraumatic growth. This is an essential element of trauma treatment, as survivors often struggle to imagine different ways of being and a different future for themselves.

Storytelling in Trauma Treatment

Storytelling is an ancient part of our shared humanity and a powerful way that we make sense of our experiences. It is also a powerful way to teach and learn, which is why "myths, legends, and folk tales have been a cornerstone of teaching in every culture" (Cajete, 2017, p. 116). Integrating storytelling into treatment is also a way for you to learn about your clients—their worldviews, values, needs, roles, and changes (Marchand, 2022). We learn through listening, and when a client shares their story, a powerful interpersonal exchange occurs between the client (as storyteller) and you (as listener). From this listener role, you pay attention with deep and active curiosity on multiple layers as the client tells their story. You listen as the client provides information about their inner world, which is revealed both explicitly and implicitly, both literally and symbolically (Lahad & Leykin, 2013). You listen to the themes that emerge in the story, including themes of coping and resilience, and how they relate to the client's life, such as their goals, presenting issues, and past experiences.

Storytelling has such immense therapeutic value because it provides a safe psychological distance from the client's inner world and their actual lived experiences, making it more tolerable to explore painful experiences from their past. The themes in the character's story symbolically hold a connection with the client's own story, and this connection is made more relevant and explicit through the act of storytelling (Dent-Brown & Wang, 2006). Even when the client creates a main character that is not themself, telling a story helps the client develop new perspectives on their own experiences as they reflect on the themes, conflicts, strengths, and problem-solving displayed in the story.

In addition, storytelling allows you to integrate a client's cultural perspectives and worldviews into treatment. It intuitively happens that experiences and cultural values are woven into how people tell their stories. In using the transformative journey storytelling method, any cultural values, symbols, metaphors, and worldviews revealed through the client's story can be explored as cultural resources that support their ability to navigate and recover from adversity. These cultural resources can be further enhanced and installed during the preparation phase as a way to increase readiness for reprocessing.

Steps for Using the Transformative Journey Storytelling Method

In this next section, I outline the steps for using the transformative journey storytelling method with clients and provide suggested scripts to facilitate this process, followed by a case example.

You can also find downloadable scripts, worksheets, and instructions at the QR code on this page.

Before you begin, prepare the art materials, such as paper, pencils, pens, colored pencils, and markers. Invite the client to divide any size sheet of paper into eight squares. Then guide the client through each step of the story, allowing time for them to draw or write each step of the story in the corresponding squares. Have them start by representing a character in the top left-hand corner of the paper and work their way across the top squares, then from left to right across the bottom squares. If using the printed worksheets from the QR code, each square is labeled so the client can draw or write each step of their story in the appropriate square. There is also an additional option of folding a single piece of paper into a booklet using a simple folding technique. A video demonstrating this folding technique can also be accessed using the QR code.

Step 1: Creating the Story

- **Choosing a character:** "Create a character for your story. This character can be based on you, another person (real or imagined), an animal or mythical being, or something completely imaginary. Who is this character? Where do they live? Imagine who or what is around them—maybe people, nature, plants, or animals. Represent your character in any way you'd like."

- **Goals and tasks:** "Your character is seeking something. Maybe it's something they really want to do or achieve, or maybe it's something they've lost and would like to get back. What is your character's goal? Represent this goal in any way you'd like."
- **Skills and supports:** "What skills and supports does your character have to help them reach their goal? Maybe special abilities or qualities, or perhaps something or someone to offer guidance or protection? Represent the skills and supports that help your character feel prepared for their journey in any way you'd like."
- **The obstacle:** "Imagine your character sets off on their journey toward their goal. There are adventures, along with twists and turns, and as your character continues forward, something suddenly appears and gets in their way. Maybe something threatening or scary. What is the obstacle? Represent this obstacle in any way you'd like."
- **Overcoming the obstacle:** "Your character doesn't turn around, they know they have to face and overcome this obstacle to reach their goal and complete their journey. What do they do? How do they do it? Represent how your character overcomes the obstacle in any way you'd like."
- **The ending:** "After facing and overcoming this obstacle, your character finally completes their journey and reaches their goal. What happens next in the character's life? What's different? Represent your character completing their journey in any way you'd like."
- **The client as storyteller:** "Now, you are the storyteller. I will listen to you tell your story from beginning to end. When you have finished telling your story, we will reflect on your character's journey together."

Step 2: Reflection

- **Open reflection:** "Did anything surprise you about your story?"
- **Embodying the ending:** "Imagine what it would feel like to be your character at the end of the story, when they reach their goal. What sensations do you notice in your body as you imagine that?"

- **Positive cognition:** "What words do you imagine your character saying to themself in that scene at the end, when they finally reach their goal and complete their journey?"
- **Movement:** "Is there a posture or movement that goes with those words? If so, explore that movement, noticing how it feels in your body."
- **Negative cognition:** "Now, go back in the story to the moment your character first encountered the obstacle, the ______ [*name the obstacle using the client's words from their story*]. Imagine what it would feel like to be your character in that scene, when they first encounter the obstacle. What negative words do you imagine your character saying to themself there?"
- **Pairing the positive cognition with the obstacle:** "Now, look at the obstacle in the story while you also remember how it felt to reach the goal of ______ [*name the goal using the client's words from their story*]. Now, imagine the obstacle in your mind while hearing those positive words ______ [*name the positive cognitions from the last scene identified by the client*] and making the posture or movement that goes with those positive words."
    - [*Optional: Invite the client to do dual attention BLS.*]
- **Further enhancement:** "Is there anything your character needs to know or hear to believe that they have what it takes to overcome the obstacle and complete their journey?"
    - The client can allow a helper to enter that part of the story to offer guidance or support: "Imagine that a helper or guide enters that scene in your story and lets your character know that with words or in any way that helps your character take in that message. Just imagine that happening."
    - [*Optional: Invite the client to do dual attention BLS.*]
- **Reassessing the response to the obstacle:** "How do you imagine your character feels now when they see the obstacle?"
- **Title:** "Now, think of a title for your story. Write down the title of your story." [*The title can be added into the next remaining square of the folded paper, alongside any drawings that they may like to add.*]

- **Future orientation:** "Now, imagine your character's future. What happens next in their life? If you'd like, you could write the title of the sequel to this story." [*The title can be added to the final square of the folded paper.*]

Step 3: Relating the Transformative Story to EMDR

- **Relate the client's story to trauma treatment using the metaphor of a journey:** "Our work together will also be like a journey, only that the obstacles you'll overcome are like the memories that continue to get in your way or hold you back. You will also face and overcome these obstacles, one step at a time, so you can clear your path and move toward your goals. As with any journey, it's always important to prepare beforehand. To prepare for this journey, we'll work together to strengthen your skills, supports, and resources so you can carry them with you, just like how your character ________ [*provide examples from the client's story*]."
- **Reiterate the client's role (leader) and your role (the guide):** "During this process, I will be like a guide, accompanying you and helping map out the journey, but I also trust you to lead the way to the places where you'll find the healing you need to resolve your past. Completing your journey will allow you to rewrite your story in a way that honors your courage and strength and brings new meaning and direction into your life, so you can reach your goals, just like when your character ________ [*provide examples from the client's story*]."

Case Example

The following is an example of a story drawn by a female Ethiopian client who presented with high levels of stress and anxiety due to a recent civil war in the region, as well as attachment issues around her father's alcoholism. The story is called "The Undryable Life" and is about a character who knows a lot of people but sometimes feels lonely (first square on the top). She wants to be independent because this allows her to spread joy and happiness to others; she can be a "giver" (second square on the top). The character gets her strength from the morning sun because it is a symbol of learning from mistakes, taking responsibility, and always having a new beginning. She gives herself time to rest and remembers to be grateful, knowing God is always there to help her (third square on the top). She has a full heart, but because her heart is so full of hurt, it has taken her passion away, like a beautiful flower that has slowly dried up. She knows she will have to remove the dead parts of the flower to keep growing. The sky is dim from the morning moon; there is not enough light, but she knows it will get brighter again (fourth square on the top).

When there is an obstacle, she thinks about the people who have to fight in life more than her, who have less than her. She reflects on the obstacle and takes the time she needs to learn from it. She looks for alternative ways to reach her goals and does not let negative thoughts get in her way (first square on the bottom). When she overcomes the obstacle, she becomes stronger and is able to help others. She holds their hands and helps them learn from their life chapters. She never forgets how God helped her be this person she wanted to be, and she is able to stay humble even though she gets what she wants in her life (second square on the bottom). She then titled her story (third square on the bottom) and wrote the title for a future series, called "Cherishing Life in Fulfilment" (fourth square on the bottom).

When she was asked to imagine how it would feel to be the character at the end of the story—when she reaches her goal—she described that it would be like drinking water after being thirsty, wetting her heart and her body. She also identified the following positive cognition when she imagined her character meeting her goal at the end of the story: "I am happy. I have become strong, and I know my worth." She then identified the negative cognition that she imagined her character saying to herself when she first encountered the obstacle of a heavy heart: "I am tired, I tried and tried—was it for nothing?" She then paired the positive cognition with the obstacle in her mind while doing a slow set of dual attention BLS using the butterfly hug. She imagined her mother telling the character how lovable she is and that she is enough. She expressed how her mother helped her family get through many difficulties, so her mother was the right person to tell the character that she could become more than her environment and more than her surroundings. She then imagined her mother's words and strength while doing another set of dual attention BLS. When invited to imagine how the character felt when encountering the obstacle now, the client reported feeling protected and feeling her mother's love.

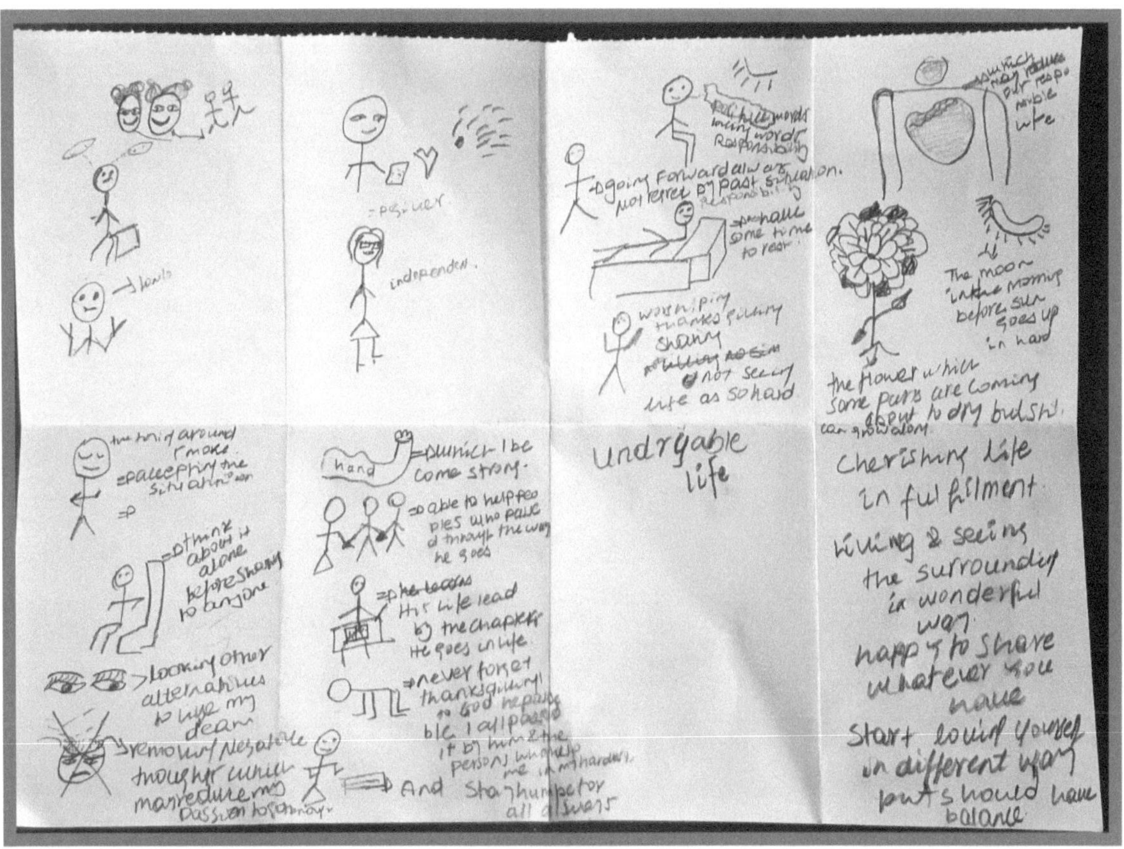

In this story, themes of grief, loss, and faith were present. She came to realize that she never let herself grieve because she believed it would mean she wasn't grateful to God for the privileges she had. For example, whenever she touched on experiences that impacted her, she would state that her situation could be much worse, as it is for many people in her country, and that she must be grateful. This activity helped her see that continuously suppressing her grief was preventing her from reaching her goal of helping people because it left her with a heavy heart. She became more open to grieving the impacts of the recent conflict, addressing the cost-of-living crisis impacting her family, and reprocessing upsetting memories in her relationship with her father.

CHAPTER 7

Enhancing Phase 2 with Body- and Nature-Based Approaches

This chapter expands on the previous one by presenting additional body- and nature-based approaches to preparation work, including a movement practice to enhance somatic awareness and present-moment orientation, known as the COME BACK tool. I also provide a polyvagal-informed lens through which to view the nervous system. Finally, I outline creative approaches for dual attention BLS and provide visual explanations and nature-based metaphors that introduce clients to the components of the assessment and reprocessing phases of EMDR, such as the validity of cognition (VOC) scale and subjective unit of disturbance (SUD) scale.

The Body and Movement in Preparation: The COME BACK Tool

In EMDR, you invite the client to attune to their body and to notice memory fragments (e.g., thoughts, beliefs, images, emotions, sensations, urges) that emerge during reprocessing. Indeed, mindfully noticing sensations is an essential part of the EMDR process, such as with questions like "Where do you feel it in your body?" and "What are you noticing now?" Although therapists often assume that clients have access to their bodies as a resource during trauma treatment, many clients have difficulty mindfully observing what is coming up in their bodies without becoming overwhelmed (Follette et al., 2015). This is especially the case for clients with complex trauma and dissociation, who often avoid or disconnect from their internal experience due to painful or unbearable sensations (Boon et al., 2016).

For these clients, it is essential to expand their window of tolerance for internal sensations during the preparation phase. That way, they have a greater capacity to tolerate and mindfully notice what is happening in their body during reprocessing. The **COME BACK tool** is one such method that can help clients come back to their bodies in a titrated and restorative way. I developed this tool with Michelli Simpson, an EMDRIA-approved consultant from Brazil, as a way to expand the reach of EMDR over telehealth (Marchand & Simpson, 2022). This approach uses an acronym to describe the skills and resources that can enhance EMDR readiness for clients with complex trauma and dissociation:

Connecting to a comforting presence

Orienting through the senses

Moving and mobilizing energy

Exploring the breath with movement and sound

Balancing and centering the body

Anchoring and grounding into the earth

Containment and closure

Kindness and compassion

In the following section, I'll walk you through strategies associated with each step of the acronym. As a note, it is not necessary to offer these strategies in any order; it is an overarching framework to teach stabilization skills that can be developed and strengthened in the preparation phase. As you use these strategies with your clients, I encourage you to simultaneously engage in the activity alongside your client, staying connected to yourself while attuning to the client's experience. This can create a shared experience that relaxes the client and enhances therapeutic rapport. In cross-cultural settings, I have found that this shared movement is especially helpful in reducing the inherent power imbalance in the therapeutic relationship and fostering a sense of playfulness and humor. It makes you available as a real presence that can provide relational safety and support, rather than a distant clinical expert.

Connecting to a Comforting Presence

You begin by inviting the client to think of someone or something that offers a comforting, calming presence, such as a specific place in nature, a spiritual presence, an animal, a person—anything at all. This part of the COME BACK tool places more emphasis on comfort and support rather than nurturance because many clients did not experience nurturance in their own attachment experiences. It also broadens the different ways in which clients can experience connection and comfort, such as through nature or spiritual figures (Marchand & Simpson, 2022).

The client can then concentrate on this comforting presence, making it as vivid as possible and noticing anything about this presence that feels comforting, such as its size or energy. To further increase a sense of connection and engagement with this presence, the client can represent it using color, symbols, lines, or images on a piece of paper. I recommend using crayons, oil or chalk pastels, or watercolors, if available, as these materials allow for more flow, movement, and expression than controlled materials like pencils or pen. The client may also like to use another medium, such as modeling clay, or they may like to create a collage by loosely assembling natural materials, such as seeds, sticks, gems, stones, shells, dried herbs, or any other natural materials that may be available.

When the client has completed their external representation of the comforting presence, they can then observe and reflect on their artwork, noticing how their body responds when looking at their creation. If the client identifies sensations such as calm, comfort, and support, you can invite them to use the butterfly hug to strengthen these associations. You can also invite the client to notice whether there is a word or phrase that goes with the comforting presence. If so, they can say that to themself as they continue to tap, or even add it to their artwork. Invite the client to engage with their comforting presence as often as feels helpful for them, either by looking at the artwork they created or by bringing the comforting presence to mind. (If the client created something that cannot be transported, like a collage from natural materials, they can take a photo of their creation to connect with it outside of the session.) The client can tap and say the word or phrase to themself as they connect to their comforting presence outside of session to take in as much comfort and connection as they would like.

Orienting Through the Senses

This part of the COME BACK tool guides the client in using the five senses—sight, sound, smell, touch, and taste—as grounding strategies. In this section, I focus on the sense of sound since it has proven to be a powerful way to ground. Many clients, including those from diverse backgrounds and in different cultural settings, respond well to the use of sound. This may be due to the connection between the inner ear and the vagus nerve, which is responsible for our ability to experience safety, connection, and recovery (Porges, 2021). When we intentionally use sound to provide calming or soothing sensory input, the nervous system responds in a powerful way.

In the COME BACK tool, the client oscillates their focus between different sounds in their environment, from far away to gradually closer to the body. When the client brings their awareness of sound to their body, they may also like to create sound using their voice or a type of instrument. For example, I have a collection of brass chimes, bells, and tuning forks that clients can use. These sounds create beautiful tones and reverberations that the client can use to increase a sense of grounding and presence. The tuning forks also harmonize, enhancing a sense of calm and peace.

Grounding with Sound Script

- **Something far:** "See whether you can hear something outside, maybe even outside the space you are in. What is the farthest sound that you can hear right now? Just notice that sound."
- **Something close:** "Now, move your attention to a sound inside the space you're in right now. You can hear my voice,

but what other sounds are there in this space? Let your ears focus on those sounds."

- **Around or from the body:** "Now, bring your attention to the sounds closest to you or to the sounds you are making. Maybe you can hear the sound of your body moving, or the sound of your breath as the air moves in and out. What is the closest sound you can hear?"
- **Creating a sound:** "You can even make a sound with your breath, such as by humming or sighing, or by experimenting with some of these bells and chimes, seeing whether there is a sound or tone that feels soothing or grounding to you right now."

Moving and Mobilizing Energy

This step of the COME BACK tool invites the client to ground through movement. Movement is an important part of regulating the nervous system, as it can release energy and tension when energy levels are too high and the client is restless and tense (in a state of **hyperarousal**), and it can increase energy when levels are too low and the client is fatigued, numb, and shutting down (in a state of **hypoarousal**). In this way, movement can meet the client in whatever physiological state they present, allowing them to move into a more balanced state of energy in which they are calm but alert.

In addition, by moving different parts of their body with a mindful, internal focus, the client can practice sensing into their body and notice shifts in sensations that slowly rebuild interoceptive awareness. This allows survivors of complex trauma to restore a sense of connection with their body. They can also practice making choices that best meet their needs in the moment based on the sensations they notice, such as what pace of movement feels good to them, which increases a sense of ownership over their bodies. This can be powerfully healing, especially for clients who have been violated.

Cross crawl and progressive muscle relaxation are two movement activities for regulating energy that are integrated into the COME BACK tool. Cross crawl uses bilateral movement to help increase energy in the body (Dennison & Dennison, 2010). This is useful at any point in treatment when the client seems to be losing a sense of present-moment orientation and is shutting down or numbing out.

Cross Crawl Script

- **Introduce cross crawl:** "Start by standing with both feet on the floor and your arms raised up at your sides like you're waving hello with both hands. Begin the movement by lifting up your left knee while moving your right hand across your body to touch your left knee. Bring your left foot back down and your right hand back up. Then lift your right knee up while moving your left hand across your body so that it touches your right knee. Continue the movement by switching left knee to right hand, then right knee to left hand. [*Demonstrate these options as you engage in the movement activity with your client.*] Try making this movement back and forth, hand to knee, hand to knee." [*If it is more comfortable for the client, they can also begin by sitting on a chair or stool, lifting one knee up to meet the opposite hand and then switching while remaining in a seated position.*]
- **Experiment with pace:** "You may like to try experimenting with different speeds. You can try speeding up your movements, making them more vigorous, or you can try slowing your movements down so that you challenge your balance a bit more."

- **Variation:** "Another way to do cross crawl is by bringing your elbow to your knee instead of your hand. You may not be able to touch your elbow to your knee, that is completely fine—we are just experimenting with different movements."
- **Check in:** "Come back to standing when you're ready. Begin to check in with your body, noticing any changes in energy levels or any other shifts in your body. Just notice, without needing to shift or change anything."

Progressive muscle relaxation is a technique that invites clients to alternate tensing and releasing different muscles in the body—starting with the feet and legs and moving up through the body, all the way to the muscles in the face and head—which moves the body into a more relaxed and settled state. Clients often respond to this practice with surprise at the shifts they notice in their bodies. I sometimes use the metaphor "feeding the bite" that I learned in security training to explain the efficacy of this approach: If a dog is biting your arm and you try to pull away, the dog only bites harder. But if you push into the bite, they let go. It is the same way with tension in our bodies. If we try to avoid and disconnect from the tension, it increases. But if we move into the tension, we can start to let it go. Progressive muscle relaxation is like moving into, rather than away from, tension so that our bodies can begin to release it. The following is a script for progressive muscle relaxation in the upper body and arms, where many people hold tension.

Progressive Muscle Relaxation Script

- **Tense the upper body and arms:** "Bring your awareness to your upper body. Notice all the muscles in your upper body: your upper back, shoulders, chest, maybe even your arms and hands. Notice all those muscles. Now, try squeezing and tensing all those muscles for 10 seconds. I will count down from 10 and when we get to 0, just let it all go. Ready? Take a breath in and hold." [*Count down from 10 while also engaging in the activity.*]
- **Release the tension:** "Okay, let it all go. Let it melt away, down into the floor, into the earth."
- **Repeat:** "Let's try that again, tensing the muscles in your upper body. Take a breath in and hold. [*Count down from 10.*] Release. Shake it out and let it all go. Okay, let's try that one more time." [*Do at least three rounds of tensing and releasing.*]
- **Check in:** "What are you noticing in your body now? Are there any other areas of your body where you notice tension, where you might like to try tensing and releasing?"

It can be helpful to invite the client to do a body scan before and after engaging in the cross crawl and progressive muscle relaxation activities to notice any changes or shifts in their sensations, such as muscle tension or energy levels.

Exploring the Breath with Movement and Sound

This step of the COME BACK tool guides the client through various trauma-sensitive ways to explore and interact with the breath. Although breathing is a powerful way to reduce stress and regulate the nervous system, many clients with complex trauma find breathing techniques to be activating, especially if they are invited to turn their attention inward too quickly. For this reason, the COME BACK tool uses an art-based square breathing activity to keep the client's awareness externally oriented while exploring the movement of the breath using lines, colors, and shapes. For this activity, I recommend offering a choice of different colored markers, if available. Markers provide a sense of control over the lines while allowing the color to flow smoothly onto the paper. Clients may also like to use oil or chalk pastels to facilitate the free movement of lines and color that can also be blended together.

Art-Based Square Breathing Script

- **Introduce square breathing:** "Making a square breath means breathing in four steps, like the four edges of a square: breathing in, pausing, breathing out, and pausing. When we're stressed, we often breathe in a line—up and down, in and out—without any pauses or space. We want to breathe in a way that gives our breath some shape, like making a square, to help our bodies calm and settle in the present moment."
- **Drawing the breath:** "Now you can try drawing your breath—literally!—by drawing a square on a piece of paper using lines and color as you breathe. [*Demonstrate drawing the steps of the square on a piece of paper.*] Think of syncing your breath up with the movement of your marker [*or another mark-making material*]. Start by making a dot somewhere in the middle of your page. From there, draw the left side of your square by moving your line upward as you breathe in . . . When you have taken in enough breath, begin drawing the top edge of the square, moving the line across the top as you pause and hold your breath . . . When you're ready to exhale, begin drawing the right side of the square as you breathe out, moving the line downward . . . And when you have completed your exhale, draw the bottom edge of the square as you pause your breath again, moving the line across the bottom to complete the square. Although this is called a square breath, you do not have to create perfect

squares, just let your lines move freely as you breathe and draw, not forcing anything. You can try this a few times: breathing in, pausing, breathing out, pausing. Just breathe and draw at your own pace, making the lines of the squares as big or as small as you'd like." [*Engage in the activity alongside the client as they draw.*]

- **Experimenting with shapes:** "You may like to experiment with different shapes and patterns as you draw, just moving your marker with your breath, giving your breath shape and space to move. Maybe your breath looks more like a rectangle or a circle—it's completely up to you how you draw your breath." [*Continue to engage in the activity alongside the client, allowing them to experiment further with lines and shapes as they breathe.*]
- **Check in:** "Check in with your body and with your breath—see whether you notice any shifts."

The following drawing is an example of an art-based square breathing drawing I made while facilitating a self-care session for professionals working on the frontlines with survivors of sexual and gender-based violence in Ethiopia. I was mindful not to draw perfect squares to model that the length of the inhale and exhale do not need to be exactly the same—the aim is to intentionally slow down our breathing while staying externally oriented and grounded in the present moment.

Balancing and Centering the Body

This practice uses balance to increase body awareness in the present moment. By guiding the client through movements that carefully challenge their sense of balance—for example, by shifting their weight back and forth from one foot to the other—the client naturally reconnects to their body in order to steady themself and not topple over. You can experiment with increasing the balance challenge by guiding the client to steady their weight on one foot while lifting the other into the air, as little or as much as they are comfortable with, in front of their body, to the side, or behind their body, and then switching sides. You can then guide the client to return to the settled place of balance by standing, spreading their weight evenly between both feet, and connecting to a feeling of centeredness in their body. The client can also be invited to represent any sensations of centeredness by using a symbol, color, image, or word so it becomes a concrete place in their body that they can return to as a resource.

Anchoring and Grounding into the Earth

This practice is based on a walking meditation, which emphasizes mindful movement and awareness of our bodies and connection to our surroundings. Thich Nhat Hanh (2024), the late Vietnamese Buddhist monk and influential Buddhist teacher, believed that the earth is sacred and that walking is a practice of being reminded of our spiritual connection to the earth. To begin this practice, invite the client to use their feet to experience being supported by the earth underneath them by standing and grounding their feet into that spot, maybe even noticing a sense of gravity like a gentle pull downward. (Again, as with all the COME BACK practices, you engage in this activity alongside your client.) You can encourage your client to bring awareness to their body, exploring any sensations of pressure by shifting their weight around on their feet and noticing where their feet make contact with the earth.

Then begin taking steps. If this practice is being done in an outdoor environment, you can walk back and forth between two points, like two stones or trees. In your office, if space allows, you can place stones down on the floor as points to move back and forth between; even five feet apart can be enough. If space is a challenge, you can take steps in any direction—forward and backward, left and right, whatever direction the client chooses to move in. Invite the client to listen to their body as they take each step, lifting their foot off the ground and then firmly replanting it, noticing where their foot makes contact with the earth, using sensations of pressure to increase a sense of groundedness and being anchored right there in that moment.

As you continue taking steps, lifting and landing your feet, encourage your client to find their rhythm by beginning to find a connection between their breath and their steps, reassuring the client that there is no rush. As they breathe in, they may take one or two steps, and as they breathe out, they may take one or two steps. With each breath, they are taking a moment to land and anchor, feeling their connection to the earth. They may also like to pair a statement with each breath, such as "I have arrived" with the inhale and "I am home" with the exhale (as suggested by Thich Nhat Hanh), or any words that feel right to them.

As you complete the practice, invite the client to come back to a settled standing position, anchoring and grounding their feet into that spot, and noticing any sensations in their body as they sense that connection to the earth beneath them, maybe even a color that goes with the energy they feel flowing up from the earth through their feet and into their body and back into the earth again. If they notice any neutral or positive sensations, they can take a moment and tap (using the butterfly hug) to allow those sensations to expand and settle.

I offer the choice for clients to do this activity with their shoes on, in their socks, or even barefoot. Clients often feel more comfortable doing this barefoot over telehealth, as they are in their own space and I am unable to see their whole body. Regardless of what the client chooses in session, I encourage them to try this barefoot between sessions and, if they can, to try it somewhere outdoors where they can directly connect to the earth and notice the textures as a way to increase a sense of groundedness. In Germany, for example, barefoot parks (or *Barfußparks*) are paths that allow people to walk barefoot along different textures, such as sand, stones, mud, and even glass. This is a popular way to support well-being and health, as it trains the muscles of the feet, stimulates blood flow, and deepens the connection with nature. Providing this information to clients can increase their curiosity and willingness to experiment with this practice barefoot and in nature.

Containment and Closure

A container is an imagined resource that acts as a secure place for any thoughts, sensations, or memory fragments that cause distress or discomfort for clients. Practicing the skill of containment is a core component of phase 2 of EMDR (preparation). Since many clients struggle to contain distressing material due to its intensity or emotional charge, our approach to containment in the COME BACK tool encourages art- and body-based strategies to support the development of this skill. For example, a client can use art materials to represent their container (e.g., by drawing a barrel or treasure box) or create an actual container that can physically hold expressions of distressing material (e.g., by decorating a wooden box or a shoe box). The client can also use objects that act as containers (e.g., a drawstring bag or basket with a lid). Once the client identifies a container, they can draw or write distressing material on a piece of paper, fold it up, and physically place it into the container (or imagine placing it into their container). After this action, the client can check in and notice how it feels to have a sense of distance from that material and even begin to tap (using the butterfly hug) to enhance any neutral or positive sensations.

Clients can also use movement, gesture, and breath to support the process of moving material into their container. For example, they can use movement to push the material away from their body, stroke it off their arms, or shake it off. You can also support the client in moving distressing material into the container by doing the movements with them. In addition, you can encourage the client to use the breath to push the material outward and into the container, such as by using the exhale to push any thoughts, feelings, or sensations out through their mouth or nose so that the container can hold it for them. The client can also use gestures to show how they would physically close the container, such as screwing a lid on it, wrapping it, burying it, passing it over to a helper, or whichever movement helps the material feel securely contained.

Kindness and Compassion

This part of the COME BACK tool is a way to help clients develop loving-kindness toward themselves to better manage and reduce the self-criticism and shame resulting from trauma. You begin by inviting the client to think about someone they care about, such as someone comforting and supportive, or even a loving animal. Encourage the client to imagine that loving presence right there with them, by their side. Gently guide them to notice any feelings that come up as they focus on this presence, such as warmth, tenderness, or perhaps kindness growing and expanding inside their heart. The client can then use art materials to create lines, colors, words, or symbols that represent any positive feelings they notice. Invite them to imagine sending these positive feelings toward this presence, or toward anyone else they think would benefit from kindness.

When the client has completed their expression of love and kindness toward someone else, you can invite them to see how it would feel to direct these same tender, warm feelings toward themself. I often invite clients to experiment with rotating their image so that the colors or lines being directed outward are now being directed toward themselves. Gently guide the client to begin sending warm kindness inward as a way to honor themself, their strengths, and their inner resources. It is helpful to normalize that we are often better at sending these feelings outward than we are at taking them inward. I often tell clients that if they notice any critical thoughts, they can send those thoughts compassion too. The client may benefit from using their breath to take in kindness and compassion a little bit at a time, with each breath, letting it reach any part of them that needs it. You can then encourage the client to add any colors, lines, or compassionate words to their image as a way to continue sending kindness toward themself.

When the client has completed their artwork, they can reflect on the image they created and notice how their body responds to it. If they notice neutral or positive sensations, they may like to do the butterfly hug to further enhance the resource of self-compassion.

Polyvagal Theory and Mapping Physiological States

Polyvagal theory, developed by Stephen Porges (2011), is an evolutionary model of the autonomic nervous system that highlights the role of the vagus nerve in promoting safety, social connection, and survival. This model has shifted our thinking around the nervous system, which was originally understood as a two-part structure that consisted of the sympathetic nervous system and the parasympathetic nervous system. This two-part system was thought to operate like an on-off switch: The **sympathetic nervous system** turned our stress-response system "on" in the face of threat and danger, while the **parasympathetic nervous system** turned it "off" once the threat was overcome or subsided, allowing us to recover and return to homeostasis.

However, polyvagal theory has expanded this understanding of the autonomic nervous system to include two separate branches of the parasympathetic nervous system (the off switch): (1) the **ventral vagal system**, which is responsible for feelings of safety and connection, and (2) the **dorsal vagal system**, which is responsible for shutting us down in the face of extreme life threat. In contrast to the sympathetic nervous system—which responds to threats by mobilizing us for action, or turning us on—the dorsal vagal system responds to threats by sending us into a state of immobilization, or turning us off. The dorsal vagal system is the oldest and most primitive branch of our stress-response system and can be seen in animals who feign death to escape from a predator.

We shift between these three primary physiological states—ventral vagal, sympathetic, and dorsal vagal states—in response to sensory cues of safety or danger in our environment. The process by which we perceive and respond to this sensory information is known as **neuroception** (Porges, 2011), and it is an entirely subconscious process. For example, if we neurocept nonverbal cues of safety and belonging from others (e.g., a friendly smile, a welcome embrace), the autonomic nervous system may shift into a state of ventral vagal safety. If we neurocept cues of judgment, criticism, or threat (e.g., a harsh tone of voice, a furrowed brow), we may shift into a sympathetic state of stress and activation. If we neurocept extreme danger or perceive a threat as inescapable or unbearable (e.g., being blocked from leaving a room or being shamed or humiliated in front of others), we may shift into a dorsal vagal state of shutdown and collapse. These shifts in physiological states are involuntary and often occur before we are even consciously aware of what our body is responding to.

A Nature-Based Metaphor to Understand the Three Autonomic States

I have found it helpful to present these three autonomic states to clients by using the metaphor of water. Water automatically shifts between three different states—liquid, solid, and gas—based on the temperature of the surrounding environment. Just as water responds to temperature, our nervous system responds to cues of safety and threat by shifting between a ventral vagal state (fluid, liquid state), a sympathetic nervous system state (boiling, gas state), and a dorsal vagal state (frozen, solid state). Using the water metaphor normalizes how the nervous system shifts states according to what it perceives. If the environment is perceived as warm, safe, and loving, we can stay in a fluid state, but if the stimulus is perceived as too hot (threatening) or too cold (too extreme, inescapable), we shift into states of survival and protection.

Understanding Our Autonomic States Through the Metaphor of Water

Ventral vagal:
Fluid, flexible, adaptive, receptive, connected, creative, integrated, playful, flow state. Inside window of tolerance (not too hot, not too cold).

Sympathetic:
Hot, mobilizing energy, activated, expanded, reactive. Outside window of tolerance (boiling point).

Dorsal vagal:
Cold, conserving energy, condensed, contracted, frozen, immobilized, fragmented. Outside window of tolerance (freezing point).

The goal of presenting this metaphor to clients is to provide them with a nonpathologizing framework through which to understand that their stress-response system is hardwired to protect them when it perceives cues as threatening in their environment (e.g., situations, people, places, sensory stimuli). This metaphor helps clients understand that shifts in physiological states are not a conscious choice but involuntary and automatic.

In addition, you can use the water metaphor to help clients understand how they can return to a state of ventral vagal safety by drawing on Deb Dana's (2018) conceptualization of glimmers. As discussed in chapter 5, triggers are reminders of the past that move us into states of protection and survival, while glimmers are the people, places, activities, skills, and other resources that reconnect us with a sense of safety and bring us out of survival states. Using the water metaphor, glimmers are resources that help clients "settle" from a boiling point or "thaw" from a freezing point to return to a state of fluidity, flexibility, openness, and safety. The following script can help you introduce the full water metaphor to clients.

Step 1: Introducing the Metaphor

- "Just as water shifts between liquid, solid, and gas states in response to the temperature of the surrounding environment, our nervous system shifts between three different states in response to cues of safety and threat in our environment. If we perceive safety, we can stay in a comfortable, warm liquid state (called a ventral vagal state). If we perceive threat, we move into a boiling state that activates us and creates steam (called a sympathetic state). If we perceive a threat that feels too extreme, ongoing, or inescapable, we move into a frozen state that shuts us down to conserve energy (called a dorsal vagal state). Let's explore these three different states so you can begin to recognize them within yourself."

Step 2: Explaining the Three States

- **Liquid (ventral vagal state):** "This state has a warm, balanced energy that is calm yet alert. We can be fluid, flexible, and receptive, like liquid that flows easily and adapts to its environment. We can experience calm and relaxation, be present and mindful, and use our highest thinking capacities like creativity and problem-solving. Being in this state also allows us to be socially connected to others because the ventral vagal system runs through the areas around our face, making it possible to tune into others and take in their social cues, such as their eye contact, tone of voice, and facial expressions."

- **Gas (sympathetic state):** "This state is like water that reaches its boiling point. There is lots of movement and energy that expands outward and needs to be released, like steam. Our bodies release stress hormones like adrenaline and cortisol, causing our heart rate and breathing to increase to help us react quickly and powerfully by fighting or fleeing. Everything speeds up. Being in this elevated state of activation and alertness over time can affect our health, but in short bursts, it helps us overcome stressors and survive threats. When this survival system is turned on, our social engagement system is turned off, so we cannot easily connect with others, experience calm, or think clearly and creatively. We are reactive, not receptive, to what is happening around us."
- **Solid (dorsal vagal state):** "This state is like water that gets so cold it freezes, helping us conserve energy by contracting and becoming solid and still, like ice. In this state, our movements stop or slow. We might still have energy in our muscles as we freeze so that we can brace and hold, or we might begin to faint or fold, in which case our heart rate and breathing slows down, and we lose energy and power from our muscles. We move into this state when 'all else fails,' and any attempts to fight or escape the threat are unsuccessful. Our shutdown response helps us prepare for the worst by protecting us from feelings of pain, aided by the release of endorphins, and by disconnecting us from our internal sensations and external reality. This ability to numb out and disconnect is an adaptive way to cope with unbearable, intolerable sensations. We can even experience fragmentation as if our awareness of the experience breaks off into different pieces. In this state, we might feel hopeless or powerless, but it is important to remember that this is a powerful survival response that helps us conserve energy so that it is available in our system when escape becomes possible again, and we can return to a liquid state."

Step 3: Understanding Triggers with the Water Metaphor

- "Sometimes the environment can be warm and safe, but we might still perceive something from the external or internal world (like a sound or even a sensation) as threatening in some way and then respond by moving into a protective state. When this happens, we are reacting to reminders of the past rather than to something happening in the present. With awareness, we can begin to recognize when our response does not match the temperature of the current situation, and we are responding to a reminder of the past and not the present. If the environment truly is hot, it is adaptive to become steam. And if the environment truly is cold, it is adaptive to become ice. But if the environment is warm, it is not helpful to stay in a boiling or frozen state. We want to be able to settle or thaw to return to a liquid state, where we can feel calm, safe, and connected."

Step 4: Creating New Response Patterns

- "Just as water has set freezing and boiling points at which it automatically shifts states, we also have internal freezing and boiling points where we respond to stimuli in specific, patterned ways. However, these are not 'set' points; often, they are based on learned patterns from the past. This means we can actually change our response patterns and increase our ability to stay in a fluid state for longer when we are safe enough to do so."

Step 5: Reflection and Identification of Glimmers

- "What does it feel like to be in a liquid state of ventral vagal safety and calm? Can you think of the last time you were in this state? What does it feel like in your body? What people, places, activities, or skills help you access this state?"
- "How would you know if you shifted into a boiling hot state of sympathetic energy? What would it feel like in your body? What people, places, activities, or skills do you use to help yourself settle and come back to a place of calm, safety, and connection?"

- "How would you know if you shifted into a frozen state of dorsal vagal shutdown? What would it feel like in your body? What people, places, activities, or skills do you use to help yourself thaw and come back to a place of calm, safety, and connection?"

By explaining this metaphor in the preparation phase, you can help clients build the skills to recognize when a reaction is a result of something in the present stirring up the past and making a threat feel present again. When clients can identify cues or signals from their body that they have shifted into a protective, survival state, they can use strategies to bring themselves back to a ventral state of safety in the present. Clients can also benefit from creating a visual or expressive representation of what it feels like to be in each state (e.g., by drawing, painting, collaging, writing, or using movement or music) to enhance their awareness of their internal states and their ability identify when they have shifted into a particular state.

Resourcing Present-Moment Orientation with Dual Attention Bilateral Stimulation

The **constant installation of present orientation and safety (CIPOS) protocol** is a strategy to titrate and restrict reprocessing work with complex trauma (Knipe, 2014). When using the CIPOS protocol, you orient the client to the present moment using dual attention BLS. For example, you might throw a soft cushion to prompt an orienting response. Once the client is feeling fully present, you add dual attention BLS to install and enhance the feeling of being in the present. You can then guide them to think about an upsetting memory for a restricted period of time (such as for five seconds) and then bring them fully back to the present moment, again installing the state of presence using dual attention BLS. This technique is a way to practice dual awareness by strengthening the client's ability to touch a distressing memory without losing orientation to the present moment.

I have found CIPOS to be an effective way to introduce clients to different forms of dual attention BLS in the preparation phase of EMDR. I like to engage my clients in present-orienting activities, such as by using any of the previous COME BACK activities, and then install a state of present orientation using different types of dual attention BLS. This allows the client to choose the materials and movements that feel good and resonant for them before moving into reprocessing work.

In working with clients, I refer to dual attention BLS as "sets of movement." This language communicates to the client that movement is one of the key elements of the EMDR healing process: We get the system (the internal river) moving, whether it is with eye movements, tapping, creating rhythm with sound, drumming, or throwing a ball back and forth. Although we generally start with eye movements, as these have the most evidence base, other rhythmic movements have a similar effect (Shapiro, 2018). In addition, more body-based forms of bilateral movement, such as drumming and dancing, can feel more familiar to clients from non-Western and Indigenous cultures, where movement is a part of many traditional healing practices (Lichtenstein et al., 2017; Ma-Kellams, 2014). However, it is nonetheless important to use whatever mode of dual attention BLS best meets the needs of your client, allowing them to maintain safety, present-moment orientation, and dual awareness.

In the following section, I introduce several creative ways you can introduce dual attention BLS to clients. You can experiment with any of these different modes of dual attention during the preparation phase to install a sense of presence and prepare the client for reprocessing. Your stance while providing dual attention BLS should always be "highly interactive, client-centered, flexible" (Shapiro, 2018, p. 114), and you should be prepared to adjust, pivot, and modify your approach according to the client's needs. This can help the client experience a feeling of being in control with the dual attention BLS and normalize movement and body-based engagement during reprocessing.

Creating Dual Attention Bilateral Stimulation with Sound and Resonance

In my office, I have an array of chimes and bells available for clients to experiment with, both for grounding as well as for dual attention BLS during reprocessing. In the following image, moving from left to right, you can see tuning forks and activators, a single chime, brass bells with various figures (such as mythical creatures and animals), and a bowl holding two Chinese meditation balls, one with a sun and the other with a moon.

One of my preferred forms of dual attention BLS uses tuning forks in a way that combines eye movement, auditory, tactile, and relational forms of dual attention BLS. I typically offer C and G tuning forks, as they produce a beautiful harmony and are sometimes referred to as yin and yang sounds, creating a perfect balance. In this method, I invite the client to sit facing me while holding the handles of two tuning forks, one in each hand, out in front of them, roughly above each leg. (Some clients prefer to have a cushion on their lap to rest their elbows on and to provide a sense of comfort and protection.) While I sit directly across from the client, facing them, I then use a mallet to tap the tuning forks back and forth in order to activate the sound as the client holds them. Not only does the client hear the resonance of the tones, but they also feel their vibrations in their hands and can track the movement of the mallet back and forth between the forks held out in front of them. When the set of movement is complete, the client can also lift the tuning forks to either side of their head to listen to the reverberation. I invite the client to breathe as the sound settles and eventually stills. I then check in by asking, "What do you notice now?" This can be a very effective way to breathe and ground between sets.

I may also invite clients to create sounds for dual attention BLS by selecting any two small brass bells from a small collection and ringing them on each side of their body, back and forth, while seated or standing. They can also change bells between sets to experiment with different sounds and harmonies that the two bells produce, which can further enhance present-moment orientation.

Another way to offer dual attention BLS that uses sound is with Chinese meditation balls, called *baoding* balls. These are small, heavy metal balls with bells inside that create beautiful sounds. The client can hold one ball in each hand and engage in dual attention BLS by rolling the balls in each palm, shaking them one by one, back and forth, or by gently tossing one ball up in the air and feeling the weight as it lands back into the palm, then gently tossing the ball in the other hand up in the air and feeling the weight as it lands on that palm, and moving back and forth. These movements produce different sounds and sensations that act as a distraction as they track what is happening internally. The weight and shape of the balls are also soothing and grounding for clients. The pair of meditation balls that I use have a sun pictured on one ball and a moon pictured on the other, which promotes a sense of harmony through the metaphor of celestial balance, as the client holds the moon in one hand and the sun in the other.

Creating Dual Attention Bilateral Stimulation with Rhythm

Creating rhythm is another engaging and interactive way to offer dual attention BLS while orienting the client to relational safety. I recommend having various shakers available in your office to experiment with. In the following image, for example, you can see the different types of materials that I have available in my office. Moving from left to right, you can see maracas with long handles; cylindrical agave wood shakers filled with seeds and two sets of egg shakers (in the first basket); three fabric juggling balls filled with sand; felted finger puppet animals, including a fox, frog, raven, and a squirrel (in the second basket); a selenite rod; a long stick with a felted finger puppet of a bird placed on its end; and two beaded drum sticks with soft leather ends made by Canadian Indigenous artist Alisha Finch. The

orange stick on the right also has a tuft of fur, which adds another visual and tactile component.

When creating a rhythm together as a form of dual attention BLS, you and the client can both shake the instruments back and forth while seated or standing. I have also found that this allows me to guide the speed of the set. Often, when I speed my rhythm up, the client naturally speeds up too, as we are creating a rhythm together. If I slow down, the client slows down with me. This allows me to lead and follow the pace of the dual attention BLS collaboratively and nonverbally. Another benefit of using shakers is that not only does the client stay attuned to you through the rhythm, but it is also a full-body experience as they feel the movement of the shakers in their hands (tactile), hear the sounds the instruments produce (auditory), and visually track the back-and-forth movement of the shakers in their hands or your hands (eye movements). You then take a pause for the client to check in and notice what is coming up between sets. You go with whatever they report and begin shaking the maracas or shakers again while the client notices what comes up internally.

Other forms of movement can be used to create rhythm too, such as tossing a ball back and forth. You and the client can sit or stand as you toss the ball to each other, changing the distance between you as well as the speed of the tosses. The client naturally tracks the ball with their eyes in order to catch it, going in a rhythmic back-and-forth pattern. I like to use soft balls that are weighted with sand, like juggling balls, though you can also make balls by filling balloons with sand, flour, or rice.

Creating Dual Attention Bilateral Stimulation with Nature-Based Materials

There are various materials you can use for dual attention BLS that integrate elements of nature. For example, I sometimes gently tap back and forth on the client's hands using a small stick or felt finger puppets of small birds and animals that provide a soft and nonthreatening tactile component. Clients often enjoy integrating these fun and playful elements into our work and may select a bird or animal that they also feel a personal connection to. I also use beaded drumsticks with soft pads on the end—both as something that can be tracked for eye movements as well as a material that can provide tactile stimulation when tapped gently back and forth on the client's palms or backs of their hands (often as their hands rest on a cushion that covers their lap).

Another way to incorporate nature-based elements into eye movements is to use a selenite wand or rod. Selenite crystal has a white, translucent appearance and was named after Selene, the Greek goddess of the moon, for how it reflects light. Holding selenite in your hand while guiding eye movements can offer a soothing and interesting visual focus while the client tracks the rod and its play of light back and forth.

Lastly, walking together in nature may provide an effective form of dual attention BLS. When you encourage the client to be mindful of the sensations of walking—the movement and pressure of their feet, as well as their surroundings—this provides a truly grounding form of dual attention BLS. Not only does this experience connect them to nature, but it also connects them to you since you and the client are walking together—often keeping the same pace and rhythm. Since dual attention BLS should be done as sets of movement, you must guide the client to internally track their experience as they walk with awareness and pause to check in, noticing what is coming up, and continue to walk.

Creating Dual Attention Bilateral Stimulation with the Body and Balance

Since the act of balancing requires us to maintain awareness of our body in space, having clients practice balancing during dual attention BLS can be very effective in helping them maintain present-moment orientation. For example, you can invite the client to stand on one leg while shaking shakers back and forth with you. When the client shifts their weight onto their one standing leg, they naturally have to connect to their body so they do not topple over. Therefore, when working with clients who struggle with present-moment orientation, practicing balance can be particularly effective (Marchand & Simpson, 2022).

Orienting the Client to the Steps of EMDR

During the preparation phase, it is important to explain the process of treatment to the client in a way that makes sense to them. However, many clinicians struggle to take the language they learned in basic training and apply it to their work with clients. This section presents language, metaphors, and images that I have found resonate with clients and help get them motivated to proceed with treatment. To begin, I often use the following shorthand to describe EDMR.

EMDR Explainer

What is EMDR?

E

EMDR is an
Evidence-based,
Eight-phase
Experiential and integrative approach to trauma recovery that helps . . .

M

Metabolize unprocessed memories and
Make new meaning using
Mindful noticing together with sets of
Movement, such as eye movements or tapping, called . . .

D

Dual attention BLS in order to
Distract the mind in the present while
Decreasing the
Distress from the past, . . .

R

Reprocessing and reshaping old memories, and
Restoring your sense of self so you can
Reclaim your
Resources, inherent worth, and future potential.

During the preparation phase, I also like to prepare clients for the next phase of healing—phase 3 (assessment)—using the acronym PILES. This acronym orients clients to the questions that you will ask them during the assessment phase. PILES represents all of the components of the distressing memory that pile up to create a mountain:

Point in time or point of distress

Image of the worst

Lesson learned or internalized about the self

Emotion

Sensation

You might notice that PILES is similar to the TICES acronym often used in EMDR, which stands for target, image, cognition, emotion, sensation. However, I tend not to use the word *target* with clients, as much of my work is in conflict settings, and the word—especially when translated into a client's native language—may feel too associated with conflict and gun violence. I prefer to use language that is as neutral as possible. You'll learn more about each component of the PILES acronym in chapter 8.

To present the PILES acronym to my clients, I use the visual image of a bundle of thread that creates a knot, or multiple knots, of associated material. You must first access and stimulate the neural network holding the memory, then you follow the threads of associated material—loosening them, teasing them out, letting them unravel. Throughout the process, you weave all the threads and loose fragments of experience in with the client's strengths, resources, and supports. The memory is no longer held in knots and tight bundles but is repatterned like a tapestry that changes the way it feels to remember it. Presenting this image to clients before they start reprocessing helps prepare them and makes the questions you ask during the assessment phase more predictable.

Opening and Activating a Memory (PILES)

Point in Time/ Point of Distress

Identify the specific **memory** being accessed and begin to activate its components (image, cognition, emotion, and sensation) one step at a time using the **phase 3 assessment** questions:

Image

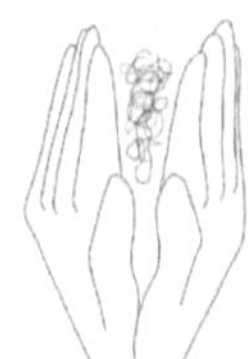

What **image** represents the worst part of that experience?

Lesson Learned About the Self/Cognition

As you think of that image now, what does it make you believe about yourself **(NC)**? And what would you rather believe about yourself **(PC)**? When you think of that image, how true do those words *[state positive cognition]* feel to you on the scale of 1–7, with 1 feeling not true at all and 7 feeling completely true **(VOC)**?

Emotion

When you think of that image of *[state image representing the worst part]* and hear those words *[state the negative cognition]*, what **emotion** do you notice now? How distressing is it on the scale of 0–10, where 0 is neutral/calm and 10 is the worst it could possibly be **(SUD)**?

Body Sensation

Where do you feel it in your **body**?

Working with Negative Cognitions

In EMDR, the **negative cognition (NC)** represents the thoughts that clients hold about themselves in relation to the trauma memory. These thoughts typically have to do with safety or survival (*I am not safe, I can't trust people*), responsibility (*I didn't try hard enough, I am to blame*), choice or control (*I am powerless, I can't trust myself to make decisions*), social belonging (*I am alone, I am different*), and core self-concept (*I am broken, I am unlovable*). When clients can begin to understand that these thoughts are not objective truths but, rather, beliefs that were planted by experiences of trauma, it creates space to challenge those thoughts during the reprocessing phase so clients can reclaim their sense of being worthy and whole.

To describe negative cognitions to clients, I find it helpful to use the metaphor of a seed that got planted into the soil of their self-concept. The client's trauma caused this seed to be buried into the soil on a deep emotional level, while similar stressful experiences in their life helped it take root and grow so that, over time, it became like a weed or invasive plant that took over. This prevented healthier plants from growing as it blocked the light and took the nutrients from more positive beliefs, making it difficult for the client to see and feel who they really are. In EMDR, you and the client work together to loosen the roots of those old beliefs so you can pull them out and create space for healthier beliefs to grow and thrive.

Presenting this metaphor helps clients begin to disidentify with their negative cognitions, which is particularly helpful in the assessment phase of EMDR, when you would typically ask, "What words go with that image that describes a negative belief you hold about yourself now?" You can instead ask, "What seed got planted in that moment, like a belief about who you are as a person?" The client can then take an objective stance as they observe and name the negative cognition that arose in response to the worst part of the memory. This objective stance can give them the space to recognize that this belief came from the experience and to begin to unlearn (or uproot) this belief.

Working with Positive Cognitions

In EMDR, the **positive cognition (PC)** represents the more helpful, positive lessons that the client has relearned about themself. Like the negative cognition, these thoughts typically fall in the categories of safety or survival (*I can trust my judgment, It is over now*), responsibility (*I did the best I could*), choice or control (*I am powerful, I have choices*), social belonging (*I am supported, I belong*), and core self-concept (*I am lovable, I am worthy of care*). When clients can unlearn the lessons of trauma—loosening and uprooting the negative cognitions—they can replace them with restorative beliefs that speak to their true nature and help them reclaim their wholeness and inherent worth.

I often present the idea of the client's core self as "the soil of the self." The soil of the self is the source of who we are; it is not a resource that can be installed or enhanced but is the essence of our being. Soil can become depleted or contaminated but regenerates with the right care and conditions. We can uproot the weeds or invasive plants (negative cognitions) and create space for new plants (positive cognitions) to grow and take root. These new beliefs cleanse and heal the soil of the self, helping it regenerate and providing a foundation for health and well-being. In phase 5 (positive installation), clients have an opportunity to water, grow, strengthen, and "fertilize" these new beliefs about the self in relation to the distressing memory.

Rating the Validity of Cognition (VOC)

In phase 3 (assessment), and again in phase 5 (positive installation), you invite the client to rate how true their positive belief feels in relation to the memory using a 7-point scale called the **validity of cognition (VOC) scale**. During the preparation phase, I introduce clients to the VOC scale with the visual metaphor of a growing seed. Sarah Tevyaw, an art therapist based in Montreal who specializes in grief and palliative care, kindly painted this visual scale for my VOC chart. On this scale, 1 is a seed that holds all the potential for growth but has not yet had the space, light, and nurturance to grow, while 7 is a flower in full bloom that feels all the way true. When a plant reaches full bloom, it can reproduce and spread its seeds by attracting pollinators with its beautiful colors. It also protects its seeds from the outside world, enclosing them until they are ready to spread. This is how clients can think about positive cognitions: When a belief is in full bloom—as in, it feels all the way true—it can spread and grow in other areas of the client's life and be carried into the future.

As I explain it to clients, "In EMDR, we remove the material that blocks the light from shining on your positive belief so that it can start taking in nutrients from the sun and soil and grow stronger as you process through the memory. We use this scale to check in on your belief and see whether we need to nurture it even more so it can feel all the way true." This visual VOC scale can help clients make sense of the numbers on the scale and connect to them in a more restorative and meaningful way. This is especially important when working with clients from diverse backgrounds because the use of scales can be culturally unfamiliar, as Paulsen and Spear Chief (2024) noted in their work with Indigenous communities.

Since many plants have healing properties, I have also found that some clients find a sense of comfort or strength when I invite them to connect with a personally or culturally meaningful plant that is not pictured on the visual VOC chart. You can simply ask your client whether there is a flower,

medicinal plant, or herb that comes to mind when they think of the positive cognition—something that might symbolize its strength, beauty, or healing properties. You can then have them notice that plant as they think of the memory and the positive cognition, rating how rooted, strong, and healthy it feels on a scale of 1–7.

Working with the Subjective Unit of Disturbance (SUD) Scale

During the preparation phase, it can also be helpful to orient clients to the **subjective unit of disturbance (SUD) scale**, which asks them to rate the intensity of their feelings after processing on a 10-point scale. To introduce this scale, I like to use the visual metaphor of a mountain with an emotional charge emanating from it, which represents the memory and the emotional charge it carries. The SUD rating represents how big the mountain *feels* to the client when they look at it now, as the emotional charge can make the mountain feel bigger than it is. With this scale, a rating of 0 or 1 means that the mountain has little to no emotional charge remaining—the mountain is scaled down to size and the presence of the mountain is neutral. In contrast, a rating of 10 is the biggest the mountain could possibly feel—it is looming, intimidating, and overpowering, with a high level of distress. The goal of this visual metaphor is to show the client that memories will always remain part of the past—and the client cannot change that—but they *can* change their relationship to these memories by decreasing their intensity and neutralizing the emotional charge they carry.

10
9
8
7
6
5
4
3
2
1
0

The Mountain of the Memory

Neutralizing the Emotional Charge of a Memory

An upsetting memory is like a mountain. It can feel overpowering and insurmountable due to the heightened emotional charge surrounding it. As we revisit and journey through the memory, we can erode and diminish the emotional charge it carries. We cannot remove a mountain, as it is a part of the past, but we can change our relationship to it and the power it holds over us.

Assessing Readiness

There are no absolute checkboxes to assess readiness when working with complex trauma. As a clinician, your goal is to determine whether the client has enough resources to safely move forward with treatment, but how can you gauge this? One way to do so is to "weigh" the client's readiness with a scale to determine whether the client's resources balance out the challenges they are facing. You do not want to stay in the preparation phase longer than is helpful for the client, or you run the risk of reinforcing avoidance.

The scale that I present here was developed in collaboration with my esteemed former colleagues at the Trauma Institute and Child Trauma Institute, Elizabeth Davis and Jessica Horder, who are both EMDRIA-approved consultants specializing in intensive trauma treatment. This scale does not use numbers but, rather, contains a spectrum of 10 different areas of functioning, ranging from one side (less ready) to the other side (more ready):

1. **Needs awareness:** Does the client neglect their needs? Or have they established regulating routines that allow them to effectively meet their needs and care for themself?
2. **Affect awareness:** Does the client numb out and disconnect from their emotions (or become easily overwhelmed by emotions)? Or can they mindfully observe and identify their emotions, using them as helpful information to guide their actions?
3. **Somatic awareness:** Is the client disconnected from their body (or easily overwhelmed by sensations)? Or are they grounded and centered in their body, able to mindfully observe and identify the sensations?
4. **Metacognitive awareness:** Does the client overidentify with their thoughts, leading them to spiral into distress, anxiety, or self-criticism? Or are they able to access different perspectives and reflect on their thoughts, challenging what is not helpful for them and developing new thinking patterns?
5. **Self-concept:** Is the client disconnected from a sense of self or experiencing self-loathing? Or can they access self-compassion and self-love?

6. **Parts or states awareness:** Is the client ignorant of their internal parts (or experiencing high conflict between parts)? Or do they have an internal awareness of their parts and can regulate these parts when they are activated?
7. **Safety:** Does the client actively engage in high-risk behaviors and place themself in situations that are unsafe? Or do they use healthy coping skills and supports to manage urges or unsafe situations?
8. **Substance use:** Does the client actively engage in substance use? Or are they able to use coping skills and supports to manage distress and urges?
9. **Supports:** Does the client have no personal or professional supports in their life? Or do they have access to and actively utilize professional and social supports?
10. **Interpersonal effectiveness:** Is the client overly boundaried, with no trust in others (or conversely lacking boundaries or the skills to assert them)? Or can they take a collaborative stance in relationships by communicating effectively and balancing the wants and needs of others with their own wants and needs?

No client needs to achieve complete functioning in all these areas before reprocessing, but you want to weigh the balance in each area and reflect on where the client's strengths, skills, resources, and supports balance out the challenges in their life. Clients often exhibit microprogress that can lead to new tipping points and functioning, but you need to be realistic about what is possible for each client given their ongoing challenges in addition to the unprocessed trauma they are managing internally. You are aiming for an overall sense of more readiness rather than less, and you want to continue shifting the balance toward readiness. However, sometimes "ready enough" is enough to begin reprocessing.

Once you feel the client is ready enough, you dip your toe into the water and begin reprocessing memories or material that are accessible and tolerable to the client. As you do so, remember that the eight phases of EMDR are not linear: You can move into the reprocessing work—restricting and modifying EMDR as needed, and engaging all of the resources that the client built up in the preparation work—and then cycle back into preparation when you need to build more psychoeducation, skills, or support.

Weighing Readiness

Needs Awareness

Can't identify own needs/ neglects needs	Feels overwhelmed by needs/judges or rejects needs	Takes steps to meet and communicate needs	Has some regulating routines established	Meets needs effectively and nurtures self/ has reparenting routines

Affect Awareness

Can't identify emotions/is numb or flat	Overwhelmed or flooded by emotions	Can identify but not tolerate emotions	Can tolerate and express emotions	Can observe and use emotions as helpful information

Somatic Awareness

Disconnected from body sensations	Triggered by body sensations	Aware of body sensations	Able to tolerate and listen to body sensations	Grounded and centered in body

Metacognitive Awareness

Lacks mindfulness/ distance from thoughts	Triggered by thoughts/ spiraling downward	Aware of thinking patterns and cognitive errors	Able to challenge unhelpful or harmful thinking patterns	Can access different perspectives/is reflective

Self-Concept

Disconnected from self, lacks self-concept, reliant on others for self-concept	Is self-loathing/ self-attacking	Aware of self-attacking tendencies/ in pre-contemplative stage	Taking steps to interrupt self-destructive thoughts, feelings, and behaviors	Self-loving and self-compassionate

Weighing Readiness

Parts/States Awareness

Ignorant of parts	Understands parts psycho-education	Uses parts language	Internally aware of parts	Can regulate parts when activated

Safety

Actively engages in high-risk behaviors	Motivated to decrease high-risk behaviors but still struggles	Able to avoid high-risk behaviors at least 50% of time	Chooses to avoid high-risk behaviors in triggering situations	Uses healthy coping skills to manage urges

Substance Use

Actively engages in substance use	Motivated to decrease use but still struggles	Able to avoid substance use at least 50% of time	Chooses to avoid substances in triggering situations	Uses healthy coping skills to manage urges

Supports

Has no personal or professional supports	Has professional supports only	Has professional supports and is building social supports	Has professional and social supports	Has professional and social supports and actively utilizes them

Interpersonal Effectiveness

Overly boundaried and does not trust others (or has no boundaries)	Aware of boundaries but lacks skills to assert or honor boundaries	Is learning interpersonal skills and aware of others' perspectives	Is applying interpersonal skills and has increased ability to consider their own and others' perspectives	Is collaborative and balances the wants and needs of self versus other

CHAPTER 8

The Mountain Metaphor of Reprocessing

Trauma memories are like mountains. Although we all have hills, valleys, and the natural ups and downs of life, some clients have endured experiences in their past that have caused mountains to form—mountains that feel too big to overcome, too difficult to move through. These towering mountains get in their way and block clients from what is on the other side. As a result, clients develop strategies to avoid the mountain, taking other routes and paths that narrow the possibilities of their life trajectory.

To overcome this fear and avoidance, clients must go back to that point in time—to the place where the mountain was formed—and journey through it. To walk clients through this process, this chapter lays out the steps of the reprocessing journey using the mountain metaphor. With this metaphor, you can take Shapiro's (2018) theory and carry it directly into your clinical work so that it makes sense to your clients, inviting them as active participants on the journey.

Mountains as Metaphors for Reprocessing

In phase 1 of EMDR, you map out the client's landscape of experience to locate the memories that create avoidance and distress and block their path to well-being. You identify the point (or period) of time when the mountain formed and prepare the client to travel back there, carrying the resources and perspectives they hold in the present. In phase 2, you help the client develop skills to ground and orient themself to the present so that when they revisit and travel through the memory in the past, they can maintain their footing in the here and now.

Since climbing a mountain is hard work, you need to help the client build the resources and strengths needed for this journey before you begin to climb. You might train on hills and move around the lowest points of a memory, gathering the resources that help the client feel prepared, powerful, and protected. When the client is ready, you go to the peak—to the highest point of distress. Throughout this process, the client is the pathfinder. While you bring the client to the top of the mountain, they know the way back down. Like with neural pathways, all paths hold information. There are many ways down a mountain, but you trust the direction the client chooses and follow where they need to go to find healing and resolution, guiding the way if they get stuck, lost, or overwhelmed.

In EMDR, you facilitate movement through the memory with dual attention BLS, helping the mind walk through pathways of association. You guide the client to rest between sets, noticing what material is presenting itself on the path and following the client's next steps. As they progress down the mountain, different aspects of the memory are visited with present-moment awareness. The client picks up and carries what needs healing, discovers new resources, and reaches different points of view and perspectives that help integration and resolution happen spontaneously. Francine Shapiro (2018) calls this "progressive stages of self-healing." You follow the client as they move the material all the way to completion—until they reach the base of the mountain where the land becomes flat and there is no more downward movement.

You go up and down the mountain as many times as you need to for the client to reach a sense of peace and resolution with the memory. You always check back at the top, at the peak, to see whether another path opens up with more material that needs attending to. If nothing new opens up and the client feels solid and strong as they view the whole memory from the peak, then you begin the journey off the mountain again.

This process changes the client's relationship to the memory. The mountain is still there, part of their inner landscape, but its emotional charge has been diminished. The client can now see the mountain's actual size and shape. By journeying through the mountain, the client has confronted what the mountain holds and cleared new pathways, eroding away the elements that are no longer helpful, letting them all roll down into the river, and making space to see the resources and strengths that were hidden before. When the client looks back at the mountain now, they can see the new perspectives, understanding, and positive beliefs that were carved out through the journey. The memory no longer blocks their way; it can rest peacefully in their past.

Titration and Resourcing from the Foothills

Using the metaphor of a mountain to represent a distressing memory is a titration strategy, as it creates a sense of distance between the client and the memory. Giving the memory a representative form contains it within the natural boundaries of a shape and size. It becomes fixed and finite. The client can then position themself in relation to the memory rather than be flooded or overpowered by it. Creating this space can allow for increased mindful awareness and greater differentiation between now and then, which is essential for dual awareness. The client can experience a sense of control as they intentionally revisit the memory from a present perspective: "The person I am right now, in the present, is revisiting that place and time in the past." This is different from intrusions and flashbacks, where the client relives and reexperiences the memory as if it were happening again in the present. In EMDR, you want to help the client revisit the past, rather than having the past intrude into the present.

Resourcing Before the Climb

When a client turns toward a memory in their mind and begins to approach it rather than avoid it, it may appear too big and too much. They even may believe the memory has power over them. For clients, thinking about going back to that point in time can be terrifying and intimidating, even after they have done the preparation work. You can shift that fear by reinforcing the client's resources before reprocessing a specific memory. This is akin to standing at the foothills, looking up at the mountain, and inviting the client to identify something in the present that they can bring with them as they climb to increase readiness to confront that specific memory. I like to invite clients to imagine a resource that can help them feel **prepared, protected, or powerful**—which is why I call this technique **3P resourcing**.

Script for 3P Resourcing

1. **Identify the resource:** "Imagine that this memory is like a big mountain in your past, and we're going to go back there and travel through it together. What would you need to have with you to feel prepared, protected, or powerful enough to make that journey?"
2. **Install the resource:** Invite the client to focus on and engage with the resource they identified, while adding slow taps or eye movements to help them connect with the resource. The client can also use art materials to enhance the resource, such as by representing it with pastels or modeling clay, or they can choose a stone or gem to represent it so they can feel and hold it in their hands: "Take a moment and really feel how you have that with you right now, in this moment."
3. **Check in:** To ensure the resource feels helpful and available to the client, ask them, "Can you feel that ______ is with you and available whenever you need it?" If so, invite them to focus on it again—"Okay, focus on that"—while optionally adding more dual attention BLS. If the resource was not accessible or not strong enough, invite the client to identify additional resources: "What else could you bring with you to feel prepared, protected, or powerful? Check in with having that with you right now, in this moment." *[Then add optional dual attention BLS.]*

4. **Begin the journey:** Vocalize that they are now ready to take the next step toward the mountain, reinforcing the past-present differentiation: "Okay, let's go back to that place and bring some healing to it."

Resourcing the client before the climb allows them to create a **memory-specific resource**—a concept developed by Ricky Greenwald (2007) with his "safety device," where the client imagines the memory as a dream and then identifies what they need to feel safe or okay going into that dream. Whatever resource the client identifies as a safety device is then installed before the assessment phase to decrease avoidance and increase readiness for that specific memory. Resourcing the client while they imagine being back in the memory—before the memory is activated—can increase a sense of courage and belief that they can take the next step.

Going to the Peak in Phase 3 (Assessment)

During the assessment phase, you go to the place in the client's mind where the memory is stored in its original form, with its raw, vivid, emotional charge. This is akin to bringing the client to the top of the mountain where they can actively recall the memory from the highest point but not yet move into the memory. From here, the client can look down at the memory from a stance of mindful noticing that is grounded in the present.

You begin the assessment from the highest point of distress because this point allows you to activate the most amount of material associated with the memory. According to Shapiro (2018), the specific aspect of the experience that you focus on (referred to as the **target memory**) acts as a **node** that is linked with other past experiences containing similar physiological information. The memory's node is like the peak of the mountain, which opens up to all the different pathways around it. The client can walk down different pathways of information, and when everything is processed through to completion, standing back at the mountain's peak is no longer distressing.

From the peak, or "pivotal place," you assess the target memory. The client identifies the image or sensory information that represents the worst part of the experience and what it makes them believe about themself now (the negative cognition). This begins to activate the material in the memory networks that needs healing, making it available for reprocessing. However, it is also important for the client to ask what they would rather believe about themself when they look at that image (the positive cognition). This is a pivot to a present-oriented perspective that can open up the memory networks in the mind that hold positive, adaptive, and updated information (e.g., *It was not my fault*, *I was just an innocent child*, *I am a good person*), making it available to support integration and resolution. I often say to clients, "From where you're at right now, looking back at that time, what would you rather believe about yourself?" to again reinforce the differentiation between past and present and keep them connected to their presently held knowledge and resources.

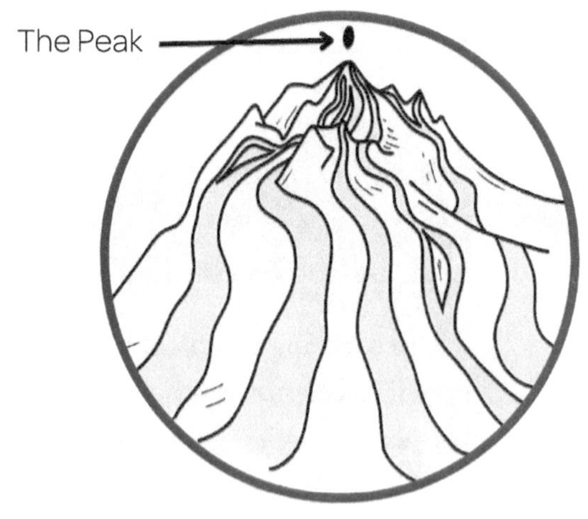

To help provide a marker of progress, you ask the client to check in with how true the updated belief *feels* to them now on a scale of 1–7 (the VOC rating). The client then assesses what they feel when they bring the image back to mind alongside the negative cognition (the emotion), how distressing it is on a scale of 0–10 (the SUD rating), and where they feel it in their body (the sensation). You then assess these different components of the memory, which opens up the way into the material, and you immediately begin moving down the mountain. You do not go up without going down, just as you do not activate the memory without then doing something to help the distress begin to shift.

As discussed in chapter 7, I like to use the acronym PILES to describe this process of going to the peak, as it orients clients to the questions that I will be asking in order to access the material that needs healing:

Point in time or point of distress

Image of the worst

Lesson learned or internalized about the self

Emotion

Sensation

Here I walk you through each aspect of PILES in more detail as it relates to the mountain metaphor of reprocessing.

Point in Time or Point of Distress

The point in time or point of distress is the specific memory or material that you focus on during reprocessing. As discussed in chapter 5, it is important to delineate between memories with as much specificity as possible by identifying key representative moments that provide a specific entry point into the distressing material that needs reprocessing. I find that referring to this distressing material as a "point in time" helps locate the memory in the past and encourages differentiation between the here and now. Sometimes I also use "point of distress" to specify the material that we are focusing on, which may not be a memory but a sensation, implicit memory, dream, or specific behavior. If your client decides on a specific label or cue word to describe the memory, make sure to use this word and to avoid describing the memory in more detail. You do not want to open up too much, too soon, or too fast:

- "Would it be okay if we begin to do some healing work on that moment when ______ [*use the client's label or language for describing the event*], focusing on just that point in time?"
    - [*If there is no memory but rather implicit material:*] "Would it be okay for us to do some healing work on that sense of _____ [*use the client's label or language for describing the material*], focusing on just that point of distress?"

Image of the Worst

During this step, you begin to activate and open up the material by asking the client to identify the image that represents the worst part of the experience. However, not all memories are encoded with an image. Some memories are held implicitly, as is the case with preverbal or generational memories, or memories that are experienced in a state of dissociation and are thus encoded without explicit markers, like time, place, and narrative. These more implicitly held memories may be more difficult to name or identify—like a mountain peak that you cannot see clearly because it is covered in mist.

In these cases, you can identify the sensory material that represents the worst part of the experience. This allows you to find a handle—something to grab hold of—so you can access and enter the material that needs healing. **Handle** is a term developed by Eugene Gendlin (1996), who speaks of it as a way into the felt sense of the body: "As with the handle of a suitcase, which brings with it the whole weight of the suitcase, the whole weight of the felt sense is brought forward by that one word or phrase when one repeats it to oneself" (p. 48). The handle can be a sensation, symbol, sound, word, or phrase—anything that helps you begin to access the memory:

- "What image would represent the worst part of that experience (or material) for you now?"
    - [*If no image:*] "What sensation, sound, or even symbol might represent the worst part of this experience now?"

Lesson Learned About the Self

Since the words *negative cognition* can feel clinical or even confusing for some clients, I prefer to use "lesson learned" with clients to describe how trauma can make them believe things about themselves that become part of their self-concept—that reflect who they think they are as a person. This language also complements the flower metaphor used to explain negative and positive cognitions in chapter 7, as it emphasizes the external nature of negative beliefs, like seeds that get planted into the soil of the self by experiences of trauma and adversity. Even though clients may feel that these beliefs are true on a deep, emotional level, it does not mean that what they learned is an objective truth about who they are:

- "Think of the image or sensation that represents the worst part of that experience . . . What does it make you believe about yourself now, like a lesson you learned about who you are as a person?"
- [*Using the flower metaphor:*] "Think of the image or sensation that represents the worst part of that experience . . . What seed got planted right there at that moment, like a belief about who you are as a person?"

Then, you invite the client to look back at that memory from the present moment and identify what they would rather believe about themself. This pivot to the positive cognition provides an opportunity for the client to take an alternative view of the memory, which sets a baseline for progress:

- "And what would you rather believe about yourself?"
- [*Using the flower metaphor:*] "If we were to loosen the roots of that belief and plant something in its place, what would that be, like something you would rather believe about yourself?"

However, some clients struggle to identify a positive cognition at this point in the process—they can only get so close to their true self or true nature—and that is okay. You want to meet them where they are. You can let the belief that more fully reflects their self-concept emerge during reprocessing. For example, at this point in treatment, a client might only be able to say, "I am not responsible for what they did to me." However, they might eventually be able to revise this statement to "I am worthy of love and care" after the reprocessing in phase 4 is complete.

Therefore, it is not productive to rework the cognitions and force them to meet certain criteria in the assessment phase. The primary goal is to activate the various components of the memory for more effective reprocessing. If the initial positive cognition feels too unrealistic or impossible to the client, their system may not integrate it, and it will not be available to help the negative cognition be updated and unlearned. The statements that have the most emotional resonance for the client are the statements I tend to go with. When the client *feels* it, it helps open up the right pathways for healing in the mind.

If the client still struggles to identify a positive cognition, you can prompt them further toward a positive belief, such as:

- "If you could unlearn that lesson [*state the negative cognition*], what belief about you would it make space for?"

Once you've identified a positive cognition, you invite the client to rate how true their positive belief feels using the 7-point VOC scale. As described in chapter 7, I like to present the VOC scale using the visual metaphor of a seed that is growing, where 1 is a seed that holds all the potential for growth but does not yet feel true, while 7 is a flower in full bloom that feels all the way true. Although the VOC scale uses numbers to rate the client's belief in the positive cognition, you want the client to notice and rate their embodied, gut-level response to the positive statement. In other words, you want them to rate how believable the thought *feels*, as opposed to how objectively true it is:

- "When you think of the image that represents the worst part of the experience, and you hear those words [*state the positive cognition*], how true do they feel now? Is it like a 1, like a seed of a belief that hasn't started to grow, or like a 7, all the way true, where the belief feels deeply rooted and in full bloom?"

Emotion

At this point, you ask the client to name the emotion they are feeling as they bring to mind the worst part of the memory and the negative cognition:

- "As you think of the image of [*state the worst part*] and hear those words [*state the negative cognition*], what emotional response do you notice now?"

You then ask them to rate how intense their distress level is on a 10-point SUD scale. Recall from chapter 7 that the SUD rating represents how big the mountain (i.e., the trauma memory) *feels*, where 0 or 1 means that the mountain has little to no emotional charge remaining and 10 means the mountain is as intimidating and overpowering as it could possibly feel:

- "How distressing is it on a scale of 0–10, where 0 is neutral or calm and 10 is the worst it could possibly feel?"
- [*Using the mountain metaphor:*] "How big would you say it feels to you right now on a scale of 0–10, where 0 is neutral or calm, like

a mountain that is just part of the landscape, and 10 is the worst it could possibly feel, like looking up at a mountain that feels huge and overpowering, with as much intensity and emotional charge as it could possibly have? How big does it *feel*?"

Sensation

Finally, you invite the client to notice where they feel the distress in their body. At this point, the primary components of the memory have been activated, and you do not want the client to explore the sensations or sit with them any longer than need be. Keeping momentum is essential to ensuring that the client does not sink into the memory and become flooded or lose dual attention. This last question of the assessment phase is focused only on where the client is noticing the distress:

- "Where do you feel it in your body?"

Once you identify the location of the sensation, transition into phase 4 to begin reprocessing.

Transitioning into Phase 4 (Desensitization and Reprocessing)

Phase 3 (assessment) is only done when the client has the time, readiness, and energy to move directly into phase 4 (desensitization and reprocessing). Once the client is ready to transition into this phase, it is important to provide an explanation of the process. The following script is a way to introduce reprocessing in a way that continues to build on the mountain metaphor:

- "Now that we have climbed up to the peak of this memory, we can begin to follow its pathways down. We will do sets of movement, like eye movements and tapping, to help your mind and body move through whatever presents itself along the path. We will take rests in between each set of movement for you to check in and notice any new information or insights that arise—continuing to move in the direction that helps you find healing and resolution. If you want to stop or come out of the memory completely, just raise your hand like a stop signal. We can pause and rest at any time."

Traveling Through the Pathways: Phase 4 (Desensitization and Reprocessing)

Once you help the client transition into this phase, you begin the process of moving back down the mountain, allowing the client to journey through the various pathways that are connected to the peak of the memory. As a therapist, you know where the top and the bottom of the mountain are, but the paths in between are the client's to choose. Remember that you play the role of a guide, helping the client when they need your support, but you trust the client to lead the way.

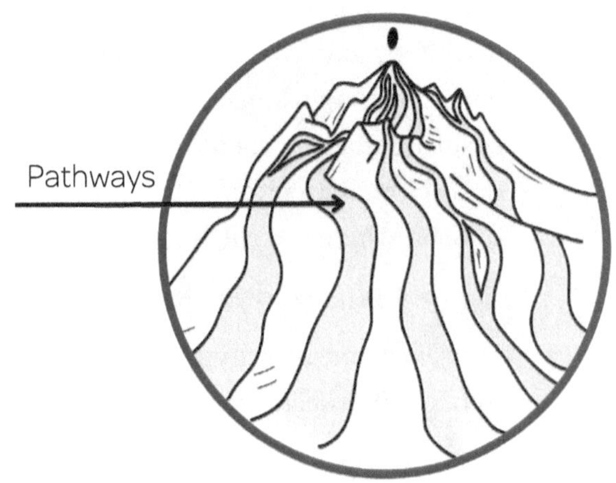

As the client moves along associated memory pathways, they encounter elements of the memory—thoughts, feelings, sensations, and sensory perceptions, such as sounds, smells, and images—that have been stored and stuck in a past state, with the same vividness, emotional charge, and perspectives that were encoded at the time of the event. To stimulate movement through this material, you introduce sets of dual attention BLS that typically range between 15 to 60 seconds in length. With each set, the distressing information is moved further along the neurophysiological pathway toward neural integration and adaptive resolution (Shapiro, 2018).

Facing and following this material can be challenging, as the terrain can get rough, steep, dark, and scary. If so, you might have to get more active in helping the client navigate those tough spots and stay connected to their present resources. You may offer interweaves to nudge the client toward the information and insights that help move them through the rough patches. If they get stuck and cannot progress any further, or they get lost, you go with them back to the top of the mountain and journey back down, often allowing them to access the material that needs healing from a different route.

The client clears new pathways through the memory, uncovering the stored and stuck material and opening the way for it to merge and intersect with the pathways that hold adaptive information, such as resources, present perspectives, and supports. According to Shapiro (2018), insight and integration occur when neural networks link up with each other. These intersections of insight and integration create new associative pathways throughout the memory that change the way it is recalled and remembered.

The use of dual attention BLS throughout the journey helps the client maintain orientation to the here and now and to a present perspective on the past, which is a powerful form of adaptive information. There is a lot that the client knows now that they did not know then. The client brings this present perspective—such as knowing that they are not stuck, that that situation is over now—back into the past. As the client journeys down the mountain with their present perspective, they begin to see the past from different angles and reach new vantage points that spontaneously change how they feel toward the memory. In turn, the perspectives that the client held at the time the mountain was formed become updated. For example, a client who was abused in childhood—and who felt responsible for this mistreatment—can now assign appropriate levels of responsibility to the adults who caused them harm. These new understandings can open up pathways of compassion for the younger self who had no control over the situation they were forced to endure and sometimes even toward the adults who, due to their own histories and life circumstances, were not able to meet the client's needs for safety, nurturance, and love.

The client can then begin to make sense of their past as well as their own responses at the time, given the resources and choices they had available to them. This is the power of bringing the present perspective into the past: The client's updated understanding of choice, safety, boundaries, responsibility, developmental needs, and all the current adaptive information that they carry can come in and challenge the old beliefs and perceptions held on the mountain. The client arrives at a deeper understanding that they got through it; they were just a child, it was never their burden to carry, and it was never their fault. This transforms the mountain and erodes old beliefs, changing the landscape of the past and their relationship with the memory.

Finding Resolution at the Bottom: The Peaceful Place

As I've discussed, it is important to follow the client's pathways of free association during reprocessing, meaning that you trust that whatever needs healing or attention on the mountain will manifest along the path as the client moves through it, bringing it to resolution as it merges and pairs with positive material. Throughout this process, there is a natural direction and momentum downward: The level of distress associated with the memory decreases as the client descends the mountain toward well-being and resolution. They are clearing out the paths, rolling what is no longer needed down into the river to be transformed and released. Your role is to follow the client's associative pathways toward healing and completion, to the foot of the mountain—the base—where there is no more movement and no more change. You listen for when it seems the client has reached this place of peace—allowing the client's mind to walk around that place for two sets of dual attention BLS to make sure nothing new emerges—and then bring the client back up to the top of the mountain, back to the peak you started at.

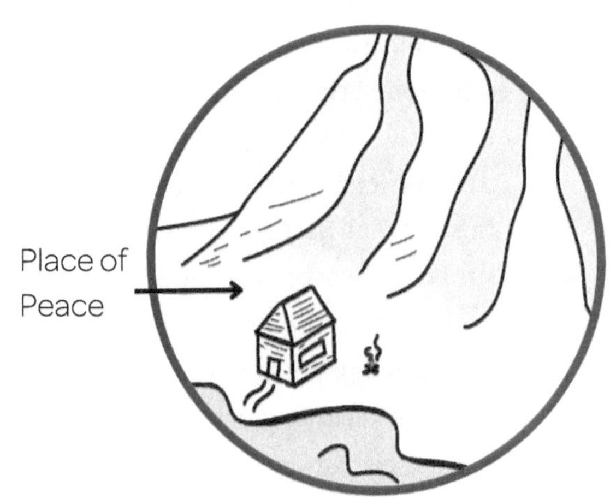

Returning to the Peak

The purpose of returning to the peak is to see whether any new material emerges. From the top of the mountain, the client can look around and notice whether new pathways have opened up. Although you already started this process with PILES in the assessment phase, here you do not want to return the client to any other component of the memory (not the image, lesson learned, emotion, or sensation)—only back to the peak, to that specific memory or point in time. This ensures that you are not restricting the client's associations with the memory:

- "Go back to the top of the memory, to that place we started from (or that ____-year-old time), and see what comes up for you now."

After bringing the client back up to the top of the memory, like the peak of the mountain, you again invite them to notice what comes up. You listen for new pathways of associative material to open up. When the memory is reprocessed and the material on the mountain has been brought to resolution, the client may not report any new information. They may instead report that the memory feels neutral, that it has lost its vividness and emotional charge, and that it is less overpowering. If the client reports no further distress or new information, do one or two sets of dual attention BLS. This is like giving the client's mind a chance to walk around the top of the mountain to look for any more material that needs healing. If something emerges, follow it down a pathway. If not, invite the client to rate their SUD level in relation to the memory. If it is a 0, do one or two more sets to let that strengthen and settle and then move to phase 5 (positive installation). If the client's SUD is more than 0, you focus on what is getting in the way—"What is in the way of this memory feeling neutral and in the past?"—and then follow whatever the client reports down another pathway toward resolution and then return to the peak to check the SUD again. You continue up and down the mountain—repeating the cycle of peak, pathways, peaceful place, and back up to the peak—until you have moved all the material toward peace, completion, and resolution.

The Art and Rhythm of Movement and Pauses

During the reprocessing phases, you use dual attention BLS, like eye movement and tapping, to stimulate the AIP system and get stuck material moving again. Unlike resourcing in phase 2—which involves the use of slow, short sets of dual attention BLS to enhance positive feelings—you generally go for long and fast sets of dual attention BLS during reprocessing, as fast as the client can comfortably manage.

You start with 24 passes but may do more or less based on the client's needs, process, and preferences. You should not concentrate on counting but should rather stay attuned to the client's nonverbal cues as they proceed through the material. This includes their pace of breathing, changes in complexion, and other nonverbal cues such as facial gestures, posture, and muscle tension. You are looking for signs of distress (e.g., eyes widening), shifts in movement or posture (e.g., their shoulders starting to drop), or resolution (e.g., a sigh or relaxed muscles).

If there is distress, you continue with dual attention BLS so the client can keep working through the material. When you observe signs of relief and resolution, you let the client pause and check in. This is the art of EMDR: the process of attuning and listening to the client from a place of trust and curiosity. You keep it collaborative, creative, and experimental. You change it up according to the client's needs—for example, by switching the speed and forms of dual attention BLS (e.g., sound, body, tactile, auditory). If you notice the client losing dual awareness and slipping too far into the memory, you might pull them more into the present through movement, balancing, standing up, smelling oil, and increasing distraction.

While keeping the momentum is essential during reprocessing, you also need to pause to breathe, check in, and notice what is emerging on the path. This is the rhythm of EMDR reprocessing: moving, pausing, and moving again. For this reason, it is more effective to do sets of movement (or dual attention BLS) as opposed to continuous dual attention BLS all the way down the mountain. According to Shapiro (2018), taking breaks between sets is important because it gives the client a chance to pause and reflect on their internal experience, maybe even verbalizing what they notice to you, which fosters further integration of the shifts and changes they notice. In contrast, if reprocessing takes place too quickly—in other words, if you allow the client to run down the mountain too fast—the client may not be able to fully integrate and make sense of their responses.

Therefore, it is important to facilitate pauses between sets. When you pause and check in, you invite the client to verbalize whatever feels most important or stands out to them. The question that you ask between sets is "What are you noticing now?" or "What is coming up for you now?" This is an open invitation for the client to notice any aspect of their internal experience that is arising. They are free to follow what feels most salient to them. In doing so, they provide the direction and clear the pathways down the mountain. Once the client reports what they are noticing, you facilitate movement again with phrases such as "notice that" or "go with that" and immediately begin dual attention BLS.

This is different from talk therapy. You are not talking, interpreting, or rephrasing what the client reports. With talk therapy, the client has to think about your words and process your interpretations—evaluating how much they resonate or not—which can move the client away from their own experience. Your goal as an EMDR therapist is to let the client come to their own interpretations and let the meaning unfold.

Following the Flow of Free Association

In EMDR, you follow the client's lead—trusting that whatever emerges is important to the healing process—because every memory that arises is, in some way, associated with the target memory (Shapiro, 2018). You let the associative material manifest and the meaning unfold so the client can make the connections that allow for healing. Sometimes you may find yourself wondering, *How will this help bring healing to the memory we started with?* You do not always need to know the answer to that. You accompany the client with curiosity and trust, following what Shapiro calls "the connective link," like a thread that weaves these fragments of experiences together.

Throughout this process, you are always listening for change. Any change is indicative of movement toward resolution. You do not need the client to provide an in-depth description of what the changes are; you just need to know that the material is shifting and moving in some way. If the material is no longer changing, you need to know whether it is stuck in a place of distress, like a rough patch (at which point you use a strategy for blocked processing or an interweave) or whether it has simply reached a place of resolution at the bottom of the mountain (at which point you would return to the original target, or the peak of the mountain).

Patterns of Change

Since memories are stored in a state-dependent way, whatever was present at the time of the traumatic event—whether internally (e.g., thoughts, emotions, sensations) or externally (e.g., images, sounds, voices, smells, words, tastes)—can get locked into the memory and stored in their original state. As you start to unlock these fragments of the memory, they reemerge and express themselves by coming into present-moment experience. As the client maintains orientation to the present and to their resources, the material naturally and spontaneously begins to change.

The process of change can look and sound different for each client and each memory, so it is important that you stay open to diverse patterns of processing. For example, some clients have difficulty with visualization, so they may connect to the memory and to their internal experiences primarily through narrative accounts or through sensations. Nonetheless, you can expect certain patterns of change during processing, as outlined by Shapiro (2018), which is why the following section provides an overview of the changes that can occur in the images, sounds, cognitions, emotions, physical sensations, and narrative account of the event. I have also included a discussion of younger self-states that can emerge and change during reprocessing. Throughout this section, I offer suggestions on how to move the material along when it gets stuck or feels overwhelming in any of these areas.

Images

During reprocessing, the vividness of images can get stripped away and be harder to access. They might become darker, brighter, or smaller. You can help the client feel a sense of control over the images if the emotional charge is too high by inviting them to manipulate the image in a way that makes it more tolerable. This also helps reinforce that the memory is just a memory, like an imprint of an experience, that can be modified and manipulated in the present as the actual event in the past is over. To do so, you can invite the client to:

- "Look at that image as if through binoculars, seeing it far away. You can adjust the focus so it is sharp or blurry."
- "Just continue to move through that scene like you are in a protective bubble. Nothing can touch you, just let those images pass by."
- "Put up a protective layer, such as a sheet of plexiglass, and see the images through it."
- "Watch the scene play out like it's on a screen in a theater or on your phone, like watching a movie."

- "Make that image or scene black and white or sepia tone, like an old photograph."
- "Put the image as far away as it needs to be, in another city, another continent, another planet, another universe—as far as way as you need it to be."
- "Just let those images resurface so they can flow into the present. Just observe as they move and float by."

Sounds

During reprocessing, the auditory components of the memory may become prominent. Distressing noises may arise with the volume going up or down, such as the sound of a crash, gunshots, or yelling. For some clients, it can be helpful to use auditory forms of dual attention BLS, such as the client tapping back and forth with their index fingers on or around the tragus part of their ears (the small bump in front of the ear canal). Another option is using tuning forks, chimes, or shakers as described in chapter 7.

In addition, the client may be able to vocalize feelings and needs that were suppressed at the time of the event. It is important to let the client's words emerge in the language in which they were thought or spoken at the time. Offer permission for the client to express themself in their native language, even if you do not understand it. If the client gets stuck, you can nudge any suppressed thoughts or feelings toward vocalization with questions such as:

- "If that person were here right now, in this room, what might you say to them?"
- "If your adult self could go back and enter that scene, what would they say? What would they do?"

Cognitions

With reprocessing, the perspective that a client takes in relation to the memory can change. Updated adult perspectives can provide adaptive information that contradicts the beliefs held at the time of the event, such as a child's perspective of being in control or responsible. The client may be able to imagine other people's motivations, thoughts, and perspectives in a new way. They may also begin to understand their own behaviors and protective responses at the time of the trauma, realizing that they did the best they could with what they had. This can lead to insight, understanding, and sometimes even compassion. If the client gets stuck on cognitions, you can ask:

- "Looking back on it now, why do you think you acted in that way? How do you make sense of that now? [*Or, if about someone else:*] Looking back on it now, why do you think they acted in that way? How do you make sense of that now?"
- "How do you think that behavior helped you get through that time?"
- "What do you know now that you didn't know then?"
- "What knowledge would you carry back to that time if you could?"

In this phase, clients can also rely on cognition as a defensive strategy, trying to analyze the material that arises without letting it move through to completion so that they do not have to feel it. If the client's intellectualizing is preventing the material from moving, you can ask:

- "It can be helpful to talk it through, but let's also try feeling it so that things can shift on a deeper level."
- "When you think of that (or when you say that), where do you feel it in your body?"
- "How would it be to stand back and observe that feeling without needing to fully understand it, just acknowledge it?"

In addition, the client may uncover negative cognitions that are closer to the core self than the original negative cognition identified in the assessment phase. For example, the client may identify "I cannot trust myself" as a negative cognition in the assessment phase, but then during the reprocessing, a deeper and perhaps more painful belief may come to the surface, such as "I am a failure." These underlying beliefs can block the processing work if they are not explored and given an opportunity to shift. To help these beliefs begin to shift, you can ask:

- "When did you learn to believe that about yourself?"
- "When did you first learn that ________ [*about yourself, others, or the world*]?"

Emotions

Reprocessing can cause emotions to emerge and increase or decrease in intensity. There can be layers of emotions from anger to grief that might even feel contradictory to the client. I often tell my clients, "We are complex beings, we are allowed to experience more than just one emotion at a time." Helping your client mindfully notice their emotions—letting them ebb and flow, as emotions naturally do—can support their release. You can remind your client that these emotions are from the past, from that memory, and that they are being expressed now because they were unable to be expressed back then. If emotions become blocked or begin to flood the client, you can provide questions or supportive statements such as:

- "Where do you feel that in your body? Notice its shape, size, temperature, texture, or density." [*The client may benefit from externally representing the feeling or sensation by drawing it or using any form of creative expression to increase emotion regulation and encourage curiosity.*]
- "What does that emotion need? Is there an action it would like to take? Go ahead and let that happen." [*The client can express the need or action in the moment, or imagine it happening in their mind.*]
- "Place a hand where you notice that emotion in your body, just noticing it and validating it without needing to change it."
- "Notice that emotion as it comes in and rolls out, like a wave, which is the natural movement of emotions."
- "Can you observe—from where you're at right now—that these feelings are coming up from that old time? They are a part of the memory just like an image is part of a memory. Let them surface and move through."
- "Notice how that emotion is from that old memory, a response to what was happening then. Let it move through, you don't have to hold on to anything from that time."

Sensations

Since sensations are stored in a state-dependent way, the client may notice an increase or decrease in heartbeat, breathing, muscle tension, pain, or pressure during reprocessing. This reflects the physiological states of protection (e.g., fight, flight, freeze, shutdown) that occurred at the time of the trauma. With dual attention, you want the client to mindfully observe that these states are emerging into the present from that time in the past. You also want them to notice where these sensations are felt. For example, sensations in the gut may be indicative of shutdown, shame, or extreme threat. As you let these sensations move through, they can be released. Sensations stuck in the throat may need to be released through sound or verbalization. Sensations in the eyes may need to be released through tears. If at any point the sensations become blocked or feel overwhelming, you can provide questions or supportive statements such as:

- "What does that sensation need right now? Is there anything that it needs to hear, say, or do? Okay, let that happen."
- "If that sensation could speak, what would it say?"
- "Is there an urge to act or move that comes with that sensation? Let your body follow that urge (or imagine yourself doing that)."
- "Can you notice how that sensation is part of the memory, just like an image is part of a memory?"
- "There are many ways that our bodies release sensations, such as through movement, tears, and verbal expression. Let that sensation move through. Where does it want to go? Just follow it."
- "What would it look like to attend to that pain [*or other sensation*] right now, perhaps with some stretching, movement, or self-massage?"
- "Can you observe with me how your body is shutting down? These are protective responses from that old time. Let's try to bring some energy in. Maybe let's stand up together for this next set (or let's try throwing this soft ball back and forth for this next set)."

The Narrative

During reprocessing, the narrative of the incident can unfold chronologically like a story or sequence of events. New adaptive aspects that the client did not think of may start to emerge—for example, the client may see how they survived or escaped the event, or they may identify helpers who supported them at that time. You can help the story move toward resolution by linking the story up to the ending, when things were okay again and when things felt over. Helpful questions to facilitate this process are:

- "What happened next? What happened after that?"
- "What did you need right there in that moment? Who or what could best provide that (or do that)? Go with that, just letting that scene unfold."
- "When did things start to feel okay again after that? When could you feel it was over?"

Younger Parts of the Self

When the client goes back and revisits the memory—the time and place of the trauma—they naturally encounter younger parts of themself, or self-states, that are stuck on the mountain, reliving the event without knowing that it is over. These younger parts hold different aspects of the memory, such as unmet needs, beliefs, physiological states of protection, sensory fragments, and an understanding of the event based on younger developmental perspectives. The younger self that the client encounters in the memory does not necessarily need to be a child. For example, I was working with an adult woman whose younger self had experienced medical trauma two years before she began working with me. The healing work happens when the client can meet the needs of their younger self (such as the need for safety and comfort), offer updated perspectives, and bring them off the mountain and into the present so they can see that the trauma is no longer happening and feel that it is over.

To do so, it is useful to slow down the work and offer these younger parts compassion, validation, and updating by orienting them to the present circumstances. It can also be helpful to meet unmet needs back in that time—for example, by revisiting certain events with the client's adult or older self there as a support or advocate—before inviting the younger self to leave that past time. You can build compassion and understanding toward the client's younger self with questions such as:

- "How old were you then? Notice that _____-year-old, there in that moment, in that memory. Can you see them? What are they doing? What are they feeling and thinking?"

- "How do you respond to seeing them there? [*If positive:*] Notice that feeling and just extend it to them, seeing whether they can receive it and take it in."
- "Is there anything that this ___-year-old wants you to know or wants to share with you? What is your response to that? Does what they shared make sense to you? [*If positive:*] Can you let them know that, that you understand them?"
- "What did that ____-year-old need back at that time? Maybe something they needed to know, to hear, or to have happen? Who or what could best provide that for them? Just imagine that happening, allowing their needs to finally get met after all this time."
- "Is there anything they need you to do for them? Perhaps something now, or even something back at the time? Would it be okay to let that happen? You can even enter that past scene as you now, as your adult self, and just see how that scene unfolds."
- "Does that ____-year-old know that time is over? Do they know that those things aren't happening anymore?"
- "Do they know that they are not stuck there? That that time is over now?"
- "How can you show them that that time is over? Could you show them something in your life, your room, your home? Maybe a pet or something you think they might like to see?"
- "Because that event is, in fact, over, they don't need to stay back there in that time and place. Where would they like to go instead? Would it be okay to let them go there?"
- "Would they like to be there with you in the present? Is it okay to let them be with you there?"

Restricting the Range of Movement

If a client is not able to tolerate the free-associative process that allows their mind to "go where it needs to go" and to move between different experiences, then it is appropriate to restrict the reprocessing by doing EMD or EMDr instead, which are both ways to provide increased stabilization and dual attention by keeping the range of associations restricted (Shapiro, 2018).

EMD fully restricts reprocessing by staying at the specific memory—at the point in time. Using the mountain metaphor, you can conceptualize EMD as staying at the peak of the mountain. You do not let the client's mind fully enter any pathway but, rather, move around the peak one set of dual attention BLS at a time to desensitize their response to it. This process of desensitization aims to bring down the overall level of distress that the client feels in relation to the memory.

EMDr, in contrast, allows for reprocessing but restricts free association by bringing the client back to the specific memory—to the point in time or point of distress—after a few sets. Using the mountain metaphor, this is like going down a pathway for a few sets but returning to the peak before the client reaches the bottom of the mountain (the place of peace and resolution). This keeps the client's mind closer to the target memory so that it feels more predictable and prevents overwhelm.

When using EMDr, one way to know when to return to the target is to listen for adaptive associations or pairings. When an adaptive association has been made, you can invite the client to bring that back to the top of the mountain, back to the memory:

- "What you just said is really valuable. Carry that back with you to the place you started from, that point in time. Keep that resource or new knowledge close at hand. What do you notice now? Has anything changed? Go with that."

As is the case at any point of reprocessing, you must reinforce the client's agency to say no and immediately stop the process if the client indicates they do not want to proceed. When a client sets a limit and you are able to honor that limit, it creates a new positive experience that can also serve as adaptive information to support integration and resolution.

Incomplete Reprocessing: Grounding Container and Closure

The likelihood of needing to contain material at some point during reprocessing is high unless you are using an intensive therapy model in which you set aside several hours to fully reprocess the memory without needing to break between sessions. Remember that reprocessing work encompasses phases 4 through 6, which means that we are still on the mountain. If you end a session before a client has reached a SUD rating of 0, a VOC rating of 7, and a clear body scan, then the reprocessing is incomplete, and you have to gently come off the mountain in order to safely and adequately contain the memory and close the session.

Containers provide a secure place to put away any distressing images, thoughts, feelings, and sensations in relation to the memory. Containing the memory at the end of an incomplete reprocessing session allows the client to fully return their attention to the present moment. It is important to reinforce to clients that containment does not mean that the memory is not important or that it needs to be avoided. Containment is not avoidance; it is a cognitive resource that helps the client intentionally create space between themself and the memory by giving it a secure place to be until there is a readiness to return to it. Unlike avoidance, where the goal is to never think about the memory, with containment, the client knows they have the support and resources needed to access it again and move it toward healing and resolution.

The following containment script invites the client to lean into the earth, spiritual supports, or objects for a more profound sense of containment and grounding. Once the material is contained, you can help prepare the client for any postprocessing changes and make a plan for them to use their grounding or coping skills outside of the session. You can then fully come off the mountain of reprocessing and into the present moment by practicing a grounding activity to close the session.

Grounding and Containment Script

1. **Shift to reflection:** "What was the most helpful, new, or even surprising thing that came up for you in our work today?" *[Optional: Do a slow, short set of dual attention BLS if it seems helpful to install this new learning.]*
2. **Begin to close:** "Let's begin to close this work, like coming off the mountain and coming all the way back to the present moment."

3. **Identify the container:** "What can hold this memory for you for now so that it is kept safe and secure until we are ready to come back to it? This could be like a particular place in nature where you know it will be protected, such as under a tree, in a body of water, or buried deep in the earth, remembering that the land knows what to do with it, and it can take as much as you need it to take. You could also hand the memory to someone or something that could help protect it, such as an animal, a spiritual figure, or an ancestor. Another option is to place it in a chest or a container of some sort, like a box or basket, that can be made out of any material, be any shape, and be any size. Let me know when you find what can hold this memory for you."
4. **Move the memory in:** "When you're ready, go ahead and move that memory and everything connected to it over into the [*name the place in nature, the protective person or presence, or the container that will hold the memory*] so that you can set it down completely."
5. **Close it up:** "When it feels right, you can add any layers or material to help it feel as secure and contained as you need it to be, knowing that you will come back to it when you have the time, support, and resources needed to give it your full attention."
6. **Butterfly hug:** "Notice how your body responds to this memory being held and contained. Where do you feel that in your body? [*If positive:*] If it feels helpful, you can cross your arms across your chest and slowly begin tapping back and forth on your chest or upper arms, noticing those positive sensations and letting them enhance and settle."
7. **Plan for grounding and stabilization:** "You stirred up and shifted a lot of things in our work today. It can take some time for things to sink back down and settle. You may notice between now and our next session that things continue to

surface and shift. You may notice new insights, thoughts, emotions, and sensations. Just as you did today, you can observe them with curiosity, giving them space to move through. You may also find it helpful to note these changes in some way so we can discuss it in our next session. If anything feels distressing, you can move them to that place of grounding or into the container and use any soothing or stabilization skills that might be helpful."

8. **Practice stabilization:** "Is there a soothing or stabilizing activity that you would find helpful in closing today's session? Perhaps some movement, breathing, or drawing? You could connect to an internal resource like your calm place, or we could take a moment and connect to a calming sound or smell right here in this space. What would be helpful for you?" [*Engage in this activity and close the session.*]

CHAPTER 9

Completing the Journey in Phases 5–8

This chapter outlines the remaining phases needed to complete the journey off the mountain. It begins by discussing how to help clients reclaim and restore beliefs about the self in the positive installation phase, using the metaphor of rocks being fused to resources (phase 5). Body-based strategies are also provided to address blocking beliefs. The body scan (phase 6) is then explored, including nature-based strategies to cleanse and clear the body after reprocessing to move residual somatic material. It is important to remember that you and the client are still "on the mountain" during phases 5 and 6—that is, you are still doing reprocessing work. However, these additional phases are meant to focus on the cognitions and the body to ensure that the belief the client holds about themself in relation to the memory is as adaptive and robust as possible and that any residual material is cleared.

This chapter also provides scripts and procedures to "come off the mountain of reprocessing" in phase 7 (closure). In EMDR, we conceptualize a complete memory as a SUD of 0, a VOC of 7, and a clear body scan. When this has been achieved, you can then close your work on the memory in phase 7 and move on to reevaluation (phase 8). This chapter conceptualizes phase 8 as the process of "revisiting the mountain" to check progress and emotional charge. To facilitate this process, I walk you through the steps and procedures needed to reevaluate incomplete and complete memories and also discuss how to decide on the next steps of treatment using the three-pronged protocol.

Phase 5 (Positive Installation)

When the client reports no further distress in relation to the memory (SUD of 0), or they report a number that is as low as it can possibly be given their current circumstances, such as a 0.5 or 1 (called an **ecological rating**), you do one or two more sets of dual attention BLS to allow that rating to strengthen and settle. These additional sets are like a bridge to phase 5. Once you complete those sets, so long as no new material emerges, you are in phase 5 and the focus narrows to the client's belief about themself in relation to the memory.

You'll recall that in phase 3 (assessment), the client already identified a positive belief they would rather have about themself in relation to the memory. However, during reprocessing in phase 4, the client may have spontaneously arrived at a deeper and more empowering belief. For this reason, you want to give the client an opportunity to rework their original positive cognition once you bridge to phase 5:

- "Bring that memory and the words [*state the positive cognition from phase 3*] to mind again. Do those words still fit, or is there a different statement that might feel even better now?"

The client then rates how true their stated positive belief feels using the 7-point VOC scale, where 1 is a seed that has the potential for growth but does not yet feel true and 7 is a flower in full bloom that feels all the way true:

- "Bring up that memory and those words [*state the original or updated positive cognition*]. How true do those words feel to you now on a scale of 1–7? Is it like a 1, like a seed of a belief that hasn't started to grow, or like a 7, all the way true, where the belief is strongly rooted and in full bloom?"

Even if the client reports a rating of 7, as true as it could possibly feel, you invite them to hold the memory and the cognition together in their mind, then add one set of dual attention BLS. This step gives the client's mind an opportunity to further link and fuse the positive cognition with the memory, nurturing and strengthening the new belief and ensuring that it will be the predominant cognition recalled alongside the memory.

You can think of the positive belief as a resource that was there all along but was not initially visible to the client, much like a river rock. When the rock is unprocessed, it is too rough and jagged to see the minerals held inside. But after being reprocessed by the movement of the river, it becomes reshaped and smoothed, and the beautiful patterns of quartz mineral running through it become polished and more predominant than the drab gray rock surrounding it. You want the client to see (and feel) their internal resources and strengths when they recall that memory:

- "Hold the memory and the words [*repeat positive cognition*] together in your mind."

Then apply dual attention BLS right away. The dual attention BLS should be long and fast, as this phase is still part of reprocessing. New pathways of associated material might open up, and the belief can continue to change and strengthen. Therefore, invite the client to report anything that comes up for them, and continue listening for change or any new material that may emerge:

- "Take a breath. What are you noticing now? Go with that."

Whatever the client reports, you add another set of dual attention BLS. If, after two sets, there is no further distress and no new pathways of associative material opening up, you invite the client to go back to the VOC scale and rate how true their stated positive belief feels now. If the client rates it at a 7, you do one or two more sets to let that strengthen and settle. When doing these sets, I sometimes say, "Let all parts of you take that new belief in." These sets are like a bridge to phase 6 (body scan). Once you complete those sets, so long as no new material emerges, you are in phase 6, and the focus narrows to the client's belief about themself in relation to the memory.

However, if there is distress and new material emerges, you process the residual distress and follow that down the new pathway with successive sets of dual attention BLS. Like in phase 4, you check in between each set to allow the client to report what they are noticing, listening for adaptive changes and strengthening of the cognition. For some clients, working with the body is a powerful way to embody and grow the positive belief, so you might encourage your client to experiment with movement or posture while adding dual attention BLS. This can also help shift any blocking material:

- "What movement or posture would embody or express that belief [*state the positive cognition*]? Okay, let's try that for the next set." [*Allow the client to experiment with their movement or posture. When they are ready, add another set of dual attention BLS.*]

You continue to let the material move toward adaptive resolution until it seems the client has reached the bottom of the mountain, where there is no more movement and no more change. You then bring the client back up the mountain to reassess the VOC rating to determine how true their stated positive belief feels now. If it is a 7, you do one or two more sets to let it strengthen and settle and move on to phase 6 (body scan). If the VOC rating is less than 7, you identify the blocking belief or material that is getting in the way of this belief feeling all the way true:

- "What gets in the way of that belief from feeling all the way true (or from being a 7)?"

As you are still on the mountain in this phase, whatever the client reports, you can encourage reprocessing by saying "go with that" again and following it toward resolution with successive sets of dual attention BLS. When there is no further movement or change, you bring the client back up to reassess the VOC rating to determine how true their stated positive belief feels now. If it is at a 7, you do one or two more sets to let that strengthen and settle, bridging to phase 6 (body scan).

As with phase 4, you go up and down the mountain as many times as necessary until you thoroughly complete the phase. Phase 5 simply provides another opportunity to catch any material that was missed in phase 4. You continue to reprocess to a VOC rating of 7 (or the highest possible rating given the client's current circumstances or existential reasoning).

If the session ends before a VOC of 7 (or ecological rating) is reached, then the reprocessing is incomplete, and you gently come off the mountain to safely and adequately contain the memory and close the session. (See the **Grounding and Containment Script** in chapter 8.)

Phase 6 (Body Scan)

In phase 6, the focus shifts entirely to the body. You invite the client to notice any sensations or physiological responses while holding both the memory and the positive cognition in their mind:

- "Bring the memory and the words [*repeat the positive cognition*] to mind again. Scan all through your body for any discomfort, tension, or other sensations that stand out to you. [*Give the client a moment to check in with their sensations.*] What do you notice?"

If a neutral, comfortable, or positive sensation is reported, do a set of dual attention BLS to let it strengthen and settle, and invite the client to repeat the body scan again to ensure it is clear. If nothing new emerges, the memory has been completely reprocessed, and you can move to closure of a complete memory (phase 7).

As you are still on the mountain in this phase, if the client reports any discomfort or distress, begin successive sets of dual attention BLS (again, long and fast), following that distress or discomfort down a new pathway toward resolution. Then, bring the client back up to the top of the mountain by inviting them to do another body scan to see what they are noticing now. It is always possible that the body scan will not be completely clear for a client. For example, there may be lingering discomfort or pain that makes sense given the client's current circumstances or conditions, in which case their response may be ecologically adaptive. The key is to identify and reprocess any further distress in relation to the memory. When a neutral, comfortable, or positive sensation is reported, do another set of dual attention BLS to let that sensation strengthen and settle and then move to closure (phase 7).

If the session ends before a clear or ecologically adaptive body scan is reached, the reprocessing is considered incomplete, and you can gently come off the mountain to contain the memory and close the session. (See the **Grounding and Containment Script** in chapter 8.)

Enhancing the Body Scan

Working with the body is a powerful way to end the reprocessing phases. For many of my clients, the body scan is not an afterthought or one last check before closure but a profound opportunity to restore a sense of internal harmony and balance. Slowing down and providing the space for the client to revel in a sense of resolution and peace in relation to the memory is a way to honor their journey. This is a moment to let their hard work integrate and consolidate on the deepest level.

After the body scan, you can ask the client what might help them integrate all those shifts and let their hard work settle. This might include:

- **A cleansing or refreshing smell, like peppermint or lavender:** "Breathe in that smell as deeply as you can, letting it move all through your body."
- **The resonance of sound, such as chimes and bells:** "Just let those vibrations move through your body, helping everything settle and come back into a place of harmony and balance."
- **Breathing and movement:** "Breathe in and out in sync with your movements—moving your arms up as you breathe in and moving your arms down as you breathe out. Just move at your own pace, letting everything come back into balance."
- **Sharing a cup of herbal tea together:** "Just sip in the healing properties of the tea, letting it cleanse and refresh the body."
- **A cleansing, grounding energy visualization:** "Imagine a grounding, cleansing energy moving up from the earth, letting it run through your body, all the way up to your head, and then back down into the earth, sweeping through and cleansing everything in its path."
- **A bonfire visualization:** "Imagine being at a bonfire, taking in the warmth, and putting anything you no longer need to carry with you from that time into the fire so it can transform it for you—the fire knows what to do with it, and the fire can help you let it all go."

Phase 7 (Closure)

In this phase, you come off the mountain of reprocessing, as the journey through the memory has been completed. There is no need to contain the memory, as the distress has been fully resolved (remember, the steps for containment are used for any incomplete reprocessing sessions between phases 4 through 6). As part of closure, you explain to clients that they may continue to notice thoughts, feelings, sensations, or new insights after the session is over. I like to use the language from the **Five *S*'s of Memory Reconsolidation** (see chapter 4), as this is just the natural process of stirring up, shifting, and resettling material in their internal river (or AIP system). It is important to encourage the client to mindfully notice as things continue to shift and move and to practice any stabilization or coping skills if there is distress. To do so, you can use steps 8–9 of the **Grounding and Containment Script** provided at the end of chapter 8.

Phase 8 (Reevaluation)

After the client has had time to allow the material to sink back down and settle in a new way, you can then move into phase 8. You always want to expect processing to continue after the session—things can shift, and new insights or material associated with the memory may open up, given that you have unblocked the AIP system, or the internal river, so that it may continue to move and flow. Therefore, in the reevaluation phase, you go back to the memory, as if you are revisiting the mountain, to assess what comes up for the client around that memory now, knowing that distress levels can go up, down, or stay stable.

You always reevaluate the work done on a memory, whether the reprocessing was incomplete and contained in the session prior (an **incomplete memory**) or whether the memory was fully reprocessed (a **complete memory**). When evaluating an incomplete memory, it is like returning to the mountain of reprocessing (phases 4–6) so you can take what still needs healing out of the container and begin to do the work on it.

Reevaluating Incomplete Memories

To begin reevaluation on an incomplete memory, you first want to check in with the client to see whether it is okay to revisit the memory and open it back up:

- "In our last session, you did a lot of work on that memory of ______ [*name the point in time, or use a neutral age anchor such as that ___-year-old time*]. Would it be okay to revisit that memory to continue to do some work on it?"

Then proceed through the following steps, depending on whether the incomplete session ended in phase 4, 5, or 6.

If the incomplete session ended in phase 4: You then start to open up the memory with a miniassessment. The purpose of this miniassessment is to identify and activate the distressing material that still needs healing:

- "When you bring that memory to mind, what picture (or other sensory element) would you say represents the worst part of that experience now? What emotions or sensations does that bring up for you? How distressing is it on a scale of 0–10? Where do you feel that in your body?"

If the client reports distress or discomfort, you go back onto the mountain and "go with that" to continue reprocessing, following whatever they report down the mountain toward resolution with sets of dual attention BLS. However, if the client reports a neutral or positive response as they bring the memory to mind—and they rate their SUD level at 0 (or an ecological rating)—do another two sets of dual attention BLS to provide the opportunity for new associative pathways to open up. If new material arises, follow it down the mountain. If no further material or distress arises, move into phase 5.

If the incomplete session ended in phase 5: If you ended the previous session in phase 5, before reaching a VOC rating of 7, return to phase 5 by reevaluating the VOC and continuing with positive installation:

- "Bring up that memory and those words [*state the original or updated positive cognition*]. How true do those words feel to you now on a scale of 1–7, where 1 is a seed of a belief that hasn't started to grow and 7 is all the way true, where the belief is strongly rooted and in full bloom?"

If the client rates the VOC as less than 7, you can ask what they think is getting in the way of it feeling all the way true. Whatever they report, you can "go with that" and begin following it down the mountain toward resolution with sets of dual attention BLS. In this phase, you are continuing to loosen the roots of the lesson the client learned about themself from the trauma and growing their new positive belief—giving it space and nurturing it until it feels like it is in full bloom, with a 7 or ecological rating. After a client rates the VOC at a 7, do two more sets of dual attention BLS to let it strengthen and settle. Again, these sets are like a bridge that brings you into the next phase.

If the incomplete session ended in phase 6: If you ended the last session in phase 6 before reaching a clear body scan, return to phase 6 by reevaluating how the body responds when pairing the memory with the positive cognition:

- "Bring the memory and the words [*repeat the positive cognition*] to mind again. Scan all through your body for any discomfort, tension, or any other sensations that stand out to you. [*Give the client a moment to check in with their sensations.*] What do you notice?"

Whatever the client reports, do sets of dual attention BLS to allow any residual sensations or physiological responses to clear. When the client reports a clear body scan (or ecologically adaptive scan), you can ask the client whether there is a movement, sound, smell, or visualization that might help them integrate all those shifts and let their hard work settle. If so, engage in that activity together and then move to closure.

Reevaluating Complete Memories: Returning to the Treatment Map

When reevaluating a complete memory, you still want to check in with the client to see whether it is okay to revisit the memory and open it back up:

- "In our last session, you did a lot of work on that memory of ______ [*name the point in time, or use a neutral age anchor such as that ____-year-old time*]. Would it be okay to revisit that memory, like traveling back to that mountain to check how you feel now in relation to that memory there in the past?"

You then want to ask questions to check whether the SUD rating of 0 is stable and see how the reprocessing work has reshaped the memory. You are checking whether all the intensity and emotional charge has been eroded off the mountain, permanently reshaping the mountain and reducing the size and power it holds over the client:

- "When you think of that memory, what comes up for you now?"
- "What feels different when you think about that memory now?"
- "Any new insights or thoughts?"
- "How big would you say the memory feels to you right now on a scale of 0–10, where 0 is neutral or calm, like a mountain that is just part of the landscape, and 10 is the worst it could possibly feel, like looking up at a mountain that feels huge and overpowering, with as much intensity and emotional charge as it could possibly have?"

If the client reports any distress or discomfort, return to the top of the mountain and follow it down the pathways toward resolution with successive sets of dual attention BLS. When a 0 or ecological rating has been reached, reassess the positive cognition, the VOC, and the body scan, ensuring that the memory has been completely reprocessed. You and the client can then return to the treatment map (the timeline or river of life) and decide what memory (or mountain) to travel to next.

Following the Three-Pronged Protocol

Moving from Past to Present

By returning to the visual timeline, which acts as a map for treatment, you and the client can collaboratively decide which memory to move to next. You then continue journeying through memories in the past and repeating the reprocessing steps for each memory. After processing all the past material to resolution, the focus can return to present distress or concerns. When shifting the focus back to the present, you can guide the client to identify a more recent point of distress when the issue, response, or pattern identified as a presenting concern got stirred up or triggered:

- "What was a recent experience when the issue of ________ [*name the specific presenting issue*] felt really present or distressing for you?"
- "Would it be okay if we worked on that experience?"

This recent representative experience then becomes another mountain to journey through. You bring the client to the peak of the mountain by assessing and activating the components (or PILES) of the recent experience (phase 3) and begin moving through the phases of reprocessing (phases 4–6) until the client reaches a SUD of 0, a VOC of 7, and a clear body scan (or ecologically adaptive ratings). If the distress feels blocked and is not able to clear, it can be helpful to do a floatback (see script in chapter 5) to identify any earlier material associated with the memory that did not get cleared and may be driving present distress.

Carrying the Positive Cognition into the Future: Future Template

When the present issue is cleared, you can then move to a future anticipated event. Invite the client to imagine a situation when that same issue, response, or pattern could get stirred up or triggered:

- "When is the next time you might experience anything having to do with ________?"

You can then invite the client to imagine carrying their new positive cognition into that future situation. They can imagine having the positive cognition in a pouch or bag so that it is available as a resource during the journey through that mountain. The positive cognition acts like the elixir in the hero's journey; it is a powerful medicine that the client returns home with from their journey, and it becomes the force of change in the present and the future. Like the elixir, the positive cognition also has a "multiplying effect" in that it ripples and spreads into other situations to bring more healing and wholeness to the client's life:

- "Imagine yourself entering that future scene, carrying with you the knowledge that you are ________ [*state the positive cognition*].

How would you feel? What would you do differently? Imagine that. Where do you feel that in your body?"

Adding slow sets of dual attention BLS here can enhance the connection the client feels to their positive cognition while imagining the future event. The client can then identify the outcome that would result from being able to access their positive cognition in the future scenario:

- "What would that change if you knew that about yourself, that you are ________ [*state the positive cognition*]? What would the outcome be? How would that feel in your body?"

Adding slow sets of dual attention BLS here can strengthen the positive sensations the client feels as they imagine their desired outcome. If they struggle to imagine themself reaching this outcome, you can help them identify missing skills and provide psychoeducation about these skills and lay out stepping stones, like an action plan, for the client to move toward developing and practicing those skills:

- "What other skills might you need to handle that situation in the way you would like to be able to? How could you develop those skills?"

The next step is to invite the client to imagine the future scenario playing out like a movie. I refer to this process as the **scan and scoop method**, where it is like taking a net and dipping it into our internal river, letting the net scan through this whole scenario, from beginning to end, moving through the water to see whether there is any material that is too big to fit through the net. If something gets caught in the net, like an uncomfortable feeling or image, you scoop it out right away and begin to break it down using dual attention BLS. When the material is resolved, you again dip the net in the water and scan it through the scenario, scooping out any distressing or uncomfortable material that gets caught in the net. You continue to scan and scoop, breaking down any material that could block the client from reaching their desired outcome, until the water runs clear, with no distress from beginning to end:

- "Imagine yourself moving through that future scenario from beginning to end—to when you ______ [*state desired outcome*]. Carry the knowledge that you are __________ [*state the positive cognition*] into the scene so you can access it at any time. If you come up against any challenges or distress—an image, thought, sensation, or anything that feels at all uncomfortable or distressing—stop and let me know."

If challenging or distressing material comes up, "scoop" it out and do successive sets of dual attention BLS until it clears.

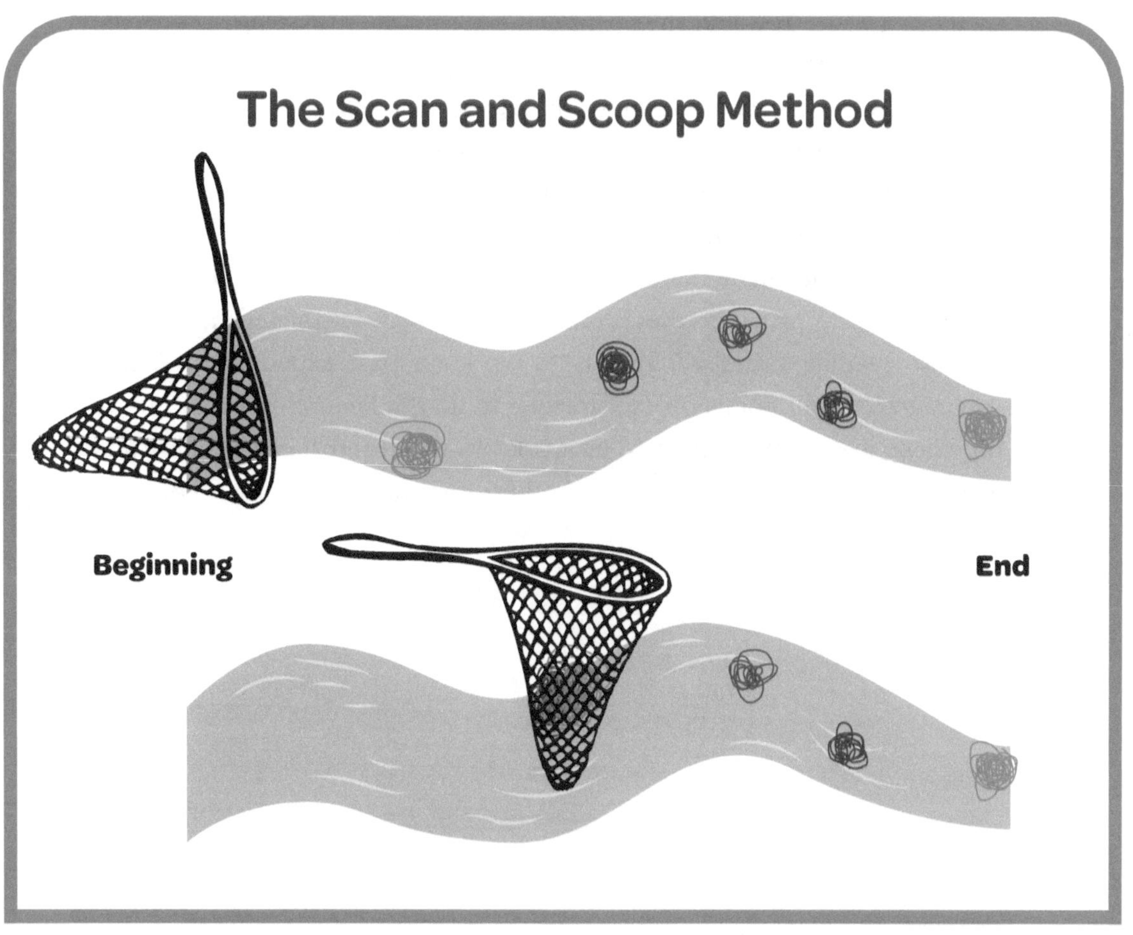

Once the water runs clear, invite the client to identify any potential challenges in the future scenario and include them in the movie. Address and reprocess any blocks or barriers to the client reaching their desired outcome by continuing to use the scan and scoop method.

After completing the future template, the material has been moved through all strands of time—past, present, and future—regarding a specific presenting issue. You and the client can again consult the map and decide where to journey to next. As stated in chapter 5, the points of distress that you and the client will focus on depend on multiple factors—it's not just about what you think will bring the client the most sustainable relief and move them toward their goals but also considerations of time, needs, readiness, level of distress tolerance, and external circumstances.

Some clients might better tolerate working with present and future distress, which provides the stabilization needed in the client's life to increase readiness and willingness to work on past experiences. Again, you can access all points on the timeline to do the healing work and move the client toward their goals. The work in one strand has a positive and generalizing effect to the work in the others, as time is interconnected.

CHAPTER 10

Working with Clusters

Clusters are a series of events or situations connected across a range or span of time by a primary theme, such as a relationship, similar repeated events, an ongoing issue, or a primary belief, sensory cue, sensation, or emotion (see chapter 5). Whereas a single event is like a mountain with a primary peak (or point of distress), clusters have multiple peaks (or points of distress), like a mountain range.

Breaking down clusters into key moments or events can allow for more effective and thorough reprocessing. For example, child sexual abuse is typically not an event that happens only once; such experiences can span years and different developmental periods and involve different components such as disclosure or legal proceedings. If you try to move through it all at once by targeting one incident that is connected to a whole period of sexual abuse, it can be overwhelming for the client. The pathways of associated material can lead the client to too many upsetting experiences within the cluster and without relief or resolution, creating discouragement or destabilization.

Working through clusters is a process of moving through one point of distress or key moment at a time, bringing it as much resolution as possible, and then moving to the next, across the peaks of the mountain range. My approach to grouping and treating clusters comprehensively is adapted from the work of Ricky Greenwald (2007), who recommends working through a cluster chronologically, from beginning to end, and then running a movie through the entire cluster to ensure all memories within the cluster have been reprocessed and the healing has generalized across all associated events. However, for some clusters (e.g., attachment-related clusters, certain health conditions), the beginning point may be at conception, at birth, or during the preverbal years. When this is the case, it is helpful to begin reprocessing using the **Resource Place** protocol described in this chapter, which is an art- and nature-based approach to reprocessing preverbal trauma.

Processing the Primary Points of Distress

During history taking, if the client identifies an event that seems connected to a cluster, you aim to identify the beginning and end points of that cluster to map it out along the timeline (see chapter 5). Knowing where the cluster falls on the timeline informs case conceptualization and target sequence planning. When you and the client consult the treatment map and decide to begin reprocessing those grouped or clustered experiences, it is advisable to start at the beginning point of the cluster, at the first memory having anything to do with the primary theme that causes distress.

The First Point of Distress

Treating the first point of distress involves moving through reprocessing (phases 4–6) on that specific memory or material. It is important to keep in mind that this point of distress is connected to other associated events in the cluster that may hold more distress, much like a higher peak along the mountain range. For example, you may find that more distressing memories arise later on through free association, which risks destabilization, or you may find that the free-associative process is too meandering through various periods of time and is not bringing relief or resolution. In these cases, it is sometimes helpful to restrict reprocessing within a cluster by returning to the specific memory or point of distress being focused on before the client reaches the end of a channel or pathway, like with EMDr (see chapter 8).

It may also happen that, when assessing the SUD level on a memory within the cluster, the client struggles to rate only the specific memory being focused on and as a result continually provides a higher SUD rating. In this case, you can help narrow the focus to only the material being focused on:

- "We know there is a lot that happened after this moment, but let's focus on just this one point in time. When you think of only that moment, how distressing does it feel on that scale of 0–10?"

The Worst Point(s) of Distress

When the first memory in a cluster has been completely reprocessed, you can invite the client to identify another worst memory in the cluster, as if they are letting their mind walk along the ridge of the mountain range to identify the next highest point of distress:

- "When you let your mind scan forward through that period of time having anything to do with ________ [*state the theme of the cluster*], what memory stands out to you as having the most heightened charge or intensity to it, maybe even the worst or biggest one?"

You can then reprocess the identified memory by first taking the client to the peak of that memory during assessment (phase 3) and then following the client as they journey down the pathways connected to that point in time, shifting and moving any distressing material they encounter toward resolution at the bottom of the mountain (phases 4–6). When this part of the mountain range (or cluster) has been completely reprocessed, you can invite the client to again let their mind walk along the ridge of the mountain range to identify any other highest points of distress:

- "When you let your mind scan forward through that period of time having anything to do with _______ [*state the theme of the cluster*], is there another memory that stands out to you as having the most heightened charge or intensity to it, maybe even the worst or biggest one?"

Any identified worst memories within the cluster can be reprocessed, beginning with assessment through to body scan (phases 3–6). Again, you can restrict reprocessing using EMDr if free association leads to overwhelm or destabilization. The client does not need to travel throughout the whole mountain range during reprocessing to bring healing to that particular point in time. With EMDr, you can travel down the pathways connected with that peak, and when the pathways wander and intersect with other parts of the mountain (other memories in the cluster) in a way that causes distress rather than healing and integration, simply bring the client back to the point of distress that you started with and see what comes up for the client now.

Last or Most Recent Point of Distress

After the worst memories in the cluster have been reprocessed, you can invite the client to identify the last or most recent experience in the cluster. If the cluster has a clear end point in the past, it can be treated as an **overcluster**, and the last memory can be identified and reprocessed:

- "What memory would you say represents the end of that period of time, maybe even the last time anything upsetting happened having to do with _______ [*state the theme of the cluster*]?"

If the issue or theme has no clear end in the past and continues into the client's current life, it can be treated as an **ongoing cluster**, and the most recent experience can be identified and reprocessed:

- "What was a recent experience when the issue of _______ [*state the theme of the cluster*] felt really present or distressing for you?"

You then reprocess the memory that the client identifies as the last or most recent event, beginning with assessment through to body scan (phases 3–6). For ongoing clusters, the end point is in the future, so you will also reprocess an additional anticipated future event after reprocessing the last or most recent event. For this, you use the steps in **Carrying the Positive Cognition into the Future: Future Template** described in chapter 9. This anticipated future event marks the end point in the next step: scan and scoop.

Scan and Scoop Through the Whole Cluster

When the first, worst, and last memories in an overcluster—or the first, worst, most recent, and anticipated future event in an ongoing cluster—have been reprocessed, you can then move to the scan and scoop method to catch any unprocessed material to allow the healing from the worst memories to generalize across the cluster:

- "Allow your mind to scan through the entire period of time having to do with __________ [*state the theme of the cluster*] from beginning to end, with the knowledge that you are _____________ [*state the positive cognition installed from each clustered memory*], just letting the healing spread throughout all of those experiences (. . . and even into the future [*if the cluster is ongoing*]). If you come up against any distress—an image, thought, sensation, or anything that feels at all uncomfortable or distressing—stop and let me know."
- [*Using the scan and scoop metaphor:*] "This is like taking a net and dipping it into the river, starting from the beginning, and scanning it through all of those memories, seeing whether it catches anything that is too big to fit through the net. If something gets caught in the net, like something uncomfortable or distressing, we'll scoop it out right away and begin to break it down and work through it. The goal is for the water to run clear, with no more discomfort or distress blocking its flow."

If challenging or distressing material comes up, scoop it out and do successive sets of dual attention BLS until it clears. Scan through the cluster again from beginning to end, scooping out any distress or discomfort and processing it. Continue to scan and scoop until the cluster runs clear, with no distress from beginning to end.

Loaf of Bread Metaphor for Clusters

Another metaphor that I have found helpful in conceptualizing working through clustered experiences is the loaf of bread metaphor. Thinking of a cluster as a loaf of bread, you never want to work with the whole loaf at once. In history taking, you only need to identify the "end pieces" of the bread—the beginning and end points—to get a sense of where the bread is located and its size, but you do not need to start breaking it down and digesting it yet.

When you are ready to work through that cluster, you can begin to "slice it thin" and find the individual slices between the end pieces that hold the most substance (i.e., the moments or primary points of distress that the client identifies as holding the most intensity or emotional charge). *Slicing it thin* is a phrase used by Shirley Turcotte, the developer of IFOT, when describing a titrated approach to working with complex trauma: You cannot work with all of it at once; you have to slice it thin. In carrying this metaphor into work with clients, I provide this explanation:

- "When we are ready for reprocessing, we have to break the experience down and slice it thin. If we try to digest everything all at once, it will get stuck—it's too big. After we have worked through the end pieces and a few slices in between, we see what's left and work with that until the whole loaf has been digested."

I have found this metaphor works across various cultural contexts as an easy and relatable visual for clients to grasp. It is always important that clients understand your treatment approach so they feel in control and like active participants in the process. It is also reassuring to clients that you are taking steps to ensure their psychological and emotional safety by pacing the process and not jumping into the deep end of a memory. This step-by-step process breaks it down and follows the "slower is faster" adage when it comes to complex rather than single-episode experiences.

The Resource Place: Preverbal Protocol

Some clusters begin early in life, during the preverbal years. The cluster might be something that feels like it has always been a part of the client's life or something that they know happened during early development but do not have explicit access to it. The resource place protocol is an art- and nature-based approach to accessing and reprocessing implicitly held memories from prenatal and preverbal periods of development. It can be used when there is any indication of trauma or neglect in attachment relationships or experiences of early life disruption, such as major loss, surgeries, displacement, conflict, or any other form of trauma during the preverbal and early childhood years.

This protocol uses a seed, bean, or grain of rice to symbolically represent the beginning of the client's life. Handling the seed adds a concrete and sensory-based element to preverbal work that can increase the client's connection to the earliest stages of their development and help elicit unprocessed, implicitly held memories from those phases of life. This also provides soothing, sensory components that help ground the client in the present and support the safe accessing and reprocessing of upsetting material.

In the protocol, the client is invited to create a nurturing place for the seed, bean, or grain of rice using the art materials. Then, using the scan and scoop method, you invite the client to scan through different preverbal phases, starting from the beginning and scanning through until the end of that phase. Scanning through each developmental phase is done one stage at a time, always beginning with conception and moving forward until a certain point:

- Conception until before birth
- Conception until after birth
- Conception until age one
- Conception until age two
- Conception until age three

Whenever distress or discomfort comes up, you scoop it out right away to assess it and then move through the reprocessing phases. When no more disturbance comes up in that developmental phase, or the water runs clear, you can then extend the movie to the next phase of preverbal development, scanning through from conception to the end of that phase, scooping out and breaking down disturbance until that phase runs clear, and then extending again. This process of scanning through different developmental periods is adapted from the work of Katie O'Shea and Sandra Paulsen (2009) in their preverbal protocol *When There Are No Words*. O'Shea and

Paulsen recommend setting up the targets by time frame or in fractionated doses based on the client's capacity to help titrate preverbal work.

Creating the Resource Place

The first step of the protocol is to invite the client to create a resource place—a comforting and safe place to connect and come back to—using natural and creative materials. The resource place represents wholeness and peace at the very beginning of one's life, like a womb that can help keep the small seed or grain of rice safe and allow it to begin to grow. For some clients, their resource place represents the womb of Mother Earth, which allows them to identify a connection to something deeper than their attachment relationship growing up (which may have been insecure or unhealthy). Some clients imagine that their resource place is the womb of a nurturing figure or spiritual figure, or it may simply be a safe and comforting place to continually return to, like a refuge, during reprocessing. It is not necessary that the resource place be representative of the actual womb the client began their life in.

To facilitate the creation of this resource place, you will need the following materials: (1) a variety of seeds, beans, or grains of rice (different shades, such as white, brown, and wild rice); (2) paper; (3) a selection of drawing materials, including markers, oil or chalk pastels, or colored pencils; (4) glue; and (5) any natural or creative materials of the client's choosing. It is helpful for clients to experience not only a personal connection to the materials but also a cultural connection. For example, rice and beans are important food staples around the world and can elicit memories of cultural dishes and traditions that connect them with a sense of home, family, and place.

Once you have the materials gathered, invite the client to choose a grain of rice, bean, or seed and hold it in their palm. As they hold it, gently guide them to connect to the beginning of their life:

- "Begin by imagining yourself at the very beginning of your life, as small as a seed/bean/grain of rice, just beginning to form, with all that potential for growth. Hold the seed/bean/grain of rice in your hand, connecting with that time."

Then, using the provided art material, invite the client to create a resource place for the seed, bean, or grain of rice to begin to grow:

- "Imagine a nurturing place to keep that small seed/bean/grain of rice protected and comfortable, to allow it to begin to grow and develop. You can use the art materials to create or represent that nurturing place, such as by using colors, lines, symbols, words, or in any way you would like."

Allow the client some time to complete their artwork. When the client is ready, invite them to place the seed/bean/grain of rice on their image wherever it feels right.

I shared this protocol with an EMDR consultee, Noriko Baba, a Japanese art therapist as well as a couple and family therapist who focuses on developmental, relational, and intergenerational trauma across multiracial backgrounds. She was interested in learning this protocol and felt especially excited about the use of rice, as it holds significant cultural meaning for herself and many of the clients she works with. I walked Noriko through the steps of the protocol as a form of experiential learning and exchange. The image here is her initial resource place before doing any reprocessing work. As you can see, she placed the grain of rice on the image so that it could be cradled and have space to move and grow without being enclosed.

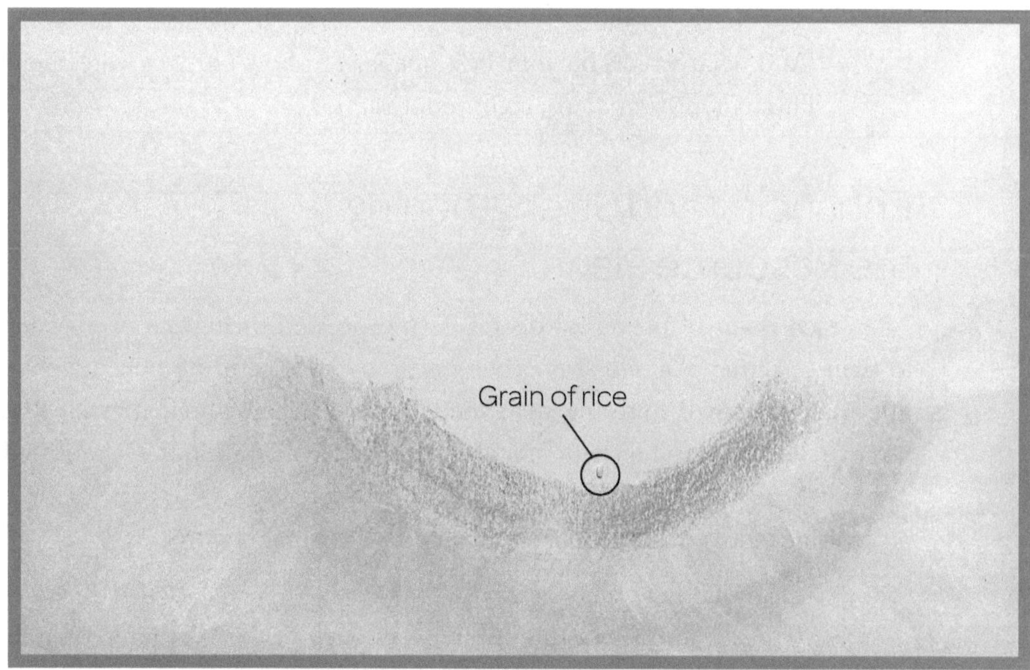

Scanning and Reprocessing the Developmental Periods

After the client creates their resource place, you guide them to mentally scan through the first phase of preverbal development (i.e., from conception until just before birth), beginning with the client being as small as the seed, bean, or grain of rice:

- "Imagine that you are watching a movie that starts right at the beginning of your life, when you are as small as that seed/bean/grain of rice. See whether you can imagine yourself beginning to develop and grow all the way until just before birth, just watching and observing all that was happening at that time. As you watch that movie, if you notice any sensations, feelings, images, or anything at all that feels distressing or uncomfortable, just stop and let me know."

Whenever the client notices any distressing or uncomfortable material—such as a thought, image, sensation, belief, or even a story—you scoop it out so that the material can be assessed and worked through right away. In other words, it becomes a target memory that is then reprocessed using phases 3 through 6 of the EMDR basic protocol. Begin by identifying where it falls on the timeline by getting the age anchor, then continue to move through the reprocessing phases:

- "And what would be your best guess as to how old you were then? Three months in utero, eight months . . . ?"

Enhancing and Strengthening the Resource Place

After each point of preverbal distress is reprocessed, bring the client back to their resource place to strengthen and modify it with the new adaptive information gained and any reclaimed positive beliefs about the self (the positive cognition). The client can add the positive cognition they identified in phase 5, as well as any other adaptive or helpful insights, to their resource place using words or symbolically through the art-making process:

- "Take that new knowledge, that you are ________ [*state the positive cognition*], and carry that all the way back to the beginning of your

> life, when you were as small as a seed/bean/grain of rice. Use the art materials to add that new belief to your resource place in any way that makes sense to you, maybe with words, color, lines, or symbols."

Leave time for art making. Once the client is done, ask them to notice how it feels, to have that knowledge about who they are right from the very beginning of their life. Invite the client to imagine themself as a developing being, as small as that seed, bean, or grain of rice, taking that in, and to notice where they feel that in their body. Then add dual attention BLS to enhance and strengthen the resource place. After this, you can invite the client to scan through that developmental period again, repeating the process until the water of the prenatal and preverbal years runs clear.

The following image was created by Noriko after reprocessing two different points of distress that came up during the process. The first point of distress occurred during the first developmental phase (conception to before birth), when she stated she felt around four or five months in utero. She described a sense of guilt or shame, as well as the image of something being deformed, like a shape that is not right. We processed through the sense of shame, which she described as a genetic awareness that she was developing differently due to a complication that resulted in her having a "misshaped" head. In exploring what that little developing being needed, she said it needed to have permission to grow in its own way and to know that it did not need to be like the others. She tapped as she shared that information with that little being, reassuring it. She felt a sense of growing and taking up space. She then placed the grain of rice back into the artwork. In doing so, she noticed that the grain itself also had a dent in it, like her developing head, and felt a tender connection toward herself as that little being as she placed it on her image.

The second point of distress occurred during Noriko's experience of coming into the world. She was born breech, and due to the number of miscarriages her mother had had, there were health complications that made this situation a medical emergency. The doctors told her mother that she would have to choose her life or the baby's life. Her mother chose her daughter's life. Fortunately, they both survived. As Noriko moved through the narrative account of the whole experience of being born, she described how she felt stuck as her mother was losing blood. Despite the atmosphere of fear and chaos around her at that time, she felt trusting and ready to come into the world with a determination not to cause harm to her mother, as her mother had chosen her to live.

At this point in her reprocessing, Noriko felt a connection with the siblings that her mother had lost through miscarriage. She felt them surrounding her and holding her hand, giving her the energy to come into the world when her mother had no more strength to get her out. She was born with an acute awareness that her mother needed to recover and could not provide nurturance for her. In exploring what that freshly born baby needed right there at that moment, she said that the baby needed space, as all of the medical professionals rushed at her and it was too much. She noted that to this day, she cannot handle attention or concern directed at her. She imagined giving her baby self the space she needed and honored her strength, her openness, and her trust toward the medical team, reassuring her baby self that she did not choose to come into the world this way but that she was able to handle it in a way that did not cause harm to anyone.

As you can see in the image on the next page, Noriko added lines like roots or veins extending through the bottom of the image, which connected to an enlarged drawing of the grain of rice with a visible dent and three sprout-like shapes extending from the grain of rice. Noriko shared that these represent her unborn baby siblings who helped her come into the world and that she feels they still help her today. This whole process helped her shift a core belief she has carried about herself of being difficult or challenging for others to handle. This helped her see that she is trusting and collaborative and that feelings of being "too much" have more to do with others than a reflection of her true self. For example, she noted that the doctors who felt fear and pulled away did so because they did not have the training or medical equipment at that time to handle the situation with confidence and not because she herself is difficult.

Once the client has run through all the preverbal years with no disturbance, you can return to the visual representation of the resource place once again—with all of the positive cognitions added to it—and invite the client to make any final changes to it should they so desire. Ask the client how true all those positive cognitions feel, and add dual attention BLS to further strengthen and install these beliefs. When the resource place is complete, the client can use glue to attach their seed, bean, or grain of rice to their artwork if they would like. You can then move on to the next

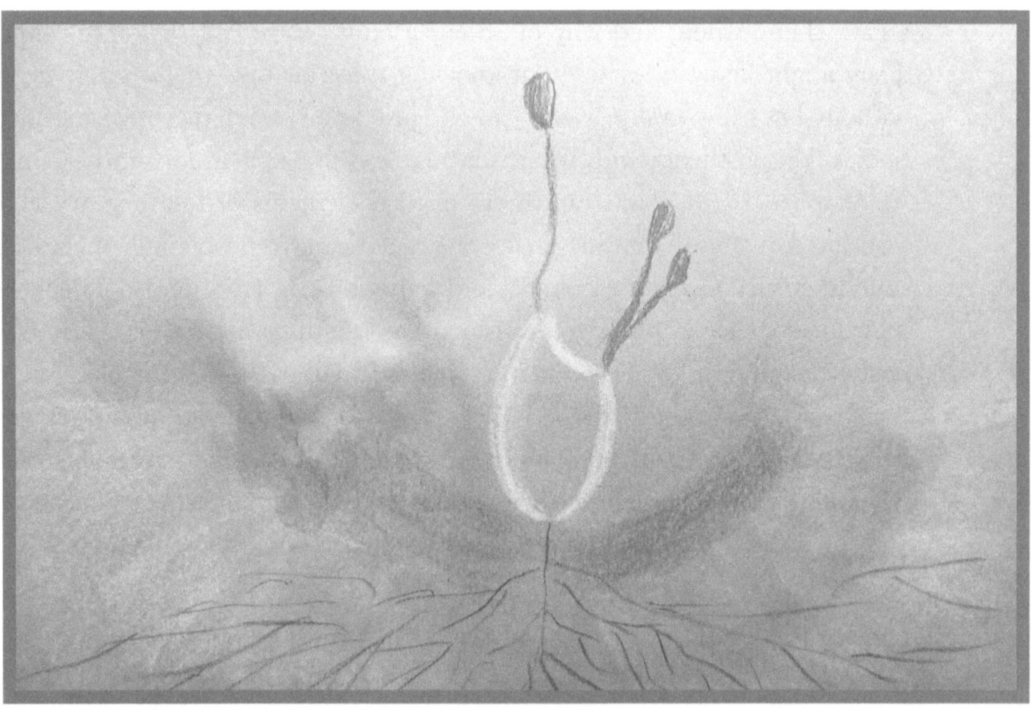

target on the timeline or treatment plan, reminding the client that they can return to this resource place any time it feels useful:

- "This is like a resource place at the beginning of your life, where you have a knowing about who you are—your deepest, truest self. You can come back to this place anytime it is helpful."

This process of scanning and scooping, and then carrying the positive cognition back to the resource place, allows the client to create a solid concept of the self that serves as a foundation they can stand on during reprocessing of later targets. Ideally, you want to do this preverbal protocol before working through any later targets related to attachment relationships, but this will depend on client readiness as well as the client's goals and needs.

Working with Implicit Memories

Sometimes clients may be reluctant to reprocess material that arises without any explicit markers, leading them to believe that it is not a "real" memory or event in their past. Other clients may question material that arises while scanning through developmental periods, as they struggle to understand it. I often reassure clients that they do not need to know all five *w*'s—the who, what, where, when, and why of an experience—to be able to reprocess it. They might know *where* without knowing *when*, or they might know *when* without knowing *who*. Or they might just know *what* they feel in their bodies. You just work with what is available in the system for reprocessing. As Shapiro (2018) points out, more explicit elements of the memory and associated material may begin to emerge during reprocessing, including sounds, smells, thoughts, feelings, and sensations. In addition, some clients may also struggle in phase 3 (assessment) to identify a negative cognition or positive cognition for the preverbal material that arises. That is okay since the client had not yet developed the capacity for language at the time of the original trauma. Again, you work with what is available and accessible and what allows the beliefs about the self to emerge during the work. Sometimes I say to clients, "We don't have to solve the memories, only resolve them."

Working with Generational Material

It is also important to be prepared for generational material that may arise during preverbal reprocessing (or when processing any memory where the origins of the distress are historical or collective). This might include experiences that the caregivers or others in the family lineage experienced, such as a sense of internalized shame or fear stemming from experiences of oppression or persecution, or feelings of complex loss and grief. Some associated material might have a generational quality, like a feeling or sensation that feels very old and deep, as if it has always been there. Generational material can also be followed to resolution and completion like any other material or point of distress by moving through phases 3–6. To identify and assess for generational material, you can invite the client to notice the sensations and do an affect scan and see what comes up:

- "How far back does that sensation go? Is that maybe even sometime before you? See whether you can let your mind float back, maybe even to a time before you, to an earlier time that felt anything like this."

You can then reprocess this material using the standard EMDR protocol and then return to the preverbal protocol (or to the memory that was originally targeted).

CONCLUSION

Many of us, even from our first practice session in basic training, recognize that EMDR is a very powerful and profound trauma treatment modality. The healing work I experienced and witnessed as a trainee was incredibly moving and left me motivated to integrate it into my work; yet when I tried to bring EMDR back to the communities I was working in, something got lost. I found myself unable to convey to clients how innate and organic the process is and often ended up resorting to overly scientific or complicated explanations to justify why moving their eyes back and forth would help their recovery. It was only by applying an ecocentric framework to EMDR that I was able to help clients and consultees feel a deeper connection to the phases of EMDR in a way that facilitated trust, healing, and cultural expression.

The work that we do as trauma therapists is important, especially as the world has seen a dramatic increase in conflict, disaster, and people on the move. Finding ways to expand the reach of EMDR is vital to responding to those affected by the world's crises, conflicts, and climate disasters that are on an upward trajectory. The role of nature in trauma treatment and healing cannot be overstated in this regard. Richard Mollica (2015), a professor of psychiatry at Harvard Medical School and the director of the Harvard Program in Refugee Trauma, teaches that healing cannot happen in the absence of nature and natural spaces. Therefore, my advice is to connect to the power of nature for your own healing and as a source of comfort and strength as you do this work.

I hope that new and seasoned clinicians alike will find a refreshing reconceptualization of EMDR in this book. I also hope to honor the legacy of Francine Shapiro by continuing to place the utmost trust in our clients' innate capacity to heal. Trusting our clients as the experts of their own healing places power back in their hands, helping equalize power differentials and resist the reenactment of trauma dynamics within the therapeutic relationship. In my experience, approaching intercultural exchange, and truly all therapeutic exchange, from a place of humility, curiosity, and respect has served me much better than a stance of competence and assumption based on expertise. As you continue this work as a helping professional, I wish you well on your continued journey of self-discovery, critical self-reflection, and learning as you navigate your relationships with each and every client and community you serve, and as you humbly accompany them along their pathways to healing.

REFERENCES

Africa, J., & Endres, A. (2009). *Towards better quality of care: Applying cultural competence and cultural humility to our daily work* [PowerPoint slides]. CAMINAR. https://www.smchealth.org/sites/main/files/file-attachments/caminarhandout0509.pdf

Al-Hroub, A. (2023). Art therapy interventions for Syrian child and adolescent refugees: Enhancing mental well-being and resilience. *Current Psychiatry Reports, 25*, 857–863. https://doi.org/10.1007/s11920-023-01474-0

Archer, D. (2021). *Anti-racist psychotherapy: Confronting systemic racism and healing racial trauma.* Each One Teach One Publications.

Archer, D. (2022). *Racial trauma recovery: Healing our past using rhythm and processing.* Each One Teach One Publications.

Archer, D. (2024). *Transforming complex trauma: Reflections on anti-racist psychotherapy.* Duppy Konkara Publications.

Artigas, L., Jarero, I., Mauer, M., López Cano, T., & Alcalá, N. (2000, September). *EMDR and traumatic stress after natural disasters: Integrative treatment protocol and the butterfly hug* [Poster presentation]. EMDRIA Conference, Toronto, ON, Canada.

Atkins, S., & Snyder, M. (2017). *Nature-based expressive arts therapy: Integrating the expressive arts and ecotherapy.* Jessica Kingsley Publishers.

Ben-Ezra, M. (2004). Trauma in antiquity: 4000 year old post-traumatic reactions? *Stress and Health, 20*(3), 121–125. https://doi.org/10.1002/smi.1003

Bennett, M. J., & Castiglioni, I. (2004). Embodied ethnocentrism and the feeling of culture. In D. Landis, J. M. Bennett, & M. J. Bennett (Eds.), *Handbook of intercultural training* (pp. 249–265). Sage.

Ben-Yehuda, N. (1980). The European witch craze of the 14th to 17th centuries: A sociologist's perspective. *American Journal of Sociology, 86*(1), 1–31. https://doi.org/10.1086/227200

Blackmore, R., Boyle, J. A., Fazel, M., Ranasinha, S., Gray, K. M., Fitzgerald, G., Misso, M., & Gibson-Helm, M. (2020). The prevalence of mental illness in refugees and asylum seekers: A systematic review and meta-analysis. *PLOS Medicine, 17*(9), Article e1003337. https://doi.org/10.1371/journal.pmed.1003337

Blum, A. (2018, February 15). *How the enlightenment separated humanity from nature.* Medium. https://medium.com/arc-digital/how-the-enlightenment-separated-humanity-from-nature-c008881a61b0

Boon, S., van der Hart, O., & Steele, K. (2016). *Treating trauma-related dissociation: A practical, integrative approach.* W. W. Norton.

Bremner, J. D. (2006). Traumatic stress: Effects on the brain. *Dialogues in Clinical Neuroscience, 8*(4), 445–461. https://doi.org/10.31887/DCNS.2006.8.4/jbremner

Brouwers, T. C., de Jongh, A., & Matthijssen, S. J. (2021). The effects of the Flash technique compared to those of an abbreviated eye movement desensitization and reprocessing therapy protocol on the emotionality and vividness of aversive memories. *Frontiers in Psychology, 12*, Article 741163. https://doi.org/10.3389/fpsyg.2021.741163

Buettner, R. (2023, June 3). *The connection between rivers and spirituality*. GeoAffairs. https://www.geoaffairs.com/connection-rivers-spirituality

Buzzell, L., & Chalquist, C. (2010). *Ecotherapy: Healing with nature in mind.* Catapult.

Cajete, G. A. (2017). Children, myth and storytelling: An Indigenous perspective. *Global Studies of Childhood, 7*(2), 113–130. https://doi.org/10.1177/2043610617703832

Campbell, J. (1949). *The hero with a thousand faces.* Princeton University Press.

Chaitanya, M. V. N. L., Baye, H. G., Ali, H. S., & Usamo, F. B. (2021). Traditional African medicine. In H. A. El-Shemy (Ed.), *Natural medicinal plants* (pp. 47–66). Intech Open.

Chentsova-Dutton, Y., & Maercker, A. (2019). Cultural scripts of traumatic stress: Outline, illustrations, and research opportunities. *Frontiers in Psychology, 10*, Article 2528. https://doi.org/10.3389/fpsyg.2019.02528

Classen, C. C., & Clark, C. S. (2017). Trauma-informed care. In S. N. Gold (Ed.), *APA handbook of trauma psychology: Trauma practice* (pp. 515–541). American Psychological Association. https://doi.org/10.1037/0000020-025

Clinebell, H. (1996). *Ecotherapy: Healing ourselves, healing the earth.* Routledge.

Comtesse, H., Ertl, V., Hengst, S. M. C., Rosner, R., & Smid, G. E. (2021). Ecological grief as a response to environmental change: A mental health risk or functional response? *International Journal of Environmental Research and Public Health, 18*(2), Article 734. https://doi.org/10.3390/ijerph18020734

Crenshaw, K. (1991). Mapping the margins: Intersectionality, identity politics, and violence against women of color. *Stanford Law Review, 43*(6), 1241–1299. https://doi.org/10.2307/1229039

Dana, D. (2018). *The polyvagal theory in therapy: Engaging the rhythm of regulation.* W. W. Norton.

Davis, E. (2022). A model for supporting complex trauma treatment integrating the power of creative arts therapies. In E. Davis, S. Jacobs, J. Fitzgerald, & J. Marchand (Eds.), *EMDR and creative arts therapies* (pp. 7–63). Routledge.

Dennison, P. E., & Dennison, G. (2010). *Brain gym.* Hearts at Play.

Dent-Brown, K., & Wang, M. (2006). The mechanism of storymaking: A grounded theory study of the 6-part story method. *The Arts in Psychotherapy, 33*(4), 316–330. https://doi.org/10.1016/j.aip.2006.04.002

DiAngelo, R. (2018). *White fragility: Why it's so hard for white people to talk about racism.* Beacon Press.

Dissanayake, E. (2015). *What is art for?* University of Washington Press.

Dobo, A. J. (2023). *The hero's journey: Integrating Jungian psychology and EMDR therapy.* Soul Psych Publishers.

Duran, E. (2019). *Healing the soul wound: Trauma-informed counseling for Indigenous communities* (2nd ed.). Teachers College Press.

Ecker, B., & Bridges, S. K. (2020). How the science of memory reconsolidation advances the effectiveness and unification of psychotherapy. *Clinical Social Work Journal, 48*(3–4), 287–300. https://doi.org/10.1007/s10615-020-00754-z

Ecker, B., Ticic, R., & Hulley, L. (2024). *Unlocking the emotional brain: Memory reconsolidation and the psychotherapy of transformational change*. Routledge.

Emerson, D. (2015). *Trauma-sensitive yoga in therapy: Bringing the body into treatment*. W. W. Norton.

Felitti, V. J., Anda, R. F., Nordenberg, D., Williamson, D. F., Spitz, A. M., Edwards, V., Koss, M. P., & Marks, J. S. (1998). Relationship of childhood abuse and household dysfunction to many of the leading causes of death in adults: The adverse childhood experiences (ACE) study. *American Journal of Preventive Medicine, 14*(4), 245–258. https://doi .org/10.1016/S0749-3797(98)00017-8

Figley, C. R., Ellis, A. E., Reuther, B. T., & Gold, S. N. (2017). The study of trauma: A historical overview. In S. N. Gold (Ed.), *APA handbook of trauma psychology: Foundations in knowledge* (pp. 1–11). American Psychological Association.

Fisher, J. (2017). *Healing the fragmented selves of trauma survivors: Overcoming internal self-alienation*. Routledge.

Follette, V. M., Briere, J., Rozelle, D., Hopper, J., & Rome, D. I. (Eds.). (2015). *Mindfulness-oriented interventions for trauma: Integrating contemplative practices*. Guilford Press.

Gendlin, E. T. (1996). *Focusing-oriented psychotherapy: A manual of the experiential method*. Guilford Press.

George, C., Main, M., & Kaplan, N. (1985). *Adult Attachment Interview (AAI)* [Database record]. APA PsycTests. https://doi.org/10.1037/t02879-000

Gersie, A. (1997). *Reflections on therapeutic storymaking: The use of stories in groups*. Jessica Kingsley Publishers.

Greenwald, R. (2007). *EMDR within a phase model of trauma-informed treatment*. Haworth.

Greenwald, R. (2013). *Progressive counting within a phase model of trauma-informed treatment*. Routledge.

Greenwald, R. (2017, November). *Flash! Trauma therapy just got easier and faster*. Trauma Institute & Child Trauma Institute. https://www.ticti.org/flash

Grossman, S., Cooper, Z., Buxton, H., Hendrickson, S., Lewis-O'Connor, A., Stevens, J., Wong, L.-Y., & Bonne, S. (2021). Trauma-informed care: Recognizing and resisting re-traumatization in health care. *Trauma Surgery & Acute Care Open, 6*(1), Article e000815. https://doi.org/10.1136/tsaco-2021-000815

Gump, J. (2010). Reality matters: The shadow of trauma on African American subjectivity. *Psychoanalytic Psychology, 27*(1), 42–54. https://doi.org/10.1037/a0018639

Gunter, R. W., & Bodner, G. E. (2009). EMDR works . . . but how? Recent progress in the search for treatment mechanisms. *Journal of EMDR Practice and Research, 3*(3), 161–168. https://doi.org/10.1891/1933-3196.3.3.161

Hanania, A. (2020). Embroidery (*tatriz*) and Syrian refugees: Exploring loss and hope through storytelling (Broderie [*tatriz*] et réfugiées syriennes: Exploration de la perte et de l'espoir à travers le récit). *Canadian Journal of Art Therapy, 33*(2), 62–69. https://doi.org/10.1080/26907240.2020.1844416

Hanh, T. N. (2024, June 17). *Thich Nhat Hanh's walking meditation.* Lion's Roar. https://www.lionsroar.com/walking-meditation-thich-nhat-hanh/#:~:text=Walking%20meditation%20is%20first%20and,body%2C%20our%20body%20is%20dead

Herman, J. (1992). *Trauma and recovery.* Basic Books.

Hinz, L. D. (2009). *Expressive therapies continuum: A framework for using art in therapy.* Routledge.

Hocoy, D. (2002). Cross-cultural issues in art therapy. *Art Therapy, 19*(4), 141–145. https://doi.org/10.1080/07421656.2002.10129683

Hook, J. N., & Davis, D. E. (2019). Cultural humility: Introduction to the special issue. *Journal of Psychology and Theology, 47*(2), 71–75. https://doi.org/10.1177/0091647119842410

Jackson, L. C. (2020). *Cultural humility in art therapy: Applications for practice, research, social justice, self-care, and pedagogy.* Jessica Kingsley Publishers.

Jarero, I., & Artigas, L. (2009). The EMDR integrative group treatment protocol. *Journal of EMDR Practice and Research, 3*(4), 287–288.

Jawaid, A., Roszkowski, M., & Mansuy, I. M. (2018). Transgenerational epigenetics of traumatic stress. *Progress in Molecular Biology and Translational Science, 158*, 273–298. https://doi.org/10.1016/bs.pmbts.2018.03.003

Kaimal, G., Ayaz, H., Herres, J. M., Makwana, B., Dieterich-Hartwell, R. M., Kaiser, D. H., & Nasser, J. A. (2017). Functional near-infrared assessment of reward perception based on visual self-expression: Coloring, doodling and free drawing. *The Arts in Psychotherapy, 55*, 85–92. https://doi.org/10.1016/j.aip.2017.05.004

Kalmanowitz, D., & Ho, R. T. H. (2016). Out of our mind: Art therapy and mindfulness with refugees, political violence and trauma. *The Arts in Psychotherapy, 49*, 57–65. https://doi.org/10.1016/j.aip.2016.05.012

Kao, H., Zhu, L., Chao, A. A., & Chen, H. Y. (2014). Calligraphy and meditation for stress reduction: An experimental comparison. *Psychology Research and Behavior Management, 7*, 47–52. https://doi.org/10.2147/PRBM.S55743

Karlsen, C. F. (1987). *The devil in the shape of a woman: Witchcraft in colonial New England.* W. W. Norton.

Kase, R. (2023). *Polyvagal-informed EMDR.* W. W. Norton.

Kezich, G. (2014). The bear and the plough: Shamanism in the Neolithic. In E. E. Djaltchinova-Malec (Ed.), *Art and Shamanhood* (pp. 95–107). Archaeobooks.

Kinsella, M. T., & Monk, C. (2009). Impact of maternal stress, depression and anxiety on fetal neurobehavioral development. *Clinical Obstetrics and Gynecology, 52*(3), 425–440. https://doi.org/10.1097/GRF.0b013e3181b52df1

Kirmayer, L. J. (2019). Cultural concepts of distress and psychiatric disorders: Understanding symptom experience and expression in context. *Transcultural Psychiatry, 56*(4), 786–803. https://doi.org/10.1177/1363461519861795

Kirmayer, L. J., Dao, T. H. T., & Smith, A. (1998). Somatization and psychologization: Understanding cultural idioms of distress. In S. Okpaku (Ed.), *Clinical methods in transcultural psychiatry* (pp. 233–265). American Psychiatric Press.

Kirmayer, L. J., Guzder, J., & Rousseau, C. (Eds.). (2014). *Cultural consultation: Encountering the other in mental health care*. Springer.

Knipe, J. (2014). *EMDR toolbox: Theory and treatment of complex PTSD and dissociation.* Springer Publishing.

Kolah, Z. (2023). *Language barriers and expressive arts therapy with refugees: A literature review* (No. 708) [Master's thesis, Lesley University]. Expressive Therapies Capstone Theses. https://digitalcommons.lesley.edu/expressive_theses/708

Lahad, M. (1992). Story-making in assessment method for coping with stress: Six piece story making and BASIC Ph. In S. Jennings (Ed.), *Dramatherapy theory and practice 2* (pp. 192–208). Routledge.

Lahad, M., & Leykin, D. (2013). Introduction: The integrative model of resiliency—"the BASIC Ph" model, or what do we know about survival? In M. Lahad, M. Shacham, & O. Ayalon (Eds.), *The "BASIC Ph" model of coping and resiliency: Theory, research and cross-cultural application* (pp. 9–30). Jessica Kingsley Publishers.

Levine, P. A. (2008). *Healing trauma: A pioneering program for restoring the wisdom of your body.* Sounds True.

Lichtenstein, A. H., Berger, A., & Cheng, M. J. (2017). Definitions of healing and healing interventions across different cultures. *Annals of Palliative Medicine, 6*(3), 248–252. https://doi.org/10.21037/apm.2017.06.16

Linklater, R. (2014). *Decolonizing trauma work: Indigenous stories and strategies.* Fernwood Publishing.

Lloyd, E. (2016, July 20). *Anansi the spider: Trickster and spirit of knowledge in African mythology.* AncientPages. https://www.ancientpages.com/2016/07/20/anansi-the-spider-trickster-and-spirit-of-knowledge-in-african-mythology

Lowrie, M. (2021, February 28). *Quebec river granted legal rights as part of global "personhood" movement.* CBC News. https://www.cbc.ca/news/canada/montreal/magpie-river-quebec-canada-personhood-1.5931067

Magsamen, S., & Ross, I. (Eds.). (2023). *Your brain on art: How the arts transform us.* Canongate Books.

Main, M., & Hesse, E. (1990). Parents' unresolved traumatic experiences are related to infant disorganized attachment status: Is frightened and/or frightening parental behavior the linking mechanism? In M. Greenberg, D. Cicchetti, & E. Cummings (Eds.), *Attachment in the preschool years: Theory, research, and intervention* (pp. 161–182). University of Chicago Press.

Ma-Kellams, C. (2014). Cross-cultural differences in somatic awareness and interoceptive accuracy: A review of the literature and directions for future research. *Frontiers in Psychology, 5*, Article 1379. https://doi.org/10.3389/fpsyg.2014.01379

Malchiodi, C. A. (2003). Art therapy and the brain. In C. A. Malchiodi (Ed.), *Handbook of art therapy* (pp. 16–24). Guilford Press.

Manfield, P., Lovett, J., Engel, L., & Manfield, D. (2017). Use of the Flash technique in EMDR therapy: Four case examples. *Journal of EMDR Practice and Research, 11*(4), 195–205. https://doi.org/10.1891/1933-3196.11.4.195

Marchand, J. (2022, Spring). The transformative journey storytelling method: A culturally responsive approach to EMDR preparation. *Go With That Magazine, 27*(2), 4–15.

Marchand, J., & Simpson, M. (2022). Inviting the body, movement, and the creative arts into telehealth: A culturally responsive model for online EMDR. In E. Davis, S. Jacobs, J. Fitzgerald, & J. Marchand (Eds.), *EMDR and creative arts therapies* (pp. 64–101). Routledge.

McHugo, G. J., Kammerer, N., Jackson, E. W., Markoff, L. S., Gatz, M., Larson, M. J., Mazelis, R., & Hennigan, K. (2005). Women, co-occurring disorders, and violence study: Evaluation design and study population. *Journal of Substance Abuse Treatment, 28*(2), 91–107. https://doi.org/10.1016/j.jsat.2004.08.009

Mehl-Madrona, L. (1997). *Coyote medicine: Lessons from Native American healing*. Scribner.

Menakem, R. (2017). *My grandmother's hands: Racialized trauma and the pathway to mending our hearts and bodies*. Central Recovery Press.

Micots, C. (2024). *Kente cloth (Asante and Ewe peoples)*. Khan Academy. https://www.khanacademy.org/humanities/art-africa/west-africa/ghana/a/kente-cloth

Mollica, R. F., Brooks, R. T., Ekblad, S., & McDonald, L. (2015). The new H5 model of refugee trauma and recovery. In J. Lindert & I. Levav (Eds.), *Violence and mental health* (pp. 341–378). Springer.

Næss, A. (1973). The shallow and the deep, long-range ecology movement: A summary. *Inquiry, 16*(1), 95–100. https://doi.org/10.1080/00201747308601682

Naff, K. (2014). A framework for treating cumulative trauma with art therapy. *Art Therapy, 31*(2), 79–86. https://doi.org/10.1080/07421656.2014.903824

Nash, G. (2019). Response art in art therapy practice and research with a focus on reflective imagery. *International Journal of Art Therapy, 25*(1), 39–48. https://doi.org/10.1080/17454832.2019.1697307

Nickerson, M. (2016). Integrating cultural concepts and terminology into the AIP model and EMDR approach. In M. Nickerson (Ed.), *Cultural competence and healing culturally based trauma with EMDR therapy: Innovative strategies and protocols* (1st ed., pp. 15–28). Springer Publishing.

O'Shea, K., & Paulsen, S. (2009). *When there are no words: EMDR for early trauma and neglect held in implicit memory*. https://emdr-belgium.be/wp-content/uploads/2017/12/When-There-Are-No-Words.-EMDR-for-Early-Trauma-and-Neglect-Held-in-Implicit-Memory.-Katie-OShea-M.S.-2009.pdf

Paton, J., & Linnell, S. (2020). Embodied wisdom in the creative arts therapies: Learning from contemporary art. In J. Higgs (Ed.), *Practice wisdom: Values and interpretations* (Vol. 3, pp. 289–298). Brill.

Paulsen, S., & Spear Chief, S. (2024). *Indigenous trauma and dissociation: Healers, psychotherapies, and the drum*. Paulsen Integrative Psychology Press.

Popky, A. J. (2005). DeTUR, an urge reduction protocol for addictions and dysfunctional behaviors. In R. Shapiro (Ed.), *EMDR solutions: Pathways to healing* (pp. 167–188). W. W. Norton.

Porges, S. W. (2011). *The polyvagal theory: Neurophysiological foundations of emotions, attachment, communication, and self-regulation*. W. W. Norton.

Porges, S. W. (2021). *Polyvagal safety: Attachment, communication, self-regulation*. W. W. Norton.

Rogers, B. A., Chicas, H., Kelly, J. M., Kubin, E., Christian, M. S., Kachanoff, F. J., Berger, J., Puryear, C., McAdams, D. P., & Gray, K. (2023). Seeing your life story as a hero's journey increases meaning in life. *Journal of Personality and Social Psychology, 125*(4), 752–778. https://doi.org/10.1037/pspa0000341

Rothschild, B. (2017). *The body remembers: Vol. 2. Revolutionizing trauma treatment*. W. W. Norton.

Sangalang, C. C., Jager, J., & Harachi, T. W. (2017). Effects of maternal traumatic distress on family functioning and child mental health: An examination of Southeast Asian refugee families in the U.S. *Social Science & Medicine, 184*, 178–186. https://doi.org/10.1016/j.socscimed.2017.04.032

Schouten, K. A., van Hooren, S., Knipscheer, J. W., Kleber, R. J., & Hutschemaekers, G. (2019). Trauma-focused art therapy in the treatment of posttraumatic stress disorder: A pilot study. *Journal of Trauma & Dissociation: The Official Journal of the International Society for the Study of Dissociation (ISSD), 20*(1), 114–130. https://doi.org/10.1080/15299732.2018.1502712

Shapiro, F. (2018). *Eye movement desensitization and reprocessing (EMDR) therapy: Basic principles, protocols, and procedures* (3rd ed.). Guilford Press.

Shebini, N. (2019). Flash technique for safe desensitization of memories and fusion of parts in DID: Modifications and resourcing strategies. *Frontiers in the Psychotherapy of Trauma and Dissociation, 3*(1), 151–164. https://doi.org/10.46716/FTPD.2019.0031

Siegel, D. J. (1999). *The developing mind: How relationships and the brain interact to shape who we are*. Guilford Press.

Siegel, D. J. (2012, September 12). *Applications of the Adult Attachment Interview with Daniel Siegel, MD* [Webinar]. PESI. https://catalog.pesi.com/item/applications-adult-attachment-interview-daniel-siegel-md-5598

Soulé, I., Littzen-Brown, C., Vermeesch, A. L., & Garrigues, L. (2022). Expanding the mind-body-environment connection to enhance the development of cultural humility. *International Journal of Environmental Research and Public Health, 19*(20), Article 13641. https://doi.org/10.3390/ijerph192013641

Speert, E. (2016, October 27). *Eco-art therapy: Deepening connections with the natural world.* American Art Therapy Association. https://arttherapy.org/eco-art-therapy-deepening-connections-natural-world/

Steele, H., & Steele, M. (2008). Ten clinical uses of the Adult Attachment Interview. In H. Steele & M. Steele (Eds.), *Clinical applications of the Adult Attachment Interview* (pp. 3–30). Guilford Press.

Steele, K., Boon, S., & van der Hart, O. (2017). *Treating trauma-related dissociation: A practical, integrative approach.* W. W. Norton.

Stepney, S. A. (2022). Multicultural and diversity perspectives in art therapy: Transforming image into substance. In M. Rastogi, R. P. Feldwisch, M. Pate, & J. Scarce (Eds.), *Foundations of art therapy* (pp. 81–122). Academic Press.

Stone, C. (2020, November/December). *The westward journeys of buttons.* AramcoWorld. https://www.aramcoworld.com/Articles/November-2020/The-Westward-Journeys-of-Buttons

Substance Abuse and Mental Health Services Administration. (2014). *SAMHSA's concept of trauma and guidance for a trauma-informed approach* (HHS Publication No. [SMA] 14-4884). https://ncsacw.acf.hhs.gov/userfiles/files/SAMHSA_Trauma.pdf

Sue, D. W., Sue, D., Neville, H. A., & Smith, L. (2022). *Counseling the culturally diverse: Theory and practice* (9th ed.). John Wiley & Sons.

Summers, J., & Vivian, D. (2018). Ecotherapy – a forgotten ecosystem service: A review. *Frontiers in Psychology, 9,* Article 1389. https://doi.org/10.3389/fpsyg.2018.01389

Talwar, S. (2007). Accessing traumatic memory through art making: An art therapy trauma protocol (ATTP). *The Arts in Psychotherapy, 34*(1), 22–35. https://doi.org/10.1016/j.aip.2006.09.001

Te Papa Tongarewa. (2024). *Tāmoko | Māori tattoos: History, practice, and meanings.* https://www.tepapa.govt.nz/discover-collections/read-watch-play/maori/tamoko-maori-tattoos-history-practice-and-meanings

Tervalon, M., & Murray-García, J. (1998). Cultural humility versus cultural competence: A critical distinction in defining physician training outcomes in multicultural education. *Journal of Health Care for the Poor and Underserved, 9*(2), 117–125. https://doi.org/10.1353/hpu.2010.0233

Tokay, E. (2023). Climate change, environmental philosophy, and anthropocentrism. In G. Pellegrino & M. Di Paola (Eds.), *Handbook of the philosophy of climate change* (pp. 361–376). Springer.

Turcotte, S., & Schiffer, J. (2014). Aboriginal focusing-oriented therapy. In G. Madison (Ed.), *Emerging practice in focusing-oriented psychotherapy: Innovative theory and applications* (pp. 48–64). Jessica Kingsley Publishers.

van der Kolk, B. A. (2014). *The body keeps the score: Brain, mind, and body in the healing of trauma.* Viking.

Wathen, C. N., MacGregor, J. C. D., & Beyrem, S. (2021). Impacts of trauma- and violence-informed care education: A mixed method follow-up evaluation with health & social service professionals. *Public Health Nursing, 38*(4), 645–654. https://doi.org/10.1111/phn.12883

Wiest, B. (2020). *The mountain is you: Transforming self-sabotage into self-mastery*. Thought Catalog Books.

Williams, C. (2019). The hero's journey: A mudmap for change. *Journal of Humanistic Psychology, 59*(4), 522–539. https://doi.org/10.1177/0022167817705499

Wong, S.-L. (2021). A model for the Flash technique based on working memory and neuroscience research. *Journal of EMDR Practice and Research, 15*(3), 174–184. https://doi.org/10.1891/emdr-d-20-00048

Yates, F. A. (1964). *Giordano Bruno and the Hermetic tradition*. University of Chicago Press.

Zadeh, R., & Jogia, J. (2023). The use of art therapy in alleviating mental health symptoms in refugees: A literature review. *International Journal of Mental Health Promotion, 25*, 1–18. https://doi.org/10.32604/ijmhp.2023.022491

Zaidel, D. W. (2005). *Neuropsychology of art: Neurological, cognitive and evolutionary perspectives* (1st ed.). Psychology Press.

ACKNOWLEDGMENTS

This book is a true collective effort. It would not have been possible without the support and guidance of many people throughout my journey. First, I would like to thank each and every client who has given me the honor of accompanying them along their path toward healing. Your trust has meant the world to me, and I am grateful to humbly continue to learn alongside you.

I want to thank my family for always believing in me, especially my children. Your openness to living and adapting to life in different cultures and communities is more support than I could ever ask for.

I also wish to thank Josée Leclerc for being my mentor at Concordia University. Your expertise and dedication to art therapy and the role of creative expression in trauma healing have greatly influenced the direction of my work. To Carol Seychuk, the director of Northern Society for Domestic Peace (NSDP), for believing in my potential. My five years at NSDP laid the most unshakable foundation for everything I do today. And to all my NSDP colleagues: You were a family to me, and I carry your love and support wherever I go.

I am immensely grateful to all of my mentors and colleagues in the field of EMDR, particularly Sue Genest, for being such a passionate EMDR trainer and for opening the door to the world of EMDR for me. To Dr. Ricky Greenwald, thank you for all the guidance you provided me while I was growing as a consultant and EMDR trainer. You are a true expert in the field, and I have been humbled to learn from you. A heartfelt thank-you to Elizabeth Davis, for your endless wisdom and friendship—I have grown under your wing and continue to learn so much from you! And to Dorothy Ashman, for your endless support of the community of EMDR therapists in Ethiopia. I have been honored to see your legacy firsthand and to play a role in carrying it forward.

I want to thank Skye Maconachie and Chau Dinh at Blue Dragon Children's Foundation in Hanoi for all the opportunities you provided me. And to Douglas Holwerda, the founder of the Hanoi Counseling Psychology Group, for mobilizing such an incredible community of mental health practitioners in Vietnam. You are a true role model of what it means to stay true to yourself in this world and to your work.

I would like to extend a special thanks to my editor at PESI, Jenessa Jackson, for your support throughout this process. Your attention to detail and generous feedback has been invaluable.

Last but not least, I would like to thank Francine Shapiro for developing a modality that has changed the lives of so many people. You gave me hope that healing is possible.

With gratitude,

Jen

THERAPIST HIGHLIGHTS

I would like to acknowledge the fellow EMDR therapists and consultees who have contributed to this book. This book would not have been possible without our meaningful exchanges and your willingness to share your knowledge, diverse perspectives, and life experiences with me. In this section, I hope to provide a way for other EMDR and trauma therapists to be able to learn from you and your expertise.

Alemayehu Tibebe: Ethiopian EMDR therapist and cofounder of Impact Ethiopia in Addis Ababa specializing in conflict-related trauma for both individuals and groups
Email: impact2ethiopia@gmail.com
Website: https://www.linkedin.com/in/alemayehu-tibebe-32b557a9

Chau Dinh: Vietnamese psychologist and EMDR therapist specializing in human trafficking and generational trauma
Email: chaupsy79@gmail.com
Website: https://www.emdria.org/directory/people/chau-dinh-ma

Elizabeth Davis: American EMDRIA basic trainer and art therapist specializing in dissociation and DID, attachment trauma, and intensive trauma therapy
Email: edaivs@ticti.org
Website: https://www.elizabethdavis-emdr.com

Jessica Horder: American EMDR therapist and consultant specializing in intensive trauma therapy for complex trauma using EMDR, parts work, and dialectical behavior therapy
Email: jessicaHorderLMHC@gmail.com
Website: https://www.emdria.org/directory/people/jessica-horder

Lacey Poltorasky: Canadian Indigenous EMDRIA-approved consultant specializing in work with Indigenous populations, race-based trauma, and generational trauma
Email: laceycreyke@gmail.com
Website: https://www.emdria.org/directory/people/lacey-poltorasky

Mulu Mekonnen: Ethiopian EMDR therapist and cofounder of Impact Ethiopia in Addis Ababa, specializing in work with conflict-affected populations
Email: impact2ethiopia@gmail.com
Website: https://www.linkedin.com/in/mulu-mkonnen-41a22499/?originalSubdomain=et

Noriko Baba: Japanese EMDR therapist living in Montreal, Canada, offering services in English, French, and Japanese, specializing in developmental, intergenerational, and racial trauma with diverse backgrounds
Email: norikoarttherapy@gmail.com
Website: https://www.norikobaba.com

Tigist Waltenigus: Ethiopian EMDR therapist and cofounder of Erq Me'ad Counselling Center in Addis Ababa, specializing in attachment, collective, and generational trauma
Email: tigistwalta@gmail.com
Website: https://et.linkedin.com/in/tigistwaltenigus

ABOUT THE AUTHOR

Jennifer Marchand, MA, CCC, CCTP-II, RCAT, is a certified trauma specialist and EMDRIA-approved consultant with over 10 years of clinical experience in a diverse range of settings and cultural contexts. She specializes in working with sexual violence, complex and conflict-related trauma, and vicarious traumatization. Based in Addis Ababa, Ethiopia, since 2021, she is dedicated to the field of global mental health and working in underserved settings.

In addition to her private practice, Jennifer supports frontline international and Ethiopian aid workers working with survivors of conflict-related sexual violence (a project funded by the German Development Cooperation GIZ). She is also a technical advisor to Medica Mondiale, an international women's rights organization, where she supports training on trauma sensitivity for health professionals in conflict-affected settings, such as Kurdistan and Kosovo. She is a returning lecturer at Heidelberg University's Public Health in Emergencies Program and an alumnus of the Harvard Refugee Trauma Program. She has also worked with Blue Dragon Children's Foundation, an organization in Hanoi, Vietnam, supporting a team of psychologists working with survivors of human trafficking.

As a registered Canadian art therapist, she integrates the creative arts into her trauma recovery work. She is also an editor and coauthor of *EMDR and Creative Arts Therapies* (2022), a book combining EMDR and the creative arts for the treatment of complex trauma with diverse populations across a range of cultural contexts.